Series Editor:
Paul Wehman, Ph.D.

The Brookes
Transition to
Adulthood Series

SELF-DETERMINATION AND
Transition
Planning

The Brookes
Transition to
Adulthood Series

SELF-DETERMINATION AND
Transition
Planning

by

Karrie A. Shogren, Ph.D.

University of Illinois at Urbana-Champaign

·P·A·U·L·H·
BROOKES
PUBLISHING Co®

Baltimore • London • Sydney

Paul H. Brookes Publishing Co.
Post Office Box 10624
Baltimore, Maryland 21285-0624
USA

www.brookespublishing.com

Typeset by Scribe, Philadelphia, Pennsylvania.
Manufactured in the United States of America by
Sheridan Books, Chelsea, Michigan.

The individuals described in this book are real people whose situations are based on the authors' actual experiences. Real names and identifying details are used by permission.

Library of Congress Cataloging-in-Publication Data

Shogren, Karrie Ann, 1980– author.
  Self-determination and transition planning / by Karrie A. Shogren, Ph.D., University of Illinois Urbana Champaign.
     pages   cm
  Includes bibliographical references and index.
  ISBN 978-1-59857-269-8 (pbk. : alk. paper)
  ISBN 1-59857-269-5 (pbk. : alk. paper)
  1. People with disabilities—Education—United States 2. Special education—United States. 3. Autonomy (Psychology)—United States. 4. Teachers—In-service training—United States. I. Title.
  LC4019.S46 2013
  371.90973—dc23   2013001002

British Library Cataloguing in Publication data are available from the British Library.

2017   2016   2015   2014   2013

10   9   8   7   6   5   4   3   2   1

Contents

Series Preface

The Brookes Transition to Adulthood Series was developed for the purpose of meeting the critical educational needs of students with disabilities who will be moving from school to adulthood. It is no longer acceptable to simply equip a student with a set of isolated life skills that may or may not be relevant to his or her adult life. Nor is it sufficient to treat the student as if he or she will remain unchanged throughout life. As we allow for growth and change in real-life environments, so must we allow for growth and change in the individuals who will operate within the environments. Today, transition must concern itself with the whole life pattern of each student as it relates to his or her future. However, integrating the two constructs of self and the real adult world for one student at a time is not always straightforward. It requires skills and knowledge. It requires a well-thought-out, well-orchestrated team effort. It takes individualization, ingenuity, perseverance, and more.

The results of these first-rate efforts can be seen when they culminate in a student with a disability who exits school prepared to move to his or her life beyond the classroom. Unfortunately, though, this does not always happen. This is because transition has become a splintered concept, too weighted down by process and removed from building on the student's aspirations and desires for "a good life." However, it does not have to be this way.

This book series is designed to help the teachers, transition specialists, rehabilitation counselors, community service providers, administrators, policy makers, other professionals, and families who are looking for useful information on a daily basis by translating the evidence-based transition research into practice. Each volume addresses specific objectives that are related to the all-important and overarching goal of helping students meet the demands of school and society and gain a greater understanding of themselves so that they are equipped for success in the adult world.

Editorial Advisory Board

About the Author

Karrie A. Shogren, Ph.D., is Associate Professor of Special Education at the University of Illinois at Urbana-Champaign. She received her doctorate in special education from the University of Kansas. Dr. Shogren has conducted extensive research in the areas of self-determination and systems of supports for people with intellectual disability. She has a specific interest in the multiple, nested factors that have an impact on student outcomes and the use of diverse methodologies to understand and explore these factors. She has published more than 45 peer-reviewed articles, is the author or coauthor of five books, and is one of the coauthors of *Intellectual Disability: Definition, Classification, and Systems of Support*, the 11th Edition of the American Association on Intellectual and Developmental Disabilities' seminal definition of intellectual disability (formerly mental retardation). Dr. Shogren has received funding from the Institute of Education Sciences to support her research. She is currently Associate Editor of *Remedial and Special Education* and *Intellectual and Developmental Disabilities*.

Preface

The transition from school to adult life can be both an exciting and intimidating time for youth and families. The changes are often exciting but can also be overwhelming. For youth with disabilities, the barriers can sometimes be higher to creating a real life in adulthood, filled with choice, control, self-determination, and meaningful and appropriate supports. However, within the field of special education, progress has been made in creating supports and services that reduce those barriers. Transition services that are results oriented and based on the vision of the future held by youth with disabilities and their families have the potential to reduce these barriers and promote meaningful outcomes.

The field has repeatedly acknowledged that student self-determination is a key part of the process. In addition to empirical research documenting the impact of self-determination on outcomes, the voices of youth and young adults with disabilities and their family members tell of the importance of self-determination in promoting meaningful outcomes. This book attempts to describe, in meaningful ways for practitioners, how teaching strategies, opportunities, and systems of support can enable students with disabilities with any level of support need to develop skills that are culturally relevant and enable them to go after—with support—the things that they want in life.

A NOTE TO THE READER

As I prepared this manuscript and considered carefully the readership, I realized I felt most comfortable speaking directly to you. Since I am an educator myself and advocate for people with disabilities, I wrote most often in the first person, using "we" to mean myself, my colleagues, and you, the reader, as a unified group working together to understand self-determination and teach young people about it.

Acknowledgments

I want to begin by acknowledging the Pinner and the Carr families. By sharing their stories and experiences with me, and through this book with education professionals across the world, they have shown us what self-determination can really mean and lead to for youth with disabilities. They have set a high standard for all of us, but a standard we know is possible to achieve, particularly using these strategies and resources they have been kind enough to share with all of us.

To Kay, Mike, Mikey, and Christy, it has been a pleasure to work with Christy for the past 2 years (and hopefully many years to come). Getting to know all of you through Christy has enriched my professional knowledge and challenged me to think outside the box.

To Jake and Jeanine, I will always treasure the friendship that I have developed with both of you and while you often thank me for being a part of the journey, I want to take this opportunity to thank you. You have enriched my life as a professional and as a person in ways that I cannot even begin to express. I look forward to more opportunities to learn and laugh together. I know some national presentations and keynotes will be on the horizon.

I would also like to thank all of the other professionals that shared their stories in this book: Kim Wolowiec Fisher, Heather Haynes, Mike Slagor, John Kelly, Sue Walter, Michel Stringer, Tony Plotner, Christy Nittrouer, Sharon Slover, and Anne Clark. Without these stories, the "real world" applications of this book would not have been nearly as rich or diverse. I would also like to thank and acknowledge all of the researchers who I have cited throughout this book that dedicate their lives to identifying ways to support the self-determination of youth with disabilities.

I would like to thank Paul Wehman for editing this series and for suggesting that I might be a valuable contributor. I'd also like to thank Rebecca Lazo, Senior Acquisitions Editor at Brookes Publishing, for her leadership in organizing the series, and Steve Plocher, Associate Editor, and Lynda Phung, Project Editor, at Brookes Publishing for supporting the development, writing, and editing of this book. I would like to thank Mike Wehmeyer, Ann Turnbull, and Rud Turnbull for their feedback and support in the process of writing this book, as well as Sharon Vaughn, who supported me with office space and breakfasts. I would like to acknowledge my colleagues at the University of Illinois, whose feedback and encouragement is always valuable. I would also like to acknowledge the tireless work of Christy Nittrouer on this book, always ensuring all the files were in the right place, and organized in the right way.

Finally, I would like to acknowledge my personal system of support, particularly Dave Angelow, who encouraged me and even pushed me to keep focused on how to make this book have the maximum impact for youth with disabilities and their families.

*To all of the youth, families, and professionals
who are working together to promote meaningful outcomes.
My hope is that everyone has access to systems of support
that enable them to be self-determining and develop the life that they desire
and that leads to happiness, fulfillment, and hope.*

1

What Is Self-Determination and Why Does It Matter in Transition?

Transition is kind of a huge deal. So when we planned his transition to adulthood, we were doing a move, a change of schools, and a change of jobs all at once. We decided up front that self-determination was going to be an integral part of the transition process. We set everything up so Michael could make choices and everything would be done with his interests and preferences in mind. We went slowly; first we just did weekends at the new location. When we actually made the move, we took him to the new school, he started his new job, and we noticed almost no behavior problems! When we had transitions in the past, like going from elementary to middle school, we've had no sleep, screaming, and aggression. But, this transition was different because we built in Michael's self-determination. We focused on his choices and preferences, even his preference for going slowly. After we made the move, there were still so many changes, but he was fine. He was able to handle all of them; I think that's the power of self-determination.

(Kay–Michael's mom, personal communication, June 5, 2012)

I have made my decision. It was a very difficult decision and after several tries to get the words out of my mouth to make such a big announcement, I decided to go through with the surgery and I will most likely have it in early to mid-June. It was pretty grown up of me to make such a huge decision, probably the hardest I've made in my life. I thought that I would focus on my education and finish my senior year in high school, get my diploma, and then have the operation because of my dedication to school. Making a decision like this really reminded me of the self-determination PowerPoint and how we talked about self-determination and decision making.

(Jake, personal communication, February 21, 2010)

Promoting student self-determination is a critical part of effective transition services (Field, Martin, Miller, Ward, & Wehmeyer, 1998b; Hasazi et al., 2005; Test, Fowler, et al., 2009). The opening quotes demonstrate that self-determination can make a real difference in the lives of individuals with disabilities and their families. Kay, whose son Michael has multiple disabilities and is receiving community-based services focused on employment, highlights how self-determination enables Michael to exert control over his world, have his preferences respected, and experience the quality of life that he desires. His family plays a key role in creating an environment that supports his self-determination. Jake, a young man with high-functioning autism who made the transition from his neighborhood high school to a local community college, describes how learning about self-determination allowed him to make adult decisions, particularly about a needed operation on his foot and figuring out when and how to schedule this operation so it did not conflict with his last semester of high school. He had to problem-solve, weigh the pros and cons of the different options, and make a decision. He used a number of skills that are central to self-determined behavior, skills he learned throughout his life while learning about self-determination.

Although most of us would personally and professionally agree that self-determination is important, we would probably also agree that it can be difficult to figure out how to support the students we work with to become self-determining. Jake and Michael are both self-determined young men, but they express their self-determination in different ways and need different supports from their families and friends. Each student we work with is unique; they each have their own profile of strengths and support needs. Plus, there are so many demands on our time and so many things that are important to teach.

This book provides strategies to make self-determination more meaningful and accessible for students with disabilities. It focuses on 1) clarifying the definition of self-determination and what it can mean to students with disabilities (Chapter 1), 2) identifying strategies to individualize self-determination instruction (Chapter 2), 3) identifying strategies to teach skills associated with self-determination (Chapters 3–6), 4) creating opportunities for expressing self-determination (Chapter 7), 5) building supports for self-determination (Chapter 8), and 6) promoting self-determination in the systems in which we work (Chapter 9). Research-based information on how to promote self-determination is blended with real stories from the lives of individuals with disabilities and their families. The stories of Michael and Jake, who were featured in the chapter's opening quotes, are followed throughout the book. Each of these individuals has been supported to develop self-determination skills and to use these skills to achieve the lives that they want. Illustrations from their lives are used to show how this has worked. Other students, parents, and professionals are heard from throughout the book to understand the real-world application of self-determination, showing that teaching self-determination skills and creating opportunities for students to practice the skills can happen for all students, regardless of their support needs (see Chapter 2). It is all about ensuring that the research-validated practices that professionals and people with disabilities and their families acknowledge are important are actually implemented in practice. The Evidence-Based Practice, Clinical Judgment, and Values research box talks about the importance of evidence-based practice that takes into account research, professional wisdom, and student and family values.

WHAT IS SELF-DETERMINATION?

Self-determination can be an elusive concept. We all have an idea of what it means to us, but we also recognize that it might not be the same for all people. People work toward different goals and want different things out of life. They make different choices and encounter different problems, which makes it confusing. How do we support all students to be self-determining if the outcomes look different for everyone? Researchers have suggested that there are essential characteristics of self-determination that apply to all students (Wehmeyer, 1997, 2003a, 2003b), and that all students can become self-determining and work toward the adult outcomes that they personally value with individualized instruction that considers personal characteristics, culture, and preferences of students and their families (Shogren, 2011).

Though critically important for students with disabilities, self-determination is relatively new to special education, with a real research focus only beginning about twenty years ago, in the 1990s.

Definition of Self-Determination in Special Education

Although it may seem like self-determination is always a topic of discussion when we are talking about the transition to adult life, the idea of self-determination for students with

Evidence-Based Practice, Clinical Judgment, and Values

A review of evidence-based practice definitions reveals a common thread: Practices should be supported by rigorous scientific research and consistently lead to positive outcomes (LaCava & Shogren, 2012). A debate exists in the field regarding the definition of *rigorous scientific research*. Some groups have emphasized specific types of research designs (e.g., the importance of randomized control trials; What Works Clearinghouse, 2008), whereas others have emphasized that diverse research designs can contribute to identifying evidence-based practices (Odom et al., 2005).

There seems to be a growing consensus, however, that a variety of research designs can contribute to the knowledge of evidence-based practice as long as the design allows for an evaluation of the degree to which an instructional practice caused a change in a student outcome. This can include group and quasi-experimental designs (Gersten et al., 2005) as well as single-subject designs (Horner et al., 2005). Cook and Cook (2011) highlighted the importance of the 1) research design, 2) quality of research studies, 3) quantity of research studies, and 4) magnitude of effect. There should essentially be a sufficient number of high-quality studies that use research designs that can document a relationship between an instructional practice such as self-determination and a student outcome. Furthermore, the effect of the instructional practice should be of sufficient magnitude to make a difference in the lives of students and their families.

Seek out instructional practices that have research to support their impact on outcomes when working with individual students to promote self-determination. But remember that research studies are not the only thing that goes into evidence-based practice. The American Psychological Association's Presidential Task Force on Evidence-Based Practice defined *evidence-based practice* as the "integration of the best available research with clinical expertise in the context of patient characteristics, culture and preferences" (2006, p. 273). Whitehurst defined *evidence-based education* as the "integration of professional wisdom with the best available empirical evidence in making decisions about how to deliver instruction" (2002, Slide 3). Consider professional wisdom and knowledge of student characteristics, family preferences, and culture to select the most appropriate intervention. Also, data must be collected to document that practices are effective with individual students. Numerous factors should be considered in promoting positive outcomes. Figure 1.1 shows factors that the special education field has suggested are important to consider when implementing evidence-based practices (National Autism Center, 2009; Prizant, 2011; Simpson et al., 2005). Figure 1.2 provides a model for using these factors when making instructional decisions.

disabilities is relatively new in the special education field. It was only in the 1990s and early 2000s that significant attention was devoted to the need to support students with disabilities to become self-determining to promote positive adult outcomes. An explosion of writing on self-determination has occurred since that time. For example, Wood and Test (2001) reviewed the literature on self-determination at the turn of the century and found that more than 800 resources, including 450 peer-reviewed articles on self-determination, were published between 1972 and 2000, with most of this literature published in the 1990s. Imagine how many more books and articles have been published since the turn of the 21st century.

Given all of this literature, we need an organizing framework for understanding the key elements of self-determination and what it can mean for students with disabilities. Because of the diverse understandings of self-determination, Field, Martin, Miller, Ward, and Wehmeyer—all researchers who developed frameworks for understanding

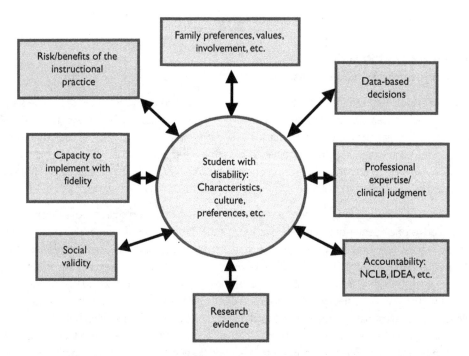

Figure 1.1. Factors to consider when using evidence-based practices. (From LaCava, P.G., & Shogren, K.A. [2012]. *Evidence-based practice and autism spectrum disorders: The intersection of research, practice, and policy.* Paper presented at the 136th Annual Meeting of the American Association on Intellectual and Developmental Disabilities, Charlotte, NC; reprinted with permission from Paul LaCava.)

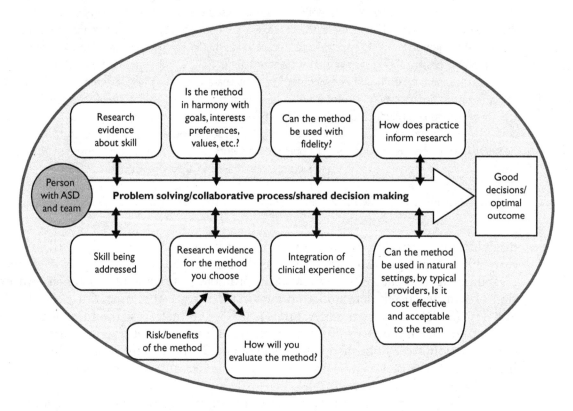

Figure 1.2. Model of implementing evidence-based practices. (From LaCava, P.G., & Shogren, K.A. [2012]. *Evidence-based practice and autism spectrum disorders: The intersection of research, practice, and policy.* Paper presented at the 136th Annual Meeting of the American Association on Intellectual and Developmental Disabilities, Charlotte, NC; reprinted with permission from Paul LaCava.)

self-determination—highlighted the evolving definition of self-determination, stating that *self-determination* is

> A combination of skills, knowledge, and beliefs that enable a person to engage in goal-directed, self-regulated, autonomous behavior. An understanding of one's strengths and limitations, together with a belief of oneself as capable and effective are essential to self-determination. When acting on the basis of these skills and attitudes, individuals have greater ability to take control of their lives and assume the role of successful adults in our society. (1998a, p. 2)

Functional Theory of Self-Determination Wehmeyer (1997, 2003b, 2005) introduced the functional theory of self-determination, one of the most cited definitional frameworks for self-determination. Wehmeyer argued that self-determination cannot simply be defined as a set of behaviors because almost any behavior can be used to exert control over one's life. He instead stated that self-determination has to be defined by the function of a person's actions or behaviors. He specifically said that self-determination is "volitional actions that enable one to act as the primary causal agent in one's life and to maintain or improve one's quality of life" (2005, p. 117). Although this definition might seem complex, breaking down the three key aspects of the definition makes it easy to see how self-determination is relevant for students with disabilities.

1. *Volitional actions:* Volitional action is purposeful and has a specific intent. Students who are self-determined are being purposeful and acting as a causal agent over their lives (Wehmeyer, 2005). Jake was being purposeful in his decision making when he opted to have his surgery (with support from his family and doctor) after the end of his senior year of high school so that he could experience his last semester with his peers.

2. *Causal agency:* Causal agents are people that make things happen in their lives. Students with disabilities are self-determining when they act with the intent of being a causal agent or of causing the things they want to happen in their lives (Wehmeyer, 2005). Michael used his behavior to express his preferences and communicate the things he wants to happen in his life (e.g., easing into changes such as a new house, school, and job).

3. *Quality of life:* Quality of life is about the hopes and dreams people have for their lives. Researchers have identified key domains of quality of life that include emotional well-being, interpersonal relations, material well-being, personal development, physical well-being, self-determination, social inclusion, and rights (Schalock et al., 2002). Each person's hopes and dreams for their quality of life are influenced by personal characteristics and environmental factors. People act in a self-determined way (i.e., with intent and as the person that makes things happen in his or her life) to improve their quality of life across these eight dimensions. Jake acted to improve not only his physical well-being by having his foot surgery but also his personal development by finishing his high school education with his class. Michael used his behavior to improve his emotional well-being by ensuring his preferences were understood and respected by his parents.

Self-determination is acting with intent to improve one's quality of life, and these actions are identified by four essential characteristics: 1) the person acted autonomously, 2) the behaviors are self-regulated, 3) the person initiated and responded in a psychologically empowered manner, and 4) the person acted in a self-realizing manner (Wehmeyer, 2003a).

This sounds deceptively simple, right? How do we enable students to be the people that make things happen in their lives, to be autonomous, to be self-regulated, to be psychologically empowered, and to be self-realizing? We focus on teaching and creating opportunities for specific skills and attitudes to develop that lead to the essential characteristics of self-determined behavior. These skills and attitudes, which Wehmeyer (2003a) called the component elements of self-determination, are listed in Table 1.1 and are discussed in greater detail in Chapters 3–6.

The importance of teaching skills, creating opportunities, and providing supports for students to use these skills to become causal agents—or people that make things happen to improve their quality of life—are the key takeaways from the functional theory. It is also important to remember the following:

The key takeaways from the functional theory of self-determination are the importance of teaching skills, creating opportunities, and providing supports for students to become people who make things happen to improve their quality of life.

- The purpose of self-determined behavior is for people to act to achieve their hopes and dreams for their lives.

- Self-determination develops over time as students develop the skills and attitudes associated with self-determination.

- Supports and accommodations are critical to developing and expressing self-determined behavior.

- Repeated opportunities and appropriate supports are critical for growing self-determination skills. These opportunities and supports will look different as students with disabilities age. Figure 1.3 shows how Jeanine, Jake's mom, thinks about her role in supporting the development of Jake's self-determination over time.

Culture and Self-Determination The role of culture is one factor that often comes up when discussing self-determination. Cultural factors may influence how individual students and their families define quality of life and their expression of self-determined behavior. Culture is not the same as categorical labels (e.g., Caucasian, Hispanic, African American), but instead is shaped by multiple factors, including gender, disability, race/ethnicity, language, and socioeconomic background. There is a small but growing body of research that examines the influence of culture on self-determination. The Self-Determination and Culture research box summarizes key findings from this body of research that inform our thinking about supporting students from diverse backgrounds to be self-determining.

Table 1.1. Skills and attitudes associated with self-determined behavior

Choice making

Decision making

Problem solving

Goal setting and attainment

Self-management (self-monitoring, self-evaluation, self-instruction, and self-reinforcement)

Self-advocacy and leadership

Internal locus of control

Perceptions of self-efficacy and positive outcome expectancies

Self-awareness and self-knowledge

Sources: Wehmeyer, 1997, 2003a, 2005.

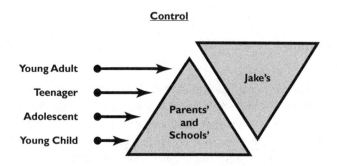

Figure 1.3. Jeanine's perceptions of her role in supporting Jake's self-determination as he grew up. (Reprinted with permission from Jake's family.)

WHY DOES SELF-DETERMINATION MATTER?

Definitions of self-determination have been provided, and factors that can influence the development and expression of self-determined behavior have been identified. Now comes the "so what" question. Why does self-determination matter? Martin, Marshall, Maxson, and Jerman provided an insightful description of the importance of self-determination for students with disabilities.

> If students floated in life jackets for 12 years, would they be expected to swim if the jackets were suddenly jerked away? Probably not. The situation is similar for students receiving special education services. All too often these students are not taught how to self-manage their own lives before they are thrust into the cold water of post-school reality. (1993, p. 4)

This quote was backed up by data from the original National Longitudinal Transition Study released in the 1990s (Blackorby & Wagner, 1996), which suggested that students with disabilities were not achieving positive postschool outcomes, especially in the domains of employment, postsecondary education, and community integration. Self-determination was identified by both researchers and self-advocates with disabilities as a key element in efforts to change these outcomes. Students needed to learn to self-determine their own lives so that they could intentionally pursue the things that mattered to them.

The Council for Exceptional Children's Division on Career Development and Transition issued a position statement on self-determination that stated that self-determination enabled students to "be more successful in education and transition to adult life" and "holds great potential to transform the way in which educational services are planned and delivered for students with and without disabilities" (Field et al., 1998b, p. 125). Researchers have established effective strategies for teaching the skills associated with self-determination (Algozzine, Browder, Karvonen, Test, & Wood, 2001; Cobb, Lehmann, Newman-Gonchar, & Alwell, 2009; Test, Fowler, et al., 2009) and identified a link between higher levels of self-determination and valued adult outcomes (Test, Mazzotti, et al., 2009; Wehmeyer & Palmer, 2003; Wehmeyer & Schwartz, 1997). The Self-Determination, School Outcomes, and Adult Outcomes research box highlights several studies that demonstrate the impact of teaching self-determination skills on school and postschool outcomes.

A growing body of research tells us we can teach self-determination skills to students and that teaching these skills affects student self-determination as well as other valued school and postschool outcomes. The affect that promoting self-determination can have on the lives of youth and young adults with disabilities and their families becomes clear when we consider research and feedback from people with disabilities and their families about the importance of self-determination.

Self-Determination and Culture

Shogren (2011) analyzed all the published literature that directly examined self-determination and culture. Unfortunately, the literature was limited. Only 10 articles that explicitly focused on the relationship between self-determination and culture were identified. The 10 articles included both theoretical and empirical examinations of how self-determination applied in diverse cultures, including Diné (Navajo), Korean, and Japanese culture, and the influence of cultural variables such as race/ethnicity, socioeconomic status, and immigration status on self-determined behavior. These articles provided initial insight into key issues to consider. Shogren identified four main themes from the literature.

1. Self-determined behavior can and does vary across cultures.

2. Self-determination as operationalized in practice often is not culturally appropriate.

3. Research must include voices and practices of diverse students and their families.

4. Change in multiple systems is needed (2011, p. 122).

The reviewed literature suggested that self-determination had universal value across cultures. Specific differences were noted, however, in how self-determined behavior was applied in different cultures. For example, Frankland, Turnbull, Wehmeyer, and Blackmountain (2004) discussed how the Diné culture valued autonomy but viewed it in the context of fulfilling family and clan roles, not individual roles. Although all of the literature included in the review suggested universal aspects of self-determination, researchers also found that, in practice, instruction to promote self-determination often did not focus on how to use self-determined behavior to achieve personally valued goals. Instead, goals were selected because they were on a form or because they were congruent with the culture of practitioners, not on the basis of the values, preferences, and interests of the student and his or her family. For example, researchers often cited independent living as a problematic domain. Goals were often written that emphasized living outside the family home, but the goal for a number of families from diverse cultures was to support the youth with a disability at home, at least for the short term (Trainor, 2005). Opportunities for students to learn and practice their self-determination skills are scarce when goals are not congruent with personal and familial values because the goals do not match desired quality-of-life outcomes.

The studies included in the review suggested that a "flexible self-determination perspective" (Shogren, 2011, p. 124) be used in schools to allow for cultural differences to be taken into account. Valenzuela and Martin (2005) provided a framework for how to include opportunities for cultural sharing and individualist and collectivist values in the *Self-Directed IEP* curriculum (Martin, Marshall, Maxon, & Jerman, 1996), which focused on teaching students to lead their individualized education program meetings. Shogren (2011) stated it was critical for teachers and transition professionals to have candid conversations with students and their families about their beliefs and practices and to think about how to make changes in the school, community, and adult service systems to ensure self-determination was understood and applied in this flexible way across the diverse systems that students and their families encounter. Family–professional partnerships are needed to understand self-determination and how it is applied in the family context (Turnbull, Turnbull, Erwin, Soodak, & Shogren, 2010). The principle of cultural reciprocity provides a framework for thinking about how to apply a flexible self-determination perspective and ensure that transition goals are linked to desired quality-of-life outcomes for students with disabilities and their families (Kalyanpur & Harry, 2012). Each student will use self-determined behavior in unique ways to be a causal agent over his or her life.

Self-Determination, School Outcomes, and Adult Outcomes

A series of studies examining the impact of teaching self-determination skills on student school and postschool outcomes were conducted (Shogren, Palmer, Wehmeyer, Williams-Diehm, & Little, 2012; Shogren, Wehmeyer, Palmer, Rifenbark, & Little, 2012; Wehmeyer, Palmer, Shogren, Williams-Diehm, & Soukup, in press; Wehmeyer, Shogren, Palmer, Williams-Diehm, Little, et al., 2012). The impact of the Self-Determined Learning Model of Instruction (SDLMI; Wehmeyer, Palmer, Agran, Mithaug, & Martin, 2000; see Chapter 5) on the self-determination, goal attainment, and access to the general education curriculum of students with intellectual and learning disabilities in secondary school was examined in one project (Shogren, Palmer, et al., 2012; Wehmeyer, Shogren et al., 2012). The SDLMI is a model of instruction that teachers can use to teach students how to use a self-regulated, problem-solving process to set and achieve valued goals. The SDLMI can be used in any educational setting with any type of goal. Teachers used it to support students to achieve academic and transition-related goals. There were 312 high school students in the project. Seventy percent of the students had learning disabilities, and 30% had intellectual disability. Each participating high school was randomly assigned to be a treatment or control campus. Teachers on the treatment campuses were trained to implement the SDLMI with students in Years 1 and 2 of the project. The control campuses conducted their normal school routine during Year 1 of the project and implemented the SDLMI during Year 2 of the project. Students with intellectual and learning disability who received instruction on the SDLMI had greater access to the general education curriculum in Year 1. They were more likely to be working on general education standards and gaining access to accommodations and modifications. In addition, students with learning disability that used the SDLMI made more progress on their academic goals, and students with intellectual disabilities made more progress on transition goals (Shogren, Palmer, Wehmeyer, Williams-Diehm, & Little, 2012). Using the SDLMI also led to significant improvements in student self-determination. Students that received instruction showed significant gains in their self-determination over time, despite having similar levels of self-determination at the beginning of the project. The greatest gains were found for students in the treatment group who received instruction using the SDLMI for 2 years (Wehmeyer, Shogren et al., 2012). These studies showed that teaching students using the SDLMI increases student self-determination and providing instruction over a longer period of time improves outcomes. Plus, it affects goal attainment and access to the general curriculum.

Wehmeyer et al. (in press) and Shogren, Wehmeyer, et al. (2012) followed 779 students with disabilities over 5 years (3 in school and 2 out of school). The schools that these students attended were assigned to a treatment or control campus. Treatment campuses could pick from numerous self-determination interventions based on what would work best on their campus. Control campuses received training on promoting family involvement—an important intervention, but one the researchers believed would not directly affect student self-determination. Students had significantly higher levels of self-determination when leaving school when they were exposed to any of the self-determination interventions (Wehmeyer et al., in press). The study also found that self-determination when leaving school predicted more positive employment and community participation outcomes, with students exposed to self-determination interventions in school having significantly more positive outcomes (Shogren, Wehmeyer, et al., 2012). These studies confirmed the affect that teaching self-determination skills can have on student self-determination, school, and postschool outcomes.

SELF-DETERMINATION AND TRANSITION PLANNING

Self-determination develops over a life span as children, youth, and adults have opportunities to learn and practice the skills associated with self-determined behavior. The way these skills are taught and the opportunities that are created may change over time. Think about how Jeanine showed her role as Jake's mom changing over time in Figure 1.1. Promoting self-determination is not something that should begin in secondary school. It is critical that the foundation be laid throughout a student's school career.

The Individuals with Disabilities Education Improvement Act of 2004 emphasizes the importance of individualized planning, and educational and vocational goals reflecting personal interests, strengths, and desires.

Promoting self-determination in the context of transition planning is critically important because this is when youth and their families are actively engaged in planning for the move from school to adult life. The Individuals with Disabilities Education Improvement Act (IDEA) of 2004 (PL 108-446) emphasizes the importance of self-determination in transition planning and defines *transition services* as

> A coordinated set of activities for a child with a disability that
>
> (A)   is designed to be a results-oriented process, that is focused on improving the academic and functional achievement of the child with a disability to facilitate the child's movement from school to post-school activities, including post-secondary education, vocational education, integrated employment (including supported employment), continuing and adult education, adult services, independent living, or community participation;
>
> (B)   *is based on the individual child's needs, taking into account the child's strengths, preferences, and interests* [emphasis added]; and
>
> (C)   includes instruction, related services, community experiences, the development of employment and other post-school adult living objectives, and, when appropriate, acquisition of daily living skills and functional vocational evaluation. (20 U.S.C. § 1401[34])

Part B of the IDEA 2004 definition of transition services emphasizes the importance of focusing on a student's strengths, preferences, interests, and needs. These strengths, preferences, interests, and needs should clearly be a key part of identifying valued post-school activities as well as selecting instruction, related services, and so forth. Assessing a student's strengths, preferences, interests, and needs and enabling each student to effectively communicate these strengths, preferences, and interests and advocate to have his or her needs met is a critical part of transition services. For this reason, promoting self-determination is key to effective transition services. The rest of this book discusses building a foundation for self-determination in students with disabilities.

2

Accommodating Individual Differences

I thought self-determination was only for people that were going to live on their own, be independent, have a job, and have someone drop in every once in a while.

(Shogren, 2012, p. 173)

I believe self-determination is a familial thing, I think it is passed down in families. We talk about how to fine tune it to each disability, why not fine tune it to each culture and family?

(Shogren 2012, p. 178)

Self-determination is often confused with being independent or achieving a specific pattern of adult outcomes (e.g., living alone, having a job, not needing paid supports), as shown in the chapter's opening quote. This quote comes from an interview project with mothers of Hispanic youth with disabilities who were in the process of making the transition from school to adult life (Shogren, 2012). The mother went on to say that when she learned more about self-determination from conferences and other families, she saw that it could be very relevant for her daughter with severe and multiple disabilities, particularly in terms of arranging her daughter's home and school environments to incorporate her choices and preferences. A different mother emphasized in the second quote that the expression of self-determined behavior and valued quality-of-life outcomes were strongly influenced by the family and felt that more work needed to be done to "fine tune" or individualize self-determination interventions based on personal values and culture. She went on to say that some of the educators she worked with excelled in this area, but many struggled.

Although self-determination can be associated with being independent or living alone, it should not be defined by specific behaviors (i.e., being independent; Wehmeyer, 2005; see Chapter 1). People with severe and multiple disabilities can be self-determining as long as the focus is on the individual intentionally making things happen to improve desired quality-of-life outcomes. These behaviors and outcomes will be different for each person with a disability, just like they are different for each person without a disability. Each person has unique values, desires, and needs that shape the job he or she wants, the place and conditions within which he or she wants to live, and the things he or she wants to do for fun. It is all about being supported to learn what those things are and figuring out how to go after them.

Students with disabilities will need and benefit from different supports to express self-determined behavior. This chapter talks about how to assess student self-determination as well as using this data in transition planning and determining appropriate supports. The chapter also discusses factors that can influence self-determined behavior and how to consider these factors when designing and implementing self-determination interventions in schools. Finally, strategies to partner with students and families to individualize self-determination interventions will be highlighted, with a vignette describing how this worked for a student who uses an augmentative and alternative communication (AAC) device.

ASSESSING STUDENT SELF-DETERMINATION

Before we can determine appropriate supports for student self-determination, we first need to understand where students are in their relative levels of self-determination. Several self-determination assessments can be used to gather data about student self-determination. Although these assessments are frequently used in research (Shogren et al., 2008), they also can provide useful information in practice to understand student's strengths and areas in need of additional support related to self-determination.

The Arc's Self-Determination Scale (Wehmeyer & Kelchner, 1995) and the AIR Self-Determination Scale (Wolman, Campeau, Dubois, Mithaug, & Stolarski, 1994) are two of the most commonly used assessments. The Arc's Self-Determination Scale was developed by Wehmeyer and colleagues and is available for free on the Beach Center web site (http://www.beachcenter.org). The Arc's Self-Determination Scale is based on the functional theory of self-determination described in Chapter 1. It is a student self-report measure, which means that it is designed for students to complete the questions (with supports, such as having the questions read aloud as needed) to provide their perspective on self-determination. The full scale includes four sections with 72 questions that assess student autonomy, self-regulation, psychological empowerment, and self-realization—the four essential characteristics of self-determination. The Adolescent Self-Determination Assessment–Short Form (Wehmeyer, Little, Lopez, & Shogren, 2011; see Figure 2.1) is a short form of the scale and includes 28 items representative of the four essential characteristics of self-determination. It is quicker to administer because it has fewer items and it still gives meaningful information about student self-determination. Information on scoring the assessment is available in Wehmeyer (2011). Figure 2.2 shows a sample student profile that could be generated from completing the Adolescent Self-Determination Scale–Short Form. This graph shows a student's scores in the different domains measured on the Adolescent Self-Determination Scale–Short Form. For example, there are a total of 50 points available. The student in this example scored around the midpoint (28 points) in overall self-determination. When we look at the subscale scores, however, we see the student scored very high in psychological empowerment and self-realization and much lower in self-regulation and autonomy. The student has strengths in self-realization and psychological empowerment but needs more support in learning skills associated with autonomy and self-regulation, including choice-making, goal-setting, and self-management skills. If you saw this profile in a student you were working with, then you could focus on providing instruction in these areas. You can administer this assessment at different points in time (e.g., the beginning and end of the school year) to see how much progress students have made in their self-determination skills to inform transition-related IEP goals for the following year.

Self-determination assessments are used with students, their families, and teachers to identify areas of strengths and need in relation to self-determination. The results help everyone involved know where to focus in order to make improvements, and maximize good results!

Adolescent Self-Determination Scale–Short Form

Michael L. Wehmeyer & Todd Little
University of Kansas

Shane J. Lopez
Clifton Strengths Institute

Karrie A. Shogren
University of Illinois

Student's name_____ Date _____

School _____ Teacher's name _____

Section I

Directions: Check the answer on each question that *best* tells how you act in that situation. There are no right or wrong answers.

1. I plan weekend activities that I like to do.

❑	❑	❑	❑
I do not do even if I have the chance	I do sometimes when I have the chance	I do most of the time I have the chance	I do every time I have the chance

2. My friends and I choose activities that we want to do.

❑	❑	❑	❑
I do not do even if I have the chance	I do sometimes when I have the chance	I do most of the time I have the chance	I do every time I have the chance

3. I write letters, notes or talk on the phone to friends and family.

❑	❑	❑	❑
I do not do even if I have the chance	I do sometimes when I have the chance	I do most of the time I have the chance	I do every time I have the chance

4. I go to restaurants that I like.

❑	❑	❑	❑
I do not do even if I have the chance	I do sometimes when I have the chance	I do most of the time I have the chance	I do every time I have the chance

(continued)

Figure 2.1. The Adolescent Self-Determination Scale–Short Form.

From Wehmeyer, M.L., Little, T.D., Lopez, S.J., & Shogren, K.A. (2011). The Adolescent Self-Determination Scale-Short Form. Lawrence: Kansas University Center for Developmental Disabilities; reprinted by permission.
In *Self-Determination and Transition Planning* by Karrie A. Shogren, Ph.D. (2013, Paul H. Brookes Publishing Co.)

5. I go to movies, concerts, and dances.

❑	❑	❑	❑
I do not do even if I have the chance	I do sometimes when I have the chance	I do most of the time I have the chance	I do every time I have the chance

6. I choose gifts to give to family and friends.

❑	❑	❑	❑
I do not do even if I have the chance	I do sometimes when I have the chance	I do most of the time I have the chance	I do every time I have the chance

7. I decorate my own room.

❑	❑	❑	❑
I do not do even if I have the chance	I do sometimes when I have the chance	I do most of the time I have the chance	I do every time I have the chance

Section IIA

Directions: Each of the following items tell the beginning and end of a story. Your job is to tell what happened in the middle of the story, to connect the beginning and the end. Read the beginning and ending for each item, then fill in the *best* answer for the middle of the story. There are no right or wrong answers. Remember, fill in the answer that you think *best* completes the story.

8. Beginning —You are meeting with your teacher and parents. You want to take a class where you can learn skills to help you work in hotel management. Your parents want you to take the Family and Child Care class. You can only take one of the classes.
   Middle — _____
   _____

   Ending — The story ends with you taking a class where you will learn hotel management.

9. Beginning — You hear a friend talking about a new job opening at the local book store. You love books and want a job. You decide you would like to work at the bookstore.
   Middle — _____
   _____
   _____

   Ending — The story ends with you working at the bookstore.

10. Beginning — Your friends are acting like they are mad at you. You are upset about this.
    Middle — _____
    _____
    _____

    Ending — The story ends with you and your friends getting along just fine.

11. Beginning — You go to your English class one morning and discover your English book is not in your backpack. You are upset because you need that book to do your homework.
    Middle — _____
    _____
    _____
    _____

    Ending — The story ends with you using your English book for homework.

12. Beginning — You are in a club at school. The club advisor announces that the club members will need to elect new officers at the next meeting. You want to be the president of the club.
    Middle — _____
    _____
    _____
    _____

    Ending — The story ends with you being elected as the club president.

13. Beginning — You are at a new school and you don't know anyone. You want to have friends.
    Middle — _____
    _____
    _____
    _____

    Ending — The story ends with you having many friends at the new school.

Section IIB

Directions: The next three questions ask about your plans for the future. Again, there are no right or wrong answers. For each question, tell if you have made plans for that outcome (by checking the appropriate box) and, if so, what those plans are and how to meet them.

14. What type of transportation do you plan to use after you graduate from high school?

❏ I have not planned for that yet   ❏ I plan to use _____
                                                  _____
                                                  _____

                                                  List four things you should do to meet this goal:
                                                  1) _____
                                                  2) _____
                                                  3) _____
                                                  4) _____

From Wehmeyer, M.L., Little, T.D., Lopez, S.J., & Shogren, K.A. (2011). The Adolescent Self-Determination Scale-Short Form. Lawrence: Kansas University Center for Developmental Disabilities; reprinted by permission.
In *Self-Determination and Transition Planning* by Karrie A. Shogren, Ph.D. (2013, Paul H. Brookes Publishing Co.)

Section III

Directions: Check the answer that *best* describes you. There are no wrong answers.

15. ❑ I usually agree with people when they tell me I can't do something. or ❑ I tell people when I think I can do something that they tell me I can't.

16. ❑ Trying hard at school doesn't do me much good. or ❑ Trying hard at school will help me get a good job.

17. ❑ It is no use to keep trying because that won't change things. or ❑ I keep trying even after I get something wrong.

18. ❑ I don't know how to make friends. or ❑ I know how to make friends.

19. ❑ I do not make good choices. or ❑ I can make good choices.

20. ❑ I will have a hard time making new friends. or ❑ I will be able to make friends in new situations.

21. ❑ My choices will not be honored. or ❑ I will be able to make choices that are important to me.

Section IV

Directions: Tell whether each of these statements describes how you feel about yourself or not. There are no right or wrong answers. Choose the one that *best* fits you.

22. It is better to be yourself than to be popular.	❑ Yes	❑ No
23. I am loved because I give love.	❑ Yes	❑ No
24. I know what I do best.	❑ Yes	❑ No
25. I like myself.	❑ Yes	❑ No
26. I know how to make up for my limitations.	❑ Yes	❑ No
27. Other people like me.	❑ Yes	❑ No
28. I am confident in my abilities.	❑ Yes	❑ No

From Wehmeyer, M.L., Little, T.D., Lopez, S.J., & Shogren, K.A. (2011). The Adolescent Self-Determination Scale-Short Form. Lawrence: Kansas University Center for Developmental Disabilities; reprinted by permission. In *Self-Determination and Transition Planning* by Karrie A. Shogren, Ph.D. (2013, Paul H. Brookes Publishing Co.)

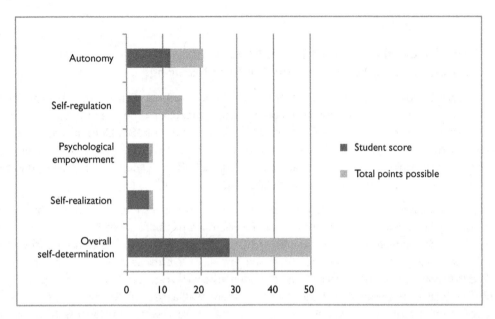

Figure 2.2. Student sample profile.

The Arc's Self-Determination Scale procedural guidelines (Wehmeyer & Kelchner, 1995) highlight how important it is to involve students and their families in using this data, suggesting students can use data from the assessment to do the following, with appropriate supports.

- Evaluate their own beliefs about themselves and self-determination.

- Work collaboratively with educators and others to identify individual areas of strength and limitations related to self-determination goals and objectives.

- Self-assess progress in self-determination over time (p. 8).

The AIR Self-Determination Scale (Wolman et al., 1994) is another commonly used assessment and is available for free at the Zarrow Center's web site (http://www.ou.edu/content/education/centers-and-partnerships/zarrow/self-determination-assessment-tools/air-self-determination-assessment.html). The AIR Self-Determination Scale provides information about student capacity and opportunity for self-determination. One of the most useful things about the AIR Self-Determination Scale is that it comes in three versions—a student, parent, and educator version. Questions focus on assessing students' knowledge, ability, and perceptions of their capacity for self-determination and the opportunities they have to build their self-determination skills at home and school. Overall self-determination scores, as well as scores for capacity and opportunity, can be calculated. The *AIR Self-Determination Scale User's Guide* has information on how to use students' scores to guide curriculum planning and how to use the parent and educator version to identify relevant IEP goals and facilitate communication between home and school. The AIR Self-Determination Scale can also provide useful information about differences in perceptions across students, educators, and parents and can be used to identify ways to create more opportunities to build self-determination skills across home and school. You might be asking, how do I decide which scale to use? Are the two scales measuring the same thing?

The What Does the Research Tell Us About What Assessments of Self-Determination Are Measuring? research box summarizes research on the relationship between these two assessments and factors to consider when choosing a self-determination assessment.

What Does the Research Tell Us About What Assessments of Self-Determination Are Measuring?

A research study was conducted with 407 high school students with intellectual disability, learning disabilities, other health impairments, emotional and behavior disorders, and autism to explore the relationship between The Arc's Self-Determination Scale and the AIR Self-Determination Scale–Student Form (Shogren et al., 2008). All of the students completed these two assessments of self-determination as part of a larger project. Their teachers also completed the AIR Self-Determination Scale–Educator Form. Unfortunately, the parents did not complete the parent form.

This study focused on learning more about the relationship between items on both scales. Were they measuring the same thing, or were they measuring different aspects of self-determination? This is important to inform the selection of measures for research and practice. A data analysis technique called structural equation modeling was used and found that The Arc's Self-Determination Scale was measuring the self-determination construct as defined by the four essential characteristics—autonomy, self-regulation, psychological empowerment, and self-realization. There was a good fit of the data to a model that specified self-determination and was made up of four factors representing the four essential characteristics. Something different was found for the AIR Self-Determination Scale–Student Form. It best represented self-determination with two factors—capacity and opportunity. This suggests that the two scales are measuring different aspects of self-determination. The two scales were only moderately correlated ($r = .5$), which further supported this finding. The relationship between scores on the student and educator forms was also examined. Weak to moderate correlations were found between the capacity and opportunity ratings on the student and educator forms ($r = .15–.21$), so students and teachers were not agreeing on student capacity and opportunities. This suggests significant discrepancies in how students and teachers are perceiving self-determination capacities and opportunities. Following are recommendations gleaned from the research.

- The AIR Self-Determination Scale gives information on assessing opportunities for self-determination, whereas The Arc's Self-Determination Scale does not. It may be useful to use the student, educator, and parent versions to get different perspectives on opportunities.

- The Arc's Self-Determination Scale is the best measure for assessing the degree to which students have started expressing the essential characteristics (e.g., the degree to which they have learned and internalized self-determination skills). It may take longer, however, to see change in student scores on The Arc's Self-Determination Scale.

- When there are discrepancies in student, educator, and parent ratings, remember that people perceive self-determination differently. No one is necessarily wrong. Discrepancies provide an opportunity for everyone to explore the capacities that might need to be enhanced and the quality of the opportunities that are being provided. It is possible that scores may become more closely aligned with ongoing education and support for self-determination for students, teachers, and parents.

UNDERSTANDING INDIVIDUAL DIFFERENCES IN SELF-DETERMINED BEHAVIOR

It is important to understand the role of personal and environmental factors in influencing student self-determination. These factors must be considered when designing self-determination interventions to address the unique needs and characteristics of students (Wehmeyer, Abery, et al., 2011).

The literature has identified numerous factors that can influence student self-determination. Wehmeyer, Abery, et al. (2011) identified several personal characteristics that influence self-determination, including culture, gender, age, and cognitive ability. Other researchers have emphasized the impact that environmental conditions such as inclusion and opportunity for making choices can have on the expression of self-determined behavior (Abery & Stancliffe, 2003; Shogren et al., 2007). The Combined Influence of Personal and Environmental Characteristics on Self-Determination research box summarizes a study looking at the combined ways that personal characteristics and environmental conditions can influence self-determination.

Combined Influence of Personal and Environmental Characteristics on Self-Determination

A multitude of personal and environmental factors can influence student self-determination. A study was conducted with 327 students with intellectual disability, learning disabilities, and other health impairments to try to understand the degree to which these factors alone or in combination predicted self-determination (Shogren et al., 2007). It examined the degree to which several personal characteristics (e.g., disability label, gender, race/ethnicity, free reduced lunch status, transition empowerment) and environmental factors (e.g., attendance at last IEP meeting, inclusion, opportunities for self-determination) predicted self-determination measured by The Arc's Self-Determination Scale and the AIR Self-Determination Scale–Student Form.

A data analysis technique called structural equation modeling was used and showed that several personal and environmental factors predicted self-determination, although these factors were different, depending on the specific assessment of self-determination. Gender, disability label, opportunity, and transition empowerment predicted self-determination on The Arc's Self-Determination Scale. None of the other factors did. Female students tended to score higher than males, and students with intellectual disability tended to score lower than the other two groups. Students who had more opportunities for self-determination and were more empowered in the transition process tended to report higher levels of self-determination. Interestingly, attendance at the last IEP meeting did not predict self-determination, but transition empowerment did, suggesting the importance of in-depth, meaningful participation in the transition planning process. None of the other factors were related to self-determination. Only disability label and transition empowerment predicted self-determination on the AIR Self-Determination Scale–Student Form. These findings

- Confirm that The Arc's Self-Determination Scale and the AIR Self-Determination Scale–Student Form are measuring different aspects of self-determination because they have different relationships with personal and environmental characteristics.

- Suggest the need for specialized supports for students with intellectual disability to increase their self-determination skills and opportunities.

- Suggest the importance of actively involving students with disabilities in transition planning because this has a significant and powerful impact on self-determination. Simply having students attend their IEP meetings as passive participants does not influence self-determination.

- Suggest that inclusion alone does not influence self-determination, and providing opportunities for self-determination is critically important.

Personal Characteristics

Researchers have consistently found a relationship between self-determination, cognitive ability, and disability label. Individuals with lower levels of cognitive ability tend to report lower levels of self-determination across studies (Shogren et al., 2007; Wehmeyer, Shogren, et al., 2012). This does not mean that students with intellectual and developmental disabilities cannot be self-determining. It means we need to provide more instruction, opportunities, and supports to allow students with intellectual disability to develop and express self-determined behavior. For example, Kay and Mike, Michael's parents (one of the students featured throughout this book), have found he does really well when information is presented to him in pictures, in words, and through songs (because he loves music). Although some students might quickly pick up on skills needed to participate in preferred activities (e.g., playing basketball for Michael), Michael needs more supports to be self-determining in these activities. Figure 2.3 shows a visual story that Michael's family developed and set to a popular tune so he could learn about playing basketball and engaging with his peers, activities he identified as preferred but in which he struggled to participate.

Researchers have also found a relationship between gender and self-determination, although this relationship has varied across cultures. For example, Shogren et al. (2007) found female adolescents with disabilities from the United States had higher levels of self-determination than males, whereas Nota, Ferrari, Soresi, and Wehmeyer (2007) found males had higher self-determination when they worked with Italian adolescents with disabilities. An individual's personal culture is defined by many diverse characteristics (see Chapter 1). Gender likely interacts with many other factors, including family and community factors, to influence self-determination. This suggests the importance of "fine tuning" self-determination instruction to each student and his or her family.

Researchers have also linked age with self-determination (Y. Lee et al., 2012). Self-determination develops as students learn skills and have opportunities and supports to practice those skills (see Chapter 1; Figure 1.3). These skills, opportunities, and supports may look different, depending on the age of the student and his or her experience with self-determination. Teaching self-determination skills is important, regardless of the age of the students with whom we are working. We have to be sensitive to the skills, opportunities, and supports that a student has (or has not) had and use this to gauge the correct ways to introduce self-determination instruction. Several researchers have provided important insight into strategies to promote self-determination across the life span, beginning in early childhood (Erwin et al., 2009; Erwin & Brown, 2003; Shogren & Turnbull, 2006).

Environmental Conditions

In addition to personal characteristics, the environments in which students with disabilities live, learn, work, and play have been found to make a difference in expressing self-determination. Researchers have found that classroom and instructional experiences may be related to students' self-determination. For example, researchers have explored the relationship between self-determination, inclusion, and access to the general education curriculum (S.H. Lee, Wehmeyer, Palmer, Soukup, & Little, 2008; Shogren et al., 2007, 2012; Zhang, 2001). Researchers have found that inclusive experiences may positively influence self-determination (Shogren et al., 2007) and access to the general education curriculum is related to self-determination (S.H. Lee et al., 2008; Shogren et al., 2012). There are still questions left to be answered. For example, it is unknown if inclusion and access predict self-determination or if self-determination predicts inclusion and access. Either way, self-determination is associated with specific classroom and instructional experiences, emphasizing the importance of teaching self-determination skills and creating opportunities for

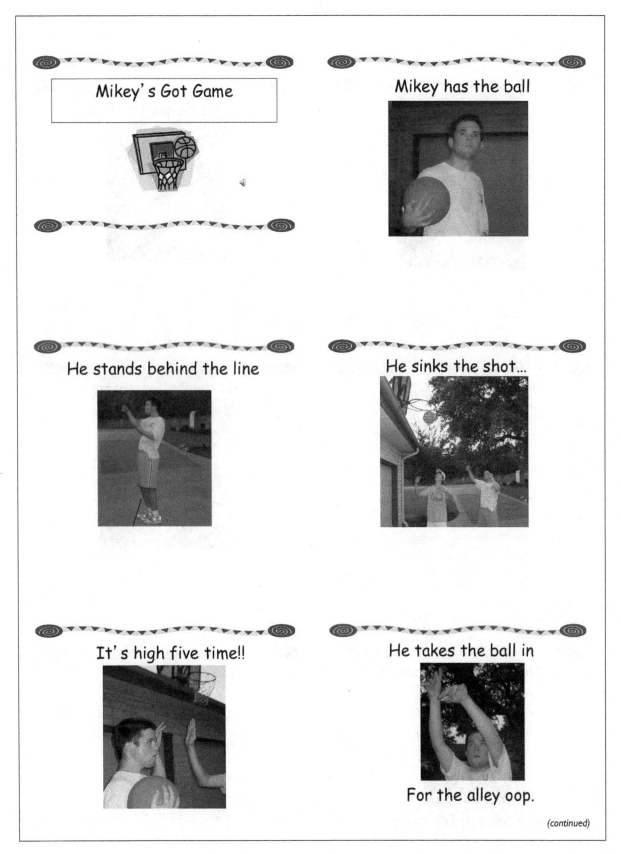

Figure 2.3.   Michael's visual story, which is set to a popular song and set up so Michael can watch on his computer. (Reprinted with permission from Michael's family.)

Figure 2.3.   *(continued)*

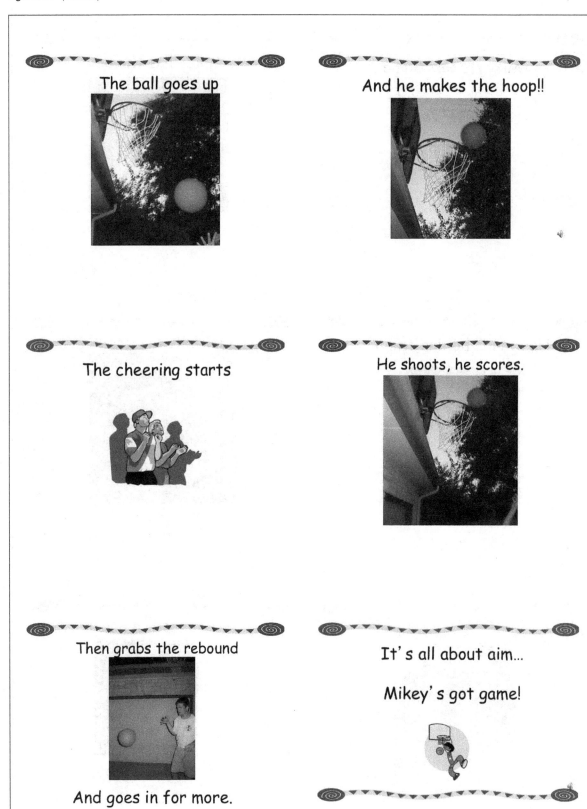

students to frequently use these skills in supportive environments. Figure 2.4 shows a paragraph Jake (one of the students featured throughout this book) wrote about himself and his strengths and his response to a question about the things that helped him overcome the difficulties he has experienced. He discusses the role of his general education peers and teachers in supporting him to be self-determining.

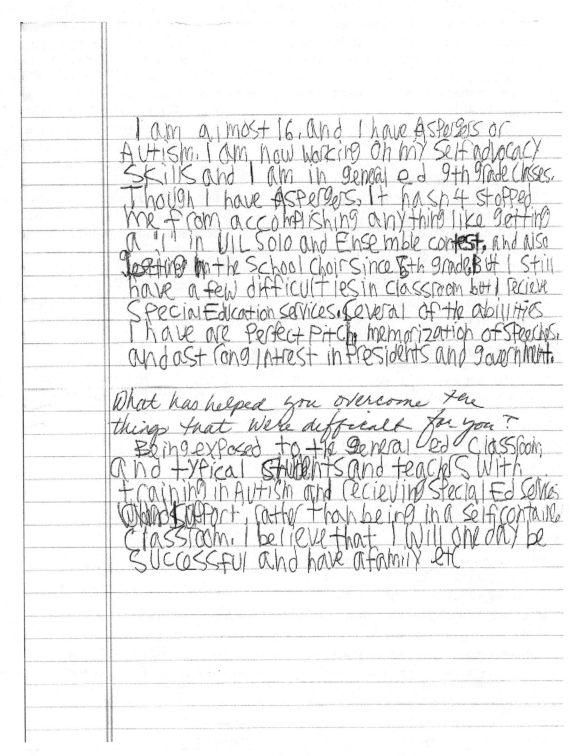

I am almost 16, and I have Aspergers or Autism. I am now working on my self advocacy Skills and I am in general ed 9th grade classes. Though I have Aspergers, it hasn't stopped me from accomplishing any thing like getting a "1" in UIL Solo and Ensemble contest, and also getting in the school choir since 8th grade. But I still have a few difficulties in classroom but I recieve Special Education services. Several of the abilities I have are perfect pitch, memorization of speeches, and a strong intrest in presidents and government.

What has helped you overcome the things that were difficult for you?
Being exposed to the general ed classroom and typical students and teachers with training in Autism and recieving special Ed servies and support, rather than being in a selfcontained classroom. I believe that I will one day be Successful and have a family etc

Figure 2.4. Jake's reflections. (Reprinted with permission from Jake's family.)

COLLABORATING WITH STUDENTS AND
FAMILIES TO PROMOTE SELF-DETERMINATION

How can we learn about and understand all of the personal and environmental factors that might influence student self-determination? Focus on building family, student, and professional partnerships around self-determination instruction (Turnbull et al., 2010). You can already see the differences in the types of supports Michael and Jake benefit from and the ways in which they express self-determination. This does not mean one of these adolescents is less self-determining. It means we must understand a variety of things about each individual to build the best supports around him or her to promote self-determination. For example, Jake's mom Jeanine knows that Jake is best able to show his knowledge of himself and his strengths and support needs (i.e., self-realization) when he can write things down and when he has question prompts in front of him (see Figure 2.4). Jake has learned this about himself over time. He will now request to write down responses or have questions written down for him. The same is true for Michael; his family blended their knowledge of his love of music, his need to see information in words and pictures, and his use of several forms of technology (e.g., computer, iPod) to identify the best way to support him to be self-determining when learning about participating in recreational events such as basketball.

Table 2.1 provides a list of questions to ask students and their families as you are learning about their views on self-determination, how they support self-determination at home, and how they think that professionals can best support self-determination. These questions should be asked during a conversational interview, but could also be added to questionnaires or surveys that are completed by students and families.

A great way to influence student self-determination is to focus on building family, student, and professional partnerships.

ACCOMMODATING INDIVIDUAL DIFFERENCES

After assessing self-determination and exploring individual and environmental characteristics that may affect self-determination, it is time to integrate this knowledge into

Table 2.1.   Starting a self-determination dialogue with families

---

1. What is your vision for the future for your family and your child?

2. What do you think defines success in adulthood?

3. How does your child learn best?

4. What supports do you provide your child at home to promote success? What works and what does not work?

5. What does self-determination mean to you and your family?

6. What does self-determined behavior look like in your home?

   a. How does your family make decisions? Who is involved?

   b. How does your family set goals? Who is involved?

   c. How does your child express his or her choices and goals? Do you talk about goals for the future at home?

   d. What types of roles does your child play at home?

   e. Have you had to advocate for your child? Does your child advocate for him- or herself? Is this important to you?

7. What role, if any, do your cultural beliefs play in how you think about self-determined behavior? Are there any family characteristics that are important for me to understand?

8. Do you actively work on teaching self-determination skills at home? If so, how?

9. Is teaching self-determination skills important to you at home and/or at school?

10. What can we do to support your and your child to achieve your goals for the future?

Sources: Erwin et al. (2009), Palmer (2010), Shogren (2012)

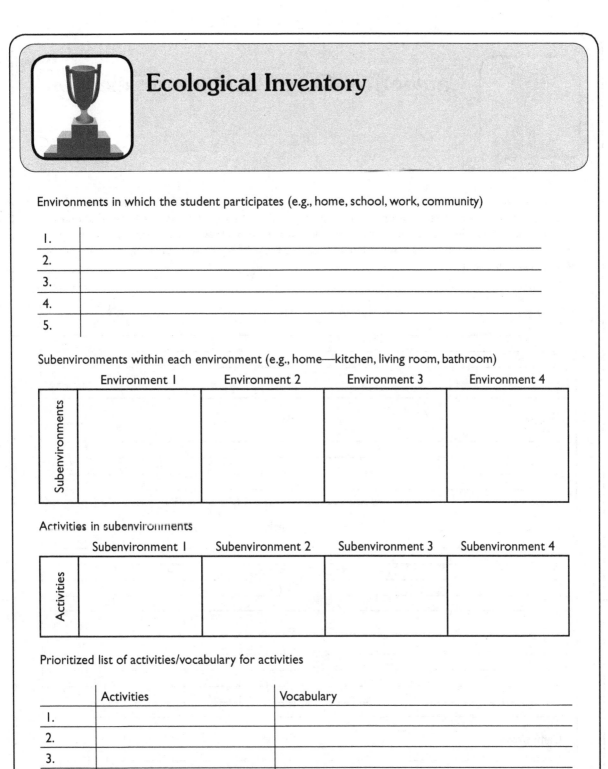

Ecological Inventory

Environments in which the student participates (e.g., home, school, work, community)

1. _____
2. _____
3. _____
4. _____
5. _____

Subenvironments within each environment (e.g., home—kitchen, living room, bathroom)

	Environment 1	Environment 2	Environment 3	Environment 4
Subenvironments				

Activities in subenvironments

	Subenvironment 1	Subenvironment 2	Subenvironment 3	Subenvironment 4
Activities				

Prioritized list of activities/vocabulary for activities

	Activities	Vocabulary
1.		
2.		
3.		
4.		
5.		

Figure 2.5. Ecological inventory.

Categorical Core Vocabulary Selection

We would like some information on common vocabulary that you use at school and home in order to develop a comprehensive inventory of language sets. Following are different categories that may fit into your life. Please help us develop a list of possible words or phrases that are commonly used in various environments within your school or home. This list will help us start building language on a communication device.

People	Places
_____	_____
_____	_____
_____	_____
_____	_____

Feelings	Food
_____	_____
_____	_____
_____	_____
_____	_____

Activities	Meals
_____	_____
_____	_____
_____	_____
_____	_____

Things	Stories
_____	_____
_____	_____
_____	_____
_____	_____

Games/toys	Other
_____	_____
_____	_____
_____	_____
_____	_____

Figure 2.6. Language inventory.

Contributed by Kim Wolowiec Fisher. *Self-Determination and Transition Planning* by
Karrie A. Shogren, Ph.D. Copyright © 2013 by Paul H. Brookes Publishing Co., Inc. All rights reserved.

developing interventions to promote self-determination. Chapters 3–6 will provide research-based strategies and practical examples of how to teach choice-making, self-management, goal-setting, and self-advocacy skills. Considering the personal characteristics and environmental factors that influence the appropriateness and potential effectiveness of the strategies is a key part of selecting the appropriate skills to teach and the strategies to use to teach these skills. Figures 1.1 and 1.2 provided a framework for thinking about these multiple factors and considering them in selecting self-determination interventions that promote the best outcomes for students. Combining feedback from students and family members on their views of self-determination and using valued outcomes and knowledge of recommended practices to teach and create opportunities for self-determination has the potential to create a win-win for everyone.

Kim Wolowiec Fisher, a former special education teacher and assistive technology specialist, highlights how self-determination became a reality for a student who used an AAC device when each of these sources of information was used to teach and create opportunities for self-determination (see Kim Wolowiec Fisher's Experiences as an Assistive Technology Specialist research box). She provides examples of how to plan with families and use diverse evidence-based instruction and assessment procedures, such as environmental inventories (Snell & Brown, 2006), to support student self-determination.

Kim Wolowiec Fisher's Experiences as an Assistive Technology Specialist

I WANT TO GO, BUT I AM SCARED, says Charlotte, an eighth-grade student, using her augmentative and alternative communication (AAC) device. Ms. Ramone, her special education teacher, replies, "Relax, Charlotte. You'll do just fine. We've practiced several times. You know you can do it, right?" YES, says Charlotte, pointing to the "yes" sign on her laptray.

A few minutes later, Charlotte and her aide, Ms. Casey, go to Charlotte's new reading class. Charlotte is joining a new inclusive language arts class and participating in a reading group with her general education peers. Charlotte utilizes a dynamic display communication device and two switches for access as her primary means of communication. Although Charlotte enjoys reading literature and relishes in the opportunity to discuss the material with her classmates, she is apprehensive about interacting with new students who are not familiar with her communication style. After Ms. Ramone had repeated discussions with Charlotte and her family and established how much they value Charlotte having opportunities to make choices, interact with peers, and take on leadership roles in inclusive, academically challenging environments—in preparation for adult life—it became clear this was the right step for Charlotte and that appropriate supports would need to be provided.

Charlotte's reading group gathers in the center of the classroom when the class begins and is ready to discuss the latest chapter of their group-read novel. Charlotte's task is to point out an important or poignant passage and discuss why it was important to her or ask a question about it to the group. The student designated as the group leader begins the discussion by reviewing what occurred in the most recent chapter and offering questions to guide the discussion. Charlotte is ready and waiting.

After three students discuss the material they prepared, the group leader looks to Charlotte and asks, "Did you find any important or poignant passages in the chapter?" Charlotte smiles and looks down at her laptray to indicate YES. The student leader does not understand, assumes Charlotte is not responding, and

(continued)

moves on to the next student. As the student begins to discuss her thoughts, everyone hears Charlotte say with her AAC device, I HAVE SOMETHING TO SAY! The group stops, shifts their gaze to Charlotte, and pauses. Charlotte smiles, giggles slightly, and then begins activating her switches in a methodical and persistent manner. Left switch two hits. Right switch one. Charlotte creates a message to share with a series of switch activations.

I DON'T LIKE START. BORING. WHY GO AMUSEMENT PARK? says Charlotte, assisted by her technology. "What was that Charlotte? Can you say it again?" says one of the group members. Charlotte accesses one of her switches again, locates the message window on her device where the created message is stored, and repeats the message. I DON'T LIKE START. BORING. WHY GO AMUSEMENT PARK? "I know! Why did they go to the amusement park anyway?" says one of Charlotte's new group members. A discussion ensues of why the characters might have gone to the amusement park and what that might foreshadow. The aide who most closely works with Charlotte monitors the situation while floating around the classroom, but does not directly intervene. Charlotte smiles.

Charlotte's success in this activity occurred after much instruction on choice and advocacy and with many supports. Charlotte had to be taught how to use her device, make choices and decisions, read and comprehend age-appropriate texts, and advocate for herself using her "attention getter" message (I HAVE SOMETHING TO SAY). She also had to be given the opportunity to participate in a new, more challenging reading class and to build relationships with her peers. Both her reading and special education teacher collaborated to identify necessary supports, including 1) relevant vocabulary added to her AAC system; 2) physical access to the classroom and to the novel (through an audiobook); and 3) preteaching about literature, asking questions, and utilizing her device to share her thoughts. Charlotte was able to participate in the reading group in the role she felt most comfortable because of these supports and the opportunity to express her needs/wants in an independent fashion.

In addition, the paraprofessional who worked with Charlotte received specific training to only assist Charlotte when absolutely necessary, giving her the opportunity to actively use her self-determination skills to gain attention, participate, and share her opinion with the group—all desired outcomes she and her family identified. Key considerations when thinking about self-determination for students such as Charlotte are both the preferences and values of Charlotte and her family. There are also practical considerations related to the activities in the environment, demands of the environment, and vocabulary that is used in those environments. In addition, her teachers did an ecological inventory of the environments when they talked to Charlotte and her family (Ecological Inventory Form, see Figure 2.5) to identify key vocabulary that could be programmed in her device (Categorical Cove Vocabulary Selection form, see Figure 2.6). This process can be used to explore environmental demands and vocabulary (or other key elements) needed for success.

Contributed by Kim Wolowiec Fisher

3

Promoting Self-Determination Skills Through Choice Making

We do not have to be told what self-determination means. We already know what it means. We already know that it is just a ten-dollar word for choice. That it is just another word for freedom. We already know that self-determination is just another word for describing a life filled with rising expectations, dignity, responsibility, and opportunity. That is just another word for having the chance to live the American Dream.

(Williams, 1989, p. 1)

I choose where to live. I like my job. I like what I do. I go to church on Sundays. I have a family. I go visit my family very often.

(Shogren and Broussard, 2011, p. 90)

The quote that opens this chapter is from a talk given by Roger Williams at a conference hosted by the Office of Special Education and Rehabilitative Services (OSERS), part of the U.S. Department of Education. The conference brought together more than 60 leaders in the disability field to plan for the future of the agency. More than half of the leaders attending the conference had disabilities, including Roger Williams. The following was written in the summary and recommendations from the meeting: "Usually, it's the professional groups, the parent organizations and government agency officials who plan for people with disabilities. It's high time you, yourselves, tell us what you need!" (OSERS, 1989, p. 3). This conference played a significant role in the emergence of self-determination as an area of emphasis in the field of special education. Between 1990 and 1996, the Office of Special Education Programs funded 26 model demonstration programs, leading to the development of definitional frameworks and interventions to promote self-determination (Ward & Kohler, 1996), many of which are discussed in this book.

Roger Williams (1989) noted that self-determination was not something new or complicated. Instead, it was about ensuring that people with disabilities be held to high expectations, treated with dignity, and provided with responsibilities and opportunities. Being able to make choices based on one's preferences and desired quality of life is fundamental to high expectations, dignity, responsibility, and opportunity. Making choices is recognized as a basic human right and a key part of the development of self-determination. Unfortunately, people with disabilities too often have restricted opportunities to make choices about their lives (Carr et al., 2002; Dunlap et al., 1994;

Houghton, Bronicki, & Guess, 1987; Stancliffe, 2001). This has likely occurred for several reasons. First, beliefs about the importance of protecting and/or controlling people with disabilities have dominated much of modern history (Smith & Wehmeyer, 2012). A lack of instruction and opportunity to participate in choice making occurs when people with disabilities are not viewed as capable of making choices. Second, methods have not been readily available to teach choice making, perhaps because of the lack of focus on teaching and creating opportunities for choice making. This has likely contributed to the research finding that special education teachers report a lack of clarity on the best ways to teach and create opportunities for choice for students with disabilities (Agran, Snow, & Swaner, 1999; Wehmeyer, Agran, & Hughes, 2000). Third, research on choice-making instruction suggests the critical importance of structured interventions that teach students how to make choices, provide multiple and repeated opportunities for choice making through the day, and allow students to experience natural consequences of their choices (Cannella, O'Reilly, & Lancioni, 2005; Lohrmann-O'Rourke & Gomez, 2001).

Research has consistently shown, however, that students with disabilities can learn and use choice-making skills to achieve valued outcomes with instruction and opportunities (Algozzine et al., 2001; Wood, Fowler, Uphold, & Test, 2005). The second quote that opened this chapter shows what choice can lead to—choosing where to live, what to do, and what relationships to emphasize—essentially being a causal agent who acts with intent to make desired things happen. The level of choice expressed by the young adult quoted at the beginning of this chapter emerged after multiple opportunities to make choices and experience consequences. Learning to identify preferences, make choices, and have diverse opportunities for choice and preference expression is fundamental to these outcomes.

Choice making is a fundamental skill that leads to self-determined behavior. This chapter introduces basic principles of expressing preferences and making choices and using strategies to infuse choice opportunities throughout instruction and supports. Examples of strategies practitioners can use to infuse choice-making opportunities throughout transition activities, with examples from real students and classrooms, are provided. The impact of choice making on transition outcomes and self-determination is illustrated.

EXPRESSING PREFERENCES AND MAKING CHOICES

Researchers have consistently identified two distinct components of the choice-making process: 1) identifying a preference and 2) engaging in behaviors that communicate the preference (i.e., the act of choosing; Reid, Parsons, & Green, 1991). Therefore, understanding what one prefers and being able to communicate those preferences are both necessary to make choices.

Identifying Preferences

How does an individual figure out what he or she prefers? How did you figure out which ice cream you liked best? Or which sandwich you preferred? Having experiences with items to determine if you like them is a key part of identifying preferences. This is true for simple choices, such as picking a favorite flavor of ice cream, and for more complex choices, such as determining a career to pursue. What strategies can be used to support students with disabilities to identify their preferences?

Self-determination isn't complicated, it's about ensuring that people with disabilities . . . are able to make choices based on their own preferences and desires.

Purpose of the Preference Assessment   It is important to understand why preferences are assessed. Lohrmann-O'Rourke, Browder, and Brown (2000) identified three reasons to conduct preference assessments.

1. Planning for the immediate context understanding students' day-to-day preferences, such as what one prefers to eat or wear, where to go for fun, and what instructional activities/materials are most engaging.

2. Planning for lifestyle enhancement supporting students to develop their knowledge of available options for work, living, continued education, and recreation. This is a key part of transition planning.

3. Planning for instruction and intervention identifying reinforcers that can be used during instruction to increase student responding.

The purpose of the preference assessment will make a difference in how you think about 1) what to include in the preference assessment, 2) where to conduct the preference assessment, 3) who will present the items/activities, and 4) how many items/activities to offer. Table 3.1 provides useful information on the factors you might need to think about. For example, if you are conducting a preference assessment for lifestyle enhancement to identify possible careers for a student, then you will want to create opportunities for the student to learn about different jobs, visit actual jobsites, and have hands-on opportunities to learn what he or she prefers. A student might think he or she wants to be a veterinarian, but until he or she sees the day-to-day activities at a clinic, he or she might not understand everything that is involved in the job. It may be another type of career involving animals that is actually in line with his or her preferences.

If you are focusing on assessing the immediate context, then emphasize exploring current routines and identifying opportunities where choice can be embedded. A great way to do this is to use the ecological inventory process discussed in Chapter 2 (see Figure 2.5). If you identify a variety of activities that a student participates in, then you can identify opportunities for him or her to choose the order of activities, peers he or she works with on activities, or materials he or she uses to complete activities. You can add in new options each day so the individual is exposed to more activities and increases his or her experiences and range of responses.

Direct versus Indirect Assessment   It is also important to think about whether the preference assessment will be a direct assessment or an indirect assessment. Hagopian, Long, and Rush (2004) described an indirect assessment as an assessment that asks others for their opinions on what people with disabilities prefer (e.g., teachers, parents, friends). A direct assessment focuses on directly observing responses that the individual with a disability makes in response to items (Hagopian et al., 2004). Direct assessments can take a variety of forms, which are covered later in this section.

An indirect assessment can be a great starting point to get information and narrow down the options that are included in a direct preference assessment (Lohrmann-O'Rourke et al., 2000). Researchers have found that it is critically important to directly assess the preferences of individuals with disabilities in addition to indirectly assessing them. Think about yourself. Is there anyone in your life, even the people that are closest to you, that could accurately identify all of your preferences, 100% of the time? Those that are close to you would likely get many things right, but would they get everything? The Research on Direct Assessment and Vocational Choices research box summarizes a research study (Martin, Woods, Sylvester, & Gardner, 2005) that documents the importance of direct

Table 3.1. Guidelines for planning for preference assessments targeting enhancing the immediate context, lifestyle enhancement, and intervention/instruction

Guideline	Immediate context	Lifestyle enhancement	Intervention/instruction
Options to offer	Determine the types of choices/decisions to be made. Assemble a list of options that are known to be preferred (e.g., interview support providers, conduct observations). Review the list to identify any similar characteristics or patterns. Assemble a list of new options based upon known preferences.	Determine the type of lifestyle decision being assessed (e.g., work, living, continued education, or recreation). Develop a profile that reflects the individual's lifestyle preferences (e.g., types of living arrangements or work conditions). Consider the person's preference for their current situation (e.g., what do they like or not like about it). Identify a range of sampling options that are consistent with the individual's lifestyle profile	Identify the target intervention or instruction situations. Assemble a list of options that are known to be preferred (e.g., interview support providers, conduct observations). Review the list to identify any similar characteristics or patterns. Assemble a list of new options based on known preferences. Consider whether the items have a discrete ending and are manageable for the instructional environment. Consider if the item should be used contingently or not.
When and where will sampling options occur?	Identify locations and routines in which the target choice-making opportunities will typically occur. Embed and distribute opportunities for the student to experience options throughout the person's day. Offer a pool of daily options from which the individual can choose. Create opportunities for new experiences that expand currently available options. Continually introduce new options for sampling over time.	Arrange opportunities to visit actual target sites (e.g., veterinarian's office). Provide repeated opportunities during typical times to experience the sampling option (e.g., visiting a veterinarian's office during work hours). Probe over time to determine if the option selected continues to be preferred.	Identify the intervention or instructional routines in which reinforcement or antecedents will occur. Offer a pool of daily options from which the individual can choose. Create opportunities for new experiences that expand currently available options. Continually introduce new options for sampling over time.
Who will present the sampling option?	Identify persons familiar to the individual and typical to the routine. Consider having several individuals present options to determine if preferences are durable across people or are person specific.	Identify persons familiar to the individual and typical to the routine. Consider having several individuals present options to determine if preferences are durable across people or are person specific. Involve individuals affiliated with the lifestyle preference (e.g., staff at veterinarian's office).	Identify a person familiar to the individual and typical to the routine. Consider having several individuals present options to determine if preferences are durable across people or are person specific.
How many options to offer?	When the individual has not yet acquired a choice response, consider offering one option at a time Use paired or group presentations for individuals with more choice-making experience. Consider the nature of the sampling option to determine if the item or event is better sampled individually or paired with other options.	Individually sample options to identify a manageable pool of options. Use paired or group presentations to make final selections.	When the student has not yet acquired a choice response consider offering one option at a time Use paired or group presentations for individuals with more choice-making experience. Consider the nature of the sampling option to determine if the item or event is better sampled individually or paired with other options.
What response will be observed?	Ask support providers or others who know the person well how they typically communicate preferences and nonpreferences. Define idiosyncratic responses that the individual currently uses to express preference; these may be either a discrete behavior or multiple behaviors. For some individuals, it may be necessary to shape an existing response or teach a new response (e.g., symbol identification) to promote preference expression. Include definitions of nonpreference (e.g., lack of response, problem behavior).		

From Lohrmann-O'Rourke, S., Browder, D.M., & Brown, F. (2000). Guidelines for conducting socially valid systematic preference assessments. *Journal of the Association for Persons with Severe Handicaps*, 25, 45–46; reprinted by permission.

assessment by highlighting differences in vocational choices made by individuals with disabilities and support providers.

Direct Assessment   Hagopian and colleagues (2004) characterized direct assessment methods as approach based or engagement based. You might put a single item (single-item presentation), two items (paired-item presentation), or multiple items (multiple-item presentation or mass-trial presentation) in front of the student during an approach-based assessment. This type of assessment works well when you are assessing preferences for foods, clothing, or other items in which the student does not need to engage with an item for a long period of time. You can then see if the student approaches the item (e.g., reaches for it, says he or she wants it, activates a microswitch). Engagement-based assessments are more useful when students need to engage with a task for a longer period of time, such as when you are assessing preferences for vocational activities, recreation and leisure activities, and instructional materials. You can measure how long the student engages in the activity or with the materials and look for differences across activities to explore which items are preferred. It is important to define engagement for each student specific to the purpose of the assessment. You might look to see which instructional materials keep the student's attention for longer periods of time, which vocational activities lead to higher levels of on-task behavior, or which video games the student plays the longest. All of these could be measures of engagement for an individual student.

Response Mode   "How will the student respond?" is one of the most important questions you need to ask, regardless of the type of assessment you are conducting. Some students might vocalize, saying, "I like the turkey sandwich best" or "I want to be a veterinarian." Other students might look at the turkey sandwich or pick a computer video of activities in a veterinarian's office using a computer mouse after watching several DVDs of occupational activities. You might also look at multiple response modes (Agran & Krupp, 2011). For example, you might start vocational assessments by giving a student a paper-and-pencil vocational assessment or asking them to verbally talk about the activities they like to do. You could then do an indirect assessment and ask key support people what they think the individual might like. You could then have the student watch computer video clips of different jobs and select those that he or she prefers. Finally, you could have the student visit actual job locations and measure his or her engagement and productivity in the real-world job situation.

The *Choose and Take Action* curriculum (Martin, Huber Marshall, & Wray, 2004; see the Research on Direct Assessment and Vocational Choices research box) uses multiple response modes and opportunities to promote self-determined vocational assessment. Students evaluate their preferences for vocational activities by watching computer videos and participating in community-based experiences, graphing their preferences over time, and learning to adjust their expectations regarding the job that they want. Martin, Mithaug, Oliphint, Husch, and Frazier (2002) found that young adults had more positive job outcomes when they went through the self-directed process, learning about their preferences, making choices and decisions, and learning to self-regulate their behavior.

Abstractness   The abstractness of the materials that are being used for preference assessments and making choices is another factor that is important to consider. We are increasingly able to take pictures or record videos of any aspect of an environment with digital and computer technology and use it to assess preferences. Sometimes it is much easier

Research on Direct
Assessment and Vocational Choices

Martin, Woods, Sylvester, and Gardner (2005) conducted a study using a self-directed vocational assessment process called Choose and Take Action (Martin, Huber Marshall, & Wray, 2004) to examine the degree to which parents, teachers, and other support providers agreed with the choices made by individuals with disabilities in terms of their vocational preferences. The Choose and Take Action software includes 20-second video clips of a variety of entry-level jobs. The student can watch between 8 and 32 videos clips during an assessment. The video clips are randomly paired with each other (a paired-item assessment). The student watches two videos at a time and picks the video he or she prefers. The videos are paired with each other until a top choice emerges. Next, the individual is asked if he or she wants to watch or try the job in the community. The program then creates a plan that shows the top settings (e.g., greenhouse, hospital, office), activities (e.g., filing, cleaning, taking care of animals), and characteristics (e.g., many people, outside, noisy) from the videos selected. The student reevaluates his or her work preferences and experiences, going through a process of regulating his or her own behavior and learning, after watching or trying the preferred settings, activities, and characteristics in the actual community site.

Martin et al. (2005) had eight individuals with cognitive disabilities go through the Choose and Take Action program. These individuals had a variety of response modes; several interacted with the program using a keyboard and mouse, one used a microswitch, and two used eye gaze and verbalizations to communicate because of a consistent lack of an augmentative and alternative communication device. Martin and colleagues then had support providers (i.e., teachers, parents, support staff) independently complete the Chose and Take Action rating forms to rank order their perceptions of the target individual's preferred setting, activities, and characteristics.

The researchers examined agreement between the rankings of support providers and target individuals. They examined the degree to which the top three settings, activities, and characteristics were the same, regardless of rank. They found that there was only 36% agreement for setting, 18% agreement for activity, and 33% agreement for characteristics. They then compared the top choice across the three areas and found even lower agreement, with 18% agreement for setting and 0% agreement for activity and characteristics.

These agreement values are low and suggest a lack of congruence in the ratings of preferred vocational activities made by individuals with disabilities and support providers. It is important to note that the majority of the target sample was relatively young. The age range was 18–48 years, with the majority between the ages of 18 and 23 years. Some of the target participants had not yet experienced any of these vocational settings, activities, or characteristics prior to watching the videos and going into the communities. It is possible that the support providers did not have a clear idea of what to expect—some of the responses of the target individuals likely surprised them.

Although information from support providers, especially family members, is important when conducting preference assessments and supporting individuals to make choices and decisions about the future, this research shows that it is important to assess preferences from the perspective of individuals with disabilities themselves. This is why supporting students to develop their skills and creating opportunities such as those described in this chapter are so important.

to show pictures of turkey sandwiches or movies of job activities to assess preferences. But, we have to remember a few things. First, we have to be sure the student understands the connection between the picture/movie and the actual activity. If students have never eaten a turkey sandwich, then they might not understand what the picture of the turkey sandwich means. Ensuring that students with severe disabilities understand the correspondence between items and images is important (Lohrmann-O'Rourke et al., 2000). As students have experience with technology (and as technology continues to improve), they can use technology to express their preferences and make simple and complex choices.

Some students, such as Michael, one of the students featured throughout this book, may not use many words to communicate. Technology can be a great way for Michael and others to make choices and express preferences. Figure 3.1 shows a screen shot from Michael's computer. Michael can interact with the pictures because his computer is a touch screen. He also uses a similar program on his iPod Touch, called Photo Mess, which is much smaller but portable. All of the pictures in the background represent Michael's schedule, and he can move pictures around to communicate his preferences. Mike and Kay, his parents, and other members of his support system are constantly taking pictures or identifying pictures that can be included on his device and organizing them into categories, such as self-help, community, chores, jobs, indoor activities, and exercise. Picture strips for each category can be pulled up on the screen to locate individual pictures that can then be dragged onto the screen and positioned into a schedule by a parent or member of his support system.

Two or more pictures can also be pulled up to the front of the screen and enlarged and Michael can make a choice about what he wants to do (e.g., take a walk, swim), and he can either point to the picture of the preferred activity or drag the picture he does not want to do off the screen. Kay says he was initially more interested in removing the

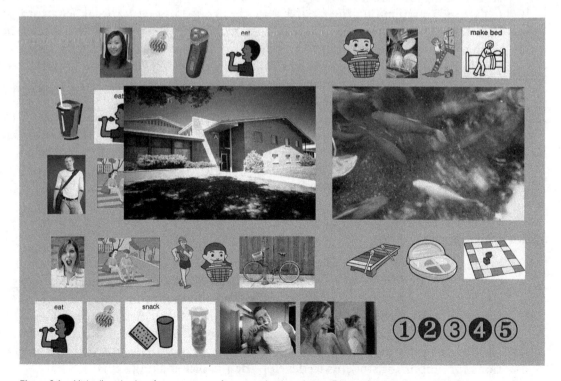

Figure 3.1. Michael's technology for expressing preferences and making choices. (Reprinted with permission from Michael's family. The Picture Communication Symbols ©1981–2013 by Mayer-Johnson LLC. All Rights Reserved Worldwide. Used with permission. Boardmaker™ is a trademark of Mayer-Johnson LLC.)

less preferred choice, but he has been more consistently selecting his preferred choice by pointing. Once Michael finishes an activity, the picture can be resized (either by pinching it with two fingers or with a verbal "zoom out" command) by his support person and placed back into the schedule. Michael then receives a token for completing the activity by dragging a picture of a token and placing it on top of the activity picture on the computer screen.

His sister Christy, an integral part of his support system, says that it was sometimes hard when he was first learning about making choices and organizing his schedule because he would want to get rid of pictures that showed work-related activities, especially new activities that he had not mastered. His support system used preference assessment (for the purpose of planning for instruction and intervention) to identify reinforcers that were motivating for Michael in completing tasks. First, these were edible reinforcers, then tokens came to have a reinforcing value so that Michael could earn things he enjoyed, such as 5–10 minutes of basketball, beanbag toss, or music. Michael generally keeps those activities in his daily schedule without problems because he sees the tokens stacked on the schedule and understands he will need to complete five activities to earn a favorite activity. He still has choice in terms of the order that he does things—even at work—which gives him more control and improves his performance.

Repeated Assessment   Michael's preferences may change over time. Each of us can probably think of careers that we may have wanted to pursue as youth that we later realized did not align with our interests and preferences as we had more experiences. We can probably also think of food or clothes that we loved at one point in our lives, but cannot imagine eating or wearing now. Therefore, it is important to frequently reassess preferences. Researchers have found that changes in preferences can be idiosyncratic to students, meaning that some students' preferences, especially in the immediate context (e.g., food, instructional materials), can change from week to week (Stafford, Alberto, Fredrick, Heflin, & Heller, 2002). Other researchers have found that preferences can change with ongoing experience and exposure to various career options, particularly for youth making career-related choices (Martin et al., 2002). It may be important to assess preferences on a weekly or even daily basis when the purpose of preference assessment is related to enhancing immediate context or instruction and intervention. This can be done by offering a pool of items for the individual to choose from with regard to meals, activities, and tasks. It is a bit more complicated when focusing on lifestyle enhancement, but ongoing probes should be built in to assess the degree to which the individual still prefers a given job and the degree to which other transition goals (e.g., going to college, living in an apartment) remain congruent with the individual's vision for his or her future.

Making Choices

Students are able to meaningfully express their preferences when they are making a choice. It is important to provide repeated opportunities for students to make choices so they can learn what they prefer and so we can work to incorporate these preferences into transition services for students with disabilities. IDEA 2004 (PL 108-446) requires that transition services be based on the individual child's needs, taking into account the child's strengths, preferences, and interests. Shevin and Klein provided five recommendations for supporting students to develop their choice-making skills.

1.   Incorporate student choice as an early step in the instruction process.

2. Increase the number of decisions related to a given activity that the student makes.

3. Increase the number of domains in which decisions are made.

4. Raise the significance in terms of risk and long-term consequences of the choices the student makes.

5. Clear communication with the student concerning areas of possible choice and the limits within which choices can be made (1984, p. 164).

Shevin and Klein (1984) and other contemporary researchers consistently stated that simply providing isolated choice opportunities is not enough. Students have to be provided with repeated opportunities to make choices in order for them to become self-determined and use choice-making skills to act as a causal agent over their lives. Jake, the other student featured throughout this book, has been supported by his parents and teachers to make choices throughout his life, ranging from relatively low-risk choices about what to wear when he was younger to what extracurricular activities to pursue as he got older (he chose choir). Jake noted, "the choices got more complicated" in high school. Jake was an active member of his IEP team and participated in making choices and decisions about what classes to take. Jake wanted to take a journalism class. One of the members of his IEP team, however, was very worried about how Jake would do in a journalism class and encouraged him not to take the class. Jake received extended time on assignments as a reasonable accommodation, but this would not work in journalism class because articles have to be ready when the paper is published. And, doing interviews requires strong social skills, which can sometimes be an area where Jake needs supports. But, Jake really wanted to take the class. He talked to his mother, they reviewed the pros and cons, and Jeanine said, "Jake was in charge. It was his decision." Jake really thought the class would help prepare him for writing in college. Plus, he considered it more interesting than the other options. Jake made the decision to take the class. Jake did have some struggles at first—meeting deadlines, working as a team, and recognizing social nuances. But, Jake found his niche with reporting on sporting events. He can remember sports facts. He knew all about his high school team's standings, points scored, leading rushers, and so forth. He was able to quickly engage with the coaches and players, and his extensive knowledge really assisted him in story writing. Jake excelled, and Figure 3.2 shows a framed picture of a newspaper article that Jake wrote that the football coach signed thanking Jake for his great reporting. One of Jake's teachers had the picture framed, knowing it was something he would treasure. Jake was able to excel because he had the opportunity to make choices and decisions about this class. He also built writing and social skills that have assisted him in his community college courses. Plus, he got to study a challenging area of the curriculum that he was very interested in and turned in outstanding stories for the newspaper.

In order to support students to be truly self-determined, repeated opportunities to make choices must be provided.

Students use decision-making skills when they begin to evaluate the pros and cons of their choices and use this information to guide them in making a decision about the best choice. Making effective decisions involves 1) identifying alternative courses of action, 2) identifying the possible consequences of each action, 3) assessing the probability of each consequence occurring, 4) choosing the best alternative, and 5) implementing the decision (Furby & Beyth Marom, 1992).

Be creative when thinking about constructing opportunities for choice making and decision making—they can be embedded everywhere. Opportunities for choices

Figure 3.2.   The outcomes of Jake's choices. (Reprinted with permission from Jake's family.)

and decisions can be embedded in academic activities, in transition activities, in social activities, and across home and school environments. Heather Haynes, a former general and special education teacher and current Assistant Professor of Special Education, provided an example of how a teacher she supervised, "Ms. Rodriquez," was able to embed choice in academic activities for students with learning disabilities in the Promoting Choice Making in Academic Settings with Students with Learning Disabilities research box.

Students can choose (and examine the pros and cons of different choices):

- Between activities
- The order of activities
- Not to participate in an activity
- Location of an activity
- Materials/reinforcers
- Goals and objectives
- Within the context of education/transition planning

Figure 3.3 includes a checklist that teachers can use as a starting point to brainstorm opportunities for choice in their classroom and in their activities with students.

Promoting Choice Making in Academic Settings with Students with Learning Disabilities

Ms. Rodriguez was very concerned about a struggling student in her collaboratively taught seventh-grade math class. Abel was born in Africa, and his native language is an African dialect. He has expressed a desire to become a professional soccer player or pursue an occupation related to athletics. He has been in the district for a number of years. Abel had a learning disability and received math instruction both in the seventh-grade general education math class and in a recovery room. In addition to number sense, equations, and problem-solving skills in math, he was working on eliminating incorrect answers and using a calculator. Abel was demonstrating a lot of frustration (e.g., off-task behavior, disrupting the class) with completing academic assignments and had occasional externalizing behaviors in class. Ms. Rodriquez was not exactly sure what to do to support Abel.

Ms. Rodriguez and the IEP team reviewed Abel's goals, accommodations, and modifications. She reflected on academic and behavioral reports and records after reviewing the IEP. She had several conversations with Abel about personal goals and preferences. Ms. Rodriquez thought that it was important for Abel to become more self-determined and feel like he had the ability to complete work in class and pursue his goals. She decided to develop and provide an intervention on choice making. She felt that this intervention would help teach self-determination skills, enable Abel to feel like he was more in control of his environment and learning, address and reinforce positive behavior, and could be provided in the context of math instruction in both the general education and recovery math class.

Ms. Rodriquez began outlining possible choices that could be provided to Abel during math instruction. He must be familiar with the options available and be provided regular, consistent choice-making opportunities in order for the intervention to be successful. Ms. Rodriquez built in additional time in her lesson plans for modeling and reinforcing specific choice-making skills within the math content. She used the lesson plan form to get started (Choice Making Checklist, see Figure 3.3). She decided to select one initial choice making opportunity to work on—having Abel select which learning strategy to apply when completing assignments and activities. She planned to build in other opportunities (e.g., choosing who to work with, choosing the order of activities) over time if the choice-making intervention was effective for Abel.

Ms. Rodriquez first taught Abel two learning strategies with a math focus. She decided to teach the DRAW strategy and the FIND strategy, which are part of the strategic instruction model. She provided instruction during the first week during Abel's daily time in the recovery room. Ms. Rodriquez reinforced the newly learned strategies in the general education classroom the following week. She then provided Abel with a small disk to keep on his desk while working. She wrote DRAW on one side and FIND on the other. Abel could pick which strategy he wanted to work with during independent work time by placing the corresponding side of the disk up. Ms. Rodriquez and the paraprofessional then supported Abel to use his chosen strategy when he was working on problems.

The team saw an immediate impact of Abel having choice over the learning strategy. He was more engaged with learning and was less frustrated when trying to solve problems with which he struggled.

Contributed by Heather Haynes.

Choice-Making Checklist

Student: _____ Class: _____

Directions: Once you have identified a student who will benefit from choice-making instruction and intervention, identify the content area and options available. These options can be integrated into content instruction and should reflect student input and preferences. Consistent, regular opportunities for practice should be provided and monitored. When providing this intervention it is important to teach, reinforce, and model choice-making activities. Use the form below to brainstorm ideas and identify appropriate options for the choice-making instruction and intervention.

Choice opportunities	Ideas
Choice of activity	
Choice to participate (or not participate) in specific activity	
Choice to end an activity	
Choice of learning strategy	
Choice of partner(s)	
Choice of method to complete an activity	
Choice of order of activities	

Figure 3.3. Choice-making checklist.

Contributed by Heather Haynes. *Self-Determination and Transition Planning* by Karrie A. Shogren, Ph.D. Copyright © 2013 by Paul H. Brookes Publishing Co., Inc. All rights reserved.

Reviews of the Research on the Relationship
Between Choice Making and Valued Outcomes

Numerous reviews on the relationship between choice and academic, vocational, and behavioral outcomes have been conducted. Each of these reviews had different purposes and included different subsets of the literature on the impact of choice-making interventions. The findings from two reviews that broadly looked at the choice literature are highlighted. Kern and colleagues (1998) examined studies published between 1975 and 1996 that focused on interventions that used choice to increase appropriate behaviors or decrease inappropriate behaviors. They found 14 studies that could be grouped in three areas, promoting choice as an antecedent intervention in 1) vocational or domestic activities; 2) academic activities; and 3) leisure, recreation, or social activities. One hundred and ten individuals with disabilities were included across the 14 studies, and most were adolescents or young adults. The majority of participants had labels of intellectual or developmental disabilities, although a subset of participants had labels of emotional or behavior disorders. Many of the studies compared the participants' behavior when choice was provided and not provided (choice versus no-choice conditions). For example, in the vocational domain individuals were given a choice of which of two nonpreferred activities to complete at a jobsite (only one needed to be completed) or when to begin a task. In the academic domain, individuals were given choice over the book they read for class or the order they completed activities when activities could be completed in any order. In the leisure, recreation, and social domains, individuals were given choice over what to watch on television and with whom to play. The majority of individuals across all of these studies demonstrated more positive outcomes when choice opportunities were provided—this was true across age, disability labels, and activities. Kern and colleagues suggest this outcome indicates "considerable generality in the pertinence of the research and the favorable findings" (p. 166).

Shogren, Faggella-Luby, Bae, and Wehmeyer (2004) examined the research that explored the impact of choice-making opportunities on behavioral outcomes. The authors identified 14 single-subject studies that implemented one of two types of choice-making interventions—providing students with choice in the order of completing tasks (62% of studies) or in whether to complete a task (38% of studies). These interventions occurred during academic, vocational, and daily living activities. The studies included 30 participants ranging in age from 4 to 50 years, with an average age of 10.4 years. Diverse disability labels were represented in the studies, including emotional disturbance (17%), autism (23%), developmental disabilities (13%), attention-deficit/hyperactivity disorder (13%), and intellectual disability (13%). Two thirds of treatment data points improved over baseline data across the studies, indicating that providing choice opportunities led to reductions in the problem behavior demonstrated by individuals with disabilities while participating in the choice opportunities. Although these results were impressive, the authors noted that the meaningfulness of the choices provided and the degree to which the choice interventions promoted lasting, comprehensive lifestyle change and self-determination needed to be further considered in the literature.

These reviews do suggest, however, that making relatively small changes to the environment (e.g., providing choice in the order in which tasks are completed or which task is completed on a given day) can lead to significant positive outcomes for individuals with disabilities. These types of choice-making opportunities can lay the foundation for introducing more choice opportunities and raising the significance of these opportunities over time, enabling students to become self-determined.

IMPACT OF CHOICE AND PREFERENCE ON OUTCOMES

This chapter has presented several strategies that can be used to assess preferences and create opportunities for students to make choices. But, the logical question is "So what?" Why does this matter for students with disabilities?

First, making choices is a basic human right and a key part of development for children and youth with and without disabilities. Second, researchers have found that providing choice opportunities to students with disabilities has significant, positive effects on academic, employment, and behavioral outcomes. For example, researchers have found that simply providing students a choice of the order in the completion of instructional activities can increase academic responses and decrease problem behaviors in students with a wide range of disabilities (Cole & Levinson, 2002; Jolivette, Wehby, & Canale, 2001; Martin, Mithaug, Cox, et al., 2003; Seybert, Dunlap, & Ferro, 1996). Researchers have also linked choice making to positive employment and transition outcomes, suggesting a relationship between choice and productivity (Lancioni, O'Reilly, & Oliva, 2002) and job tenure (Martin, Mithaug, Husch, Frazier, & Marshall, 2003). The Reviews of the Research on the Relationship Between Choice Making and Valued Outcomes research box further summarizes reviews of the literature on the relationship between choice making and valued outcomes.

Although choice making is a fundamental skill for expressing self-determined behavior, choice making is not synonymous with self-determination. Agran and Krupp (2011) cautioned teachers and support providers against thinking that choice making is the desired outcome. Agran and Krupp wrote, "Choice making initiates the self-determination process and provokes greater self-regulation by allowing individuals to make choices, act on these choices, and evaluate the resultant consequences. Choice-making is a means to achieve self-determination" (p. 574).

> *Although choice making is a fundamental skill for expressing self-determined behavior, choice making is not synonymous with self-determination.*

Agran and Krupp (2011) emphasized that choice alone does not define self-determined behavior. This is particularly important to remember for students with severe disabilities because a large majority of self-determination instruction research for this population focuses exclusively on choice (Algozzine et al., 2001). Students with severe disabilities (as all students) can develop choice-making skills, but they can also develop all of the other self-determination skills discussed in this text with the right supports. Choice-making instruction and opportunities provide an entry point for self-determination for all students, but teaching and creating opportunities for students to develop other critical skills (such as those discussed in the following chapters) are also important to enable students to become self-determining.

4

Promoting Skills Leading to Enhanced Self-Determination Through Self-Management

It's like taking the bus. I always stick with my schedule so I know what I am doing at certain times. My schedule helps me do things.

(Shogren and Broussard, 2011, p. 91)

If the children do it themselves it is much easier.

(Shogren, Lang, Machalicek, Rispoli, and O'Reilly, 2011, p. 94)

Self-management skills are critical to self-determination. Teaching and creating opportunities for students to learn strategies that allow them to manage their own learning and behavior builds the foundation for causal agency (i.e., being the person that intentionally makes things happen to achieve desired outcomes). Self-management skills, also called student-directed learning strategies, enable students to become self-regulated learners, one of the essential characteristics of self-determined behavior. Self-regulated learners are those who can "examine their environments and their repertoires of response for coping with those environments to make decisions about how to act, to act, to evaluate the desirability of the outcomes of the actions, and to review those plans as necessary" (Whitman, 1990, p. 347). Teaching self-directed learning strategies gives students the skills to know how to prompt, monitor, and evaluate their behavior, which are skills essential to self-regulation and self-determination.

The quote that opens this chapter comes from an interview project with self-advocates with intellectual disability on what self-determination means in their lives (Shogren & Broussard, 2011). This young adult was discussing how his self-determination skills enabled him to navigate in the community and get to work and to his adult education classes, and see his friends and family. He learned to ride the bus with help from teachers, family, and his support system. He did this by applying self-management skills, including those discussed in this chapter, to find out how to navigate to the bus stop, prompt himself to use his bus pass to pay the fare, monitor how many stops he needed to travel to get to his location, and evaluate things that went well and not so well on his trip. This took many instructional sessions, learning opportunities, and supports, but now this young man is able to navigate around his community with the support of self-management strategies.

Students learn to adjust their behavior to achieve desired outcomes across environments when they have opportunities to apply student-directed learning strategies. Mithaug and colleagues (Mithaug, 1993, 1996; Mithaug, Campeau, & Wolman, 2003; Wolman et al., 1994) emphasized the importance of "just-right" matches. Just-right matches are those in which students are able to match their capacities to existing opportunities. Not every situation leads to a just-right match, however. All of us have probably gotten lost when transferring buses or trying to follow directions in the car. These situations represent a mismatch between our capacity and opportunity. But, these "not-right" matches create learning opportunities. We learn what we need to do to adjust our learning or behavior to experience just-right matches. Self-management strategies are a key part of this learning. The young man whose quote opened this chapter experienced this. At first, he struggled to figure out how to identify the bus he was supposed to get on, transfer buses, and walk to the place he needed to be after getting off the bus. For a long time, another person had to ride with him and deliver prompts during each step of the process. But, his support team built up an innovative self-management system for him so that he could learn to prompt, monitor, and regulate riding the bus. He learned to follow a series of pictures that guided him to the bus stop, to check off the number of stops the bus had made so that he could get off at the right location, and to evaluate how many people he talked to on the bus to build his social skills to develop natural supports for when he had problems on the bus. This led to the bus becoming a just-right match.

Using self-management skills to promote just-right matches of capacity and opportunity can lead to benefits for the individual with a disability as well as those that are in his or her support circles. The second quote at the start of this chapter is from a teacher who was involved in a research project comparing the use of student-directed learning strategies with more traditional teacher-directed strategies (e.g., token reinforcement system) in which the teacher is in charge of prompting, monitoring, and evaluating student behavior (Shogren et al., 2011). This research project found that both student-directed and teacher-directed strategies were successful in improving students' classroom behavior and engagement in classroom activities related to math, science, and literacy. But, the teacher was much more excited about the student-directed learning strategies. Not only did she feel that the students were learning more about how to manage their own behavior, but she also felt that it reduced the demands on her time. She did not have to watch every student and try to stay on track with acknowledging and reinforcing each good behavior; instead, the students learned what good behavior was and how to reinforce themselves. Students can actually experience more consistent consequences for their behavior when they self-reinforce, which can lead to greater improvements (Wehmeyer et al., 2007).

These quotes demonstrate the potential benefits of self-management strategies. Several types of self-management strategies that can be implemented with students with disabilities to promote positive outcomes are described in this chapter. These strategies include antecedent cue regulation, self-monitoring, self-reinforcement, and self-evaluation. A description of the steps practitioners can follow to implement each strategy is provided as well as examples of how these strategies have been implemented to teach and support valued outcomes.

TEACHING SELF-MANAGEMENT SKILLS

This section talks about four strategies that enable students to self-regulate their behavior and learning. Antecedent cue regulation is the first strategy and can be implemented before a behavior, task, or activity to enable an individual to understand how to complete the behavior, task, or activity. For example, using a recipe while cooking is an antecedent strategy. The recipe provides step-by-step instructions that prompt and guide you through completing the task. The last three strategies can be thought of as consequent strategies—strategies that we implement after a behavior, task, or activity to support us to understand if we completed the behavior, task, or activity (self-monitoring), how we did, and if we need to do anything different (self-evaluation), and to recognize ourselves for completing it (self-reinforcement). These strategies are critical to adjusting our behavior and getting closer to just-right matches between capacities and opportunities.

Antecedent Cue Regulation

Antecedent cue regulation is a self-management strategy that has been extensively used with students with disabilities. This strategy involves providing a cue that enables students to guide themselves through the initiation of steps in an activity or task. Antecedent cues can include picture prompts, audio prompts, tactile prompts, and written prompts. All of us use antecedent cues. Each time we write a to-do list for ourselves, we are creating a series of written prompts to guide us through tasks that have to be completed. If you use a GPS system in your car, then this system orally and visually prompts you to get from point A to point B. It is becoming easier to build this form of support into the lives of students with disabilities because of increased access to technology, including tablet devices, iPods, and digital cameras.

It is important to identify the level of detail we need in our antecedent cues, the type of prompt that works best for us (e.g., visual, auditory, written), and the best way to present the information. Each of us probably uses varying levels of specificity in our personal to-do lists. Some individuals may break down each item on the list into a series of substeps detailing what needs to be done to complete the activity. Others may organize their written prompts at a higher level. Some of us may prefer oral and visual cues from our GPS (global positioning system); others may turn off the oral cues and simply use the visual ones. Some of us may prefer GPS, whereas others may prefer printed directions and maps.

Agran, King-Sears, Wehmeyer, and Copeland (2003) suggested the following steps in developing antecedent cue regulation systems for students.

1. Select a target behavior, activity, task, or routine. What is the activity you want to support the student to complete?

2. Break down the behavior, activity, task, or routine. Task analyze the activity, routine, or task and figure out what steps need prompts.

3. Select a type of prompt (e.g., picture, audio, tactile, written). What types of prompts does the student respond to best? Is a combination of prompts (e.g., visual and audio) needed?

4. Create a prompt for each step. Develop a prompt specific to each step based on the task analysis and type of prompt selected.

5. Decide how the prompt will be presented to the student. Figure out how you will present the prompts. Will you load them onto an iPad? Will you create a booklet with pictures? Will you record an mp3 file?

Researchers have used antecedent cue regulation to teach an array of skills to students with disabilities, including social skills (Hughes et al., 2000), transition skills (Davies, Stock, Holloway, & Wehmeyer, 2010; Van Laarhoven, Kraus, Karpman, Nizzi, & Valentino, 2010), employment skills (Davies, Stock, & Wehmeyer, 2002b, 2003), and academic skills (Cihak, Wright, & Ayres, 2010). The support team for Michael, one of the students featured throughout the book, frequently creates antecedent cue regulation systems for him to use. Figure 4.1 shows an example for doing the laundry, a task he was learning to complete at

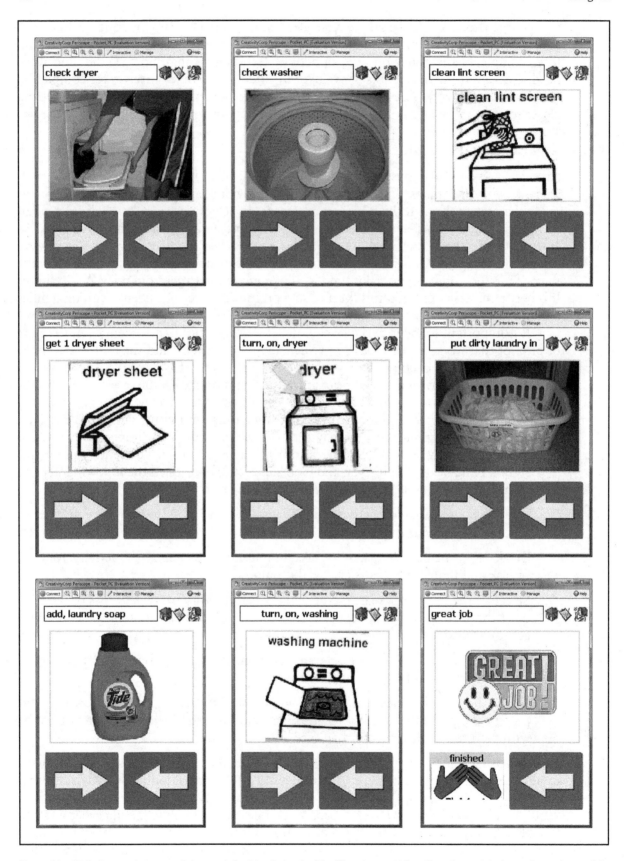

Figure 4.1. Michael's antecedent cue regulation system for doing the laundry. (*Note:* The voice personality will say the words in the text box at the top of the screen when the picture is pressed. Reprinted with permission from Michael's family and Kiba Technologies.)

home. This task is loaded on Michael's Cyrano II communication device so that he can easily carry it with him as he is going through the task. Like many of the research-based, technology-driven prompting systems (Davies, Stock, & Wehmeyer, 2002a; Davies et al., 2002b), this system prompts Michael to complete each step of the task by showing him a picture of himself correctly doing the task with a corresponding verbal prompt. He pushes arrows on his touchscreen to guide him through each step of the task, and he is provided feedback by the system on his performance of each step and at the end of the task.

Jake, the other student featured throughout the book, needs slightly different antecedent cue regulation supports. To target Jake's goals related to social skills, his mom, Jeanine, developed an antecedent cuing system to help Jake invite friends to do something. Jake was making friends at school but did not understand how to go to the next step of inviting them to do something outside of school. The script shown in Figure 4.2 helped him learn how to do this in addition to providing a tool for him to record what he decided to do (or self-monitor).

Self-Monitoring

Self-monitoring is the first consequent strategy. Researchers (Agran et al., 2003; Mace, Belfiore, & Hutchinson, 2001) commonly identify two aspects of self-monitoring: 1) self-assessment and 2) self-recording. Both skills are necessary to successfully self-monitor. The student self-assesses by learning to reliably identify whether a target behavior has occurred. The student self-records by learning to record the occurrence or nonoccurrence of their behavior. Figure 4.3 shows 10 steps that teachers can follow to teach students to self-assess and self-record. These 10 steps can be grouped into three broad categories: 1) identifying the behavior, 2) identifying the self-monitoring system, and 3) teaching the student to use the self-monitoring system.

Members of the student's support team can think about behaviors that the student needs to learn to more proficiently perform and that might have an impact across

---

Hello, this is Jake.

May I speak to _____ (name of friend), please?

Hi, _____ (name of friend). This is Jake.

Would you like to:

❏ Go to _____ (place) with me _____ (when) at _____ (time)?
   My mom or dad and I can pick you up if you like.

❏ Come over to my house to _____ (play a game, watch a movie, ride bikes)

❏ Have a sleepover at my house on _____ (day)?

(You can invite friends to do a lot of things, either at your house, their house, or somewhere else. You will need to let them know the day, date, time, and place.)

If your friend says he or she would like to do the activity you asked, you can say something such as, "Great! I need to ask my mom or dad what time we can get to your house."

If your friend says he or she cannot do the activity, then you can say something like, "Okay. Would you like to get together another time to do something together?" (Maybe you and your friend can set a time and date for another activity while you are still on the phone.)

Be sure to let your mom or dad know about your phone conversation and what you and your friend made plans to do. Have fun!

Figure 4.2. Jake's antecedent cue regulation system. (Reprinted with permission from Jake's family.)

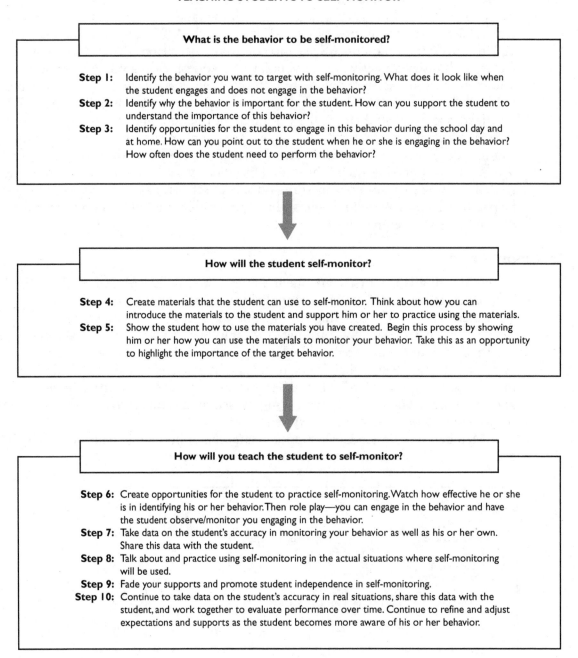

TEACHING STUDENTS TO SELF-MONITOR

What is the behavior to be self-monitored?

Step 1:   Identify the behavior you want to target with self-monitoring. What does it look like when the student engages and does not engage in the behavior?
Step 2:   Identify why the behavior is important for the student. How can you support the student to understand the importance of this behavior?
Step 3:   Identify opportunities for the student to engage in this behavior during the school day and at home. How can you point out to the student when he or she is engaging in the behavior? How often does the student need to perform the behavior?

How will the student self-monitor?

Step 4:   Create materials that the student can use to self-monitor. Think about how you can introduce the materials to the student and support him or her to practice using the materials.
Step 5:   Show the student how to use the materials you have created. Begin this process by showing him or her how you can use the materials to monitor your behavior. Take this as an opportunity to highlight the importance of the target behavior.

How will you teach the student to self-monitor?

Step 6:   Create opportunities for the student to practice self-monitoring. Watch how effective he or she is in identifying his or her behavior. Then role play—you can engage in the behavior and have the student observe/monitor you engaging in the behavior.
Step 7:   Take data on the student's accuracy in monitoring your behavior as well as his or her own. Share this data with the student.
Step 8:   Talk about and practice using self-monitoring in the actual situations where self-monitoring will be used.
Step 9:   Fade your supports and promote student independence in self-monitoring.
Step 10: Continue to take data on the student's accuracy in real situations, share this data with the student, and work together to evaluate performance over time. Continue to refine and adjust expectations and supports as the student becomes more aware of his or her behavior.

Figure 4.3.   Steps to teach students to self-monitor. (*Sources:* Agran et al., 2003; King-Sears and Copeland, 1997.)

environments. You also want to assess the student's current performance of the target behavior so you have this information available to assess the impact of the self-monitoring intervention. You then select the self-monitoring system that will be used. How will the student record his or her behavior? Will he or she respond better to paper-and-pencil methods or to technological supports? Will he or she record on an interval schedule (e.g., how often he or she is on task during 1-minute intervals) or on

Increased use of technology by ALL people is increasing the ease and acceptability for use by people with disabilities in all aspects of their lives.

completion of tasks or activities (e.g., recording the completion of 10 problems)? You can then teach the student to use the self-monitoring system.

Students can be taught in several ways to self-assess and self-record their own behavior. The study at the beginning of the chapter had students watch videos of themselves, and they were taught to correctly identify examples and nonexamples of appropriate classroom behavior (Shogren et al., 2011). The participants then self-assessed their performance of these behaviors in the classroom.

Students can also record the occurrence or nonoccurrence of their behavior in many ways. They can use simple tally sheets, programs on an iPad or computer, audio recordings, and so forth. Students can be alerted in multiple ways to self-record through audio prompts delivered through headphones, watches that are set to beep or vibrate to alert the student, or natural break points in an activity. Figure 4.4 shows a self-monitoring sheet that Jake's mom, Jeanine, developed so that he could be effective in completing his morning routine. Figure 4.5 shows a self-monitoring sheet that can be used in classrooms when students are monitoring their achievement of academic goals that they have set for themselves.

Jake first had to learn what each of these behaviors represented (see Figure 4.4). For example, Jake and his team discussed what being completely dressed meant and provided examples and nonexamples. Jake had opportunities to practice fixing breakfast and lunch with his mother. She initially modeled these activities, then provided feedback to Jake on completing these activities, and then faded her presence. Jake had a clipboard with his self-monitoring sheets, and he marked down which activities he completed each day.

Morning schedule						
Complete by:	Item	Monday	Tuesday	Wednesday	Thursday	Friday
6:45 a.m.	Get completely dressed					
7:00 a.m.	Eat breakfast*					
7:10 a.m.	Fix your lunch**					
7:20 a.m.	Brush your teeth					
7:25 a.m.	Get backpack, coat, etc.					
7:35 a.m.	Go to bus stop					
TOTALS						

ADD morning, afternoon, bedroom, bathroom, & living room checkmarks together:		
****	130–166	checkmarks- 4 hours each computer and TV time earned for Saturday & Sunday (each)
***	100–129	checkmarks- 3 hours each computer and TV time earned for Saturday & Sunday (each)
**	70–99	checkmarks- 2 hours each computer and TV time earned for Saturday & Sunday (each)
*	35–69	checkmarks- 1 hours each computer and TV time earned for Saturday & Sunday (each)

*Breakfast is eggs (boiled, scrambled, fried, etc.) or pancakes/waffles or cereal (hot or cold) or yogurt **and** milk or juice
Lunch is sandwich **and chips **and** fruit **or** yogurt **or** cheese **and** milk or juice

Figure 4.4. Jake's self-management system for the morning. (Reprinted with permission from Jake's family.)

Goal Sheet to Monitoring Progress on Classroom Goals

Name: _____

Use this goal sheet to keep track of your progress.

Goal: _____

	Monday	Tuesday	Wednesday	Thursday	Friday
Yes I met my goal for today!					
No I did not meet my goal for today.					

Figure 4.5. Goal sheet to monitoring progress on classroom goals.

Jake's mom credits the autism/behavioral support specialist from his school with educating her about how to create materials to use with Jake to support his self-determination, and she felt that the school was always open to working with her to support Jake.

The Goal Sheet to Monitoring Progress on Classroom Goals form (see Figure 4.5) is a less complex goal sheet that was used for students with disabilities to record whether they achieved their goal for the day in a research study (Shogren et al., 2012). Each student had an independent reading goal that was listed on the smartboard. The students copied their goal on the goal sheet, which they kept in their daily planners. Each day students marked if they met their reading goal. The number of students who completed their assignments each day was noted on the smartboard in the classroom, and students earned breakfast sandwiches on Fridays when the class met 80% of their goals.

A large body of research suggested the benefits of self-monitoring for students with a range of disabilities across a wide spectrum of educational outcomes. Researchers have found that self-monitoring can positively affect academic engagement and skills (Hughes, Copeland, Agran, et al., 2002; Joseph & Eveleigh, 2011; Konrad, Fowler, Walker, Test, & Wood, 2007; Mooney, Ryan, Uhing, Reid, & Epstein, 2005), social skills (Hughes, Copeland, Wehmeyer, et al., 2002; Hughes et al., 2000; Lee, Simpson, & Shogren, 2007), and behavioral outcomes (Machalicek, O'Reilly, Beretvas, Sigafoos, & Lancioni, 2007; Mancina, Tankersley, Kamps, Kravits, & Parrett, 2000). The Reviews of Research on the Relationship Between Self-Management and Valued Outcomes research box summarizes literature reviews on the impact of self-management interventions.

How accurate do students have to be when they are self-monitoring their behavior? What if they are occasionally saying they did something that they did not really do? Interestingly, researchers have often found students do not need to be completely accurate in their recording to have changes in outcomes (Reinecke, Newman, & Meinberg, 1999). It appears that the act of self-monitoring may make students more aware of their behavior, leading to changes in behavior even if the monitoring is not perfectly accurate. Wehmeyer and colleagues noted that self-monitoring

Reveals discrepancies between what we want and what we have, what we seek to achieve and how we plan to achieve it, what we have done and what we had planned to do, what we hoped to get and what we have gotten. (2007, p. 89)

This awareness enables us to seek out the just-right match for our capacities and the opportunities in our environment.

Self-Evaluation

Self-evaluation and self-reinforcement are frequently used in combination with self-monitoring strategies. Mike Slagor, vocational coordinator and former special education classroom teacher, provides an example about how these strategies can be combined (see Mike Slagor's Experiences with Self-Management Strategies research box). Self-evaluation can actually be viewed as an extension of self-monitoring because it involves going from simply recording the occurrence of a behavior, task, or activity to evaluating the quality of the behavior, task, or activity in comparison with the standard. This standard defines the expectations for performance (e.g., 80% correct, completed a task in 5 minutes, made connections with five individuals, task completed to satisfaction of employer). Evaluating one's own behavior is important to self-regulation because evaluating allows us to know if we need to adjust our behavior to meet the expectations of the environment. Students do not depend on others for evaluation when they are taught to self-evaluate, and they can

Reviews of Research on the Relationship
Between Self-Management and Valued Outcomes

Numerous research reviews have examined the impact of self-management interventions. Different reviews had different target populations and focused on different self-management strategies and different outcome domains. Overall, the reviews suggested that students with diverse disability labels can learn to self-manage, and self-management skills can have a significant and positive impact on their lives. Researchers found that self-management interventions are one of the most frequently researched self-determination interventions for students with high-incidence disabilities. Konrad and colleagues (2007) found that 88% of studies examining self-determination interventions to improve academic outcomes for students with learning disabilities included self-management strategies. The self-management interventions tended to be most effective for improving the quality of students' academic work and led to stronger effect when combined with other self-determination interventions (e.g., goal setting, choice making).

Other researchers examined the impact of self-management interventions for other high-incidence disability populations. Mooney and colleagues (2005) reviewed self-management interventions targeting academic outcomes for students with emotional and behavior disorders; they identified 22 studies with 78 participants. Students were included in the research base from grades K–12, with a slight majority of participants being in grades K–6. They found the largest number of studies implemented self-monitoring interventions. The interventions were implemented in a variety of academic domains, including math, reading, writing, and social studies instruction, and there did not appear to be differences in the impact of the intervention based on academic area. The effects of the self-management interventions were "large in magnitude and educationally meaningful" (p. 203), and there was some evidence of generalization and maintenance of outcomes.

There is also a research base on self-management for students with low-incidence disabilities, although it is not as robust as the research base for students with high-incidence disabilities. For example, Lee et al. (2007) reviewed the literature on self-management for students with autism. They identified 11 articles that examined self-management interventions and found that the majority (64%) of studies implemented some form of a comprehensive self-management intervention. Diverse materials were used for self-monitoring, including paper-and-pencil materials, token-type systems, and tangible and visible materials. Sixty-four percent of studies focused on increasing social behaviors. Self-management interventions had a large, significant impact on behavior across studies. Hughes, Korinek, and Gorman (1991) also found that self-management interventions had a significant, positive impact on employment and transition-related skills for students with intellectual disability.

Overall, these and other reviews document that self-management interventions are a powerful tool for improving the academic, social, and behavioral outcomes of students with diverse disability labels. Self-management interventions will need to be individualized for each student, target behavior, and setting, but doing so has the potential to significantly improve student outcomes, promote positive outcomes for teachers and other support people, and lead to self-regulated behavior.

learn to self-regulate their behavior. We often assume self-evaluation is always linked to self-monitoring, but this might not be internalized by students unless the step is taken to teach them to understand the criteria for evaluating the behavior, task, or activity. Adding self-evaluation into a self-management intervention can be an important step to support student self-regulation.

Agran and colleagues (2003) suggested steps similar to teaching self-monitoring when teaching self-evaluation skills, with the addition of evaluation strategies.

Mike Slagor's Experiences with Self-Management Strategies

My job involves supporting teachers working with students throughout our secondary programs around curriculum development and transition planning. Teachers in our program for individuals older than 18 were concerned about a student with a moderate intellectual disability. So they called me to brainstorm with them. This student was going to be leaving the program in about a year, and her team was very focused on developing employment skills and hopefully identifying a job where she could work during her final year of school and beyond. The student had a history of success in many work-related activities. If we placed her into a job, then she could usually learn and complete any task(s) that we put in front of her. In the past, she has shelved movies at a video store, bused tables at a restaurant, sorted books at a library, and organized clothing and food at a local pantry. But social and conversational skills have been the big issues for her across work experiences. The team was commonly finding that difficulties she had when interacting with co-workers, even in jobs where this was not a primary component (e.g., busing tables), was leading to a lack of natural support. Furthermore, the student was interested in working in some type of retail environment, so a lack of social and conversational skills could be very problematic. And, it had kept the team from trying this type of a placement in the past.

Because effective transition services means basing our work on each student's interests and preferences, the team decided to focus on the student's interests and preferences and set the student up with a paid experience at a local retail store. The employer was very open to supporting the student and was looking for a long-term, reliable worker. The team decided to give it a try and focus on teaching and building up supports around conversational and social skills. The student enjoyed conversing with people and could sustain conversations, but she was only interested in having conversations on a very narrow range of topics that she enjoyed. If the conversation deviated from any of those topics or she was prompted to talk about work-related activities, then she would get very frustrated and express it in ways that were difficult for those who were interacting with her (e.g., roll her eyes, make negative comments, "huff and puff"). These were the primary reasons co-workers in the past had identified for not wanting to spend time with her. These difficulties seemed further compounded in a retail setting, where she had to interact with customers around topics that were not in her range of interests.

The team extensively worked with her. They taught her routines for interacting with customers, and she continued to demonstrate those negative behaviors while she was implementing these routines. Sensing a risk of her losing the job, the team brainstormed and decided that the student needed to be a part of the data collection we were doing so that she could develop self-awareness of her behavior. When talking to the student about these issues, she seemed to have very limited awareness that she was engaging in the problem behaviors. We developed a contract with her that detailed her behavioral expectations in the retail environment. We provided extensive detail on these expectations and reviewed this with the student weekly, at the very least. We also developed a recording system in which the job coach recorded task completion and the student kept track of the three primary unwanted behaviors (i.e., eye rolling, making negative comments, "huffing and puffing"). This allowed her to become more aware of when she was engaging in them. Figure 4.6 is an example of her data collection sheet. The student received feedback on her productivity from her job coach and learned to review and evaluate her unwanted behaviors via modeling by the job coach. She earned reinforcers, including her paycheck, for her productivity, but we also embedded extra time at the end of her work schedule that she could earn to have a soda and talk about whatever topic she wanted. We saw quick and marked improvement. The student became much more aware of her behaviors, and there was a large and immediate reduction in the three unwanted behaviors. Her family implemented a similar system at home and also found that they were able to have much more positive interactions around a diverse array of topics. It made everyone in her life much happier and has created an opportunity for the student to have a long-term job possibility with opportunities to form natural supports and relationships.

Contributed by Mike Slagor.

Student's name: _____

Monday: Jobsite		Date:	
Times	What tasks was the student doing?	How many seconds/minutes was he or she off task?	
9:15–9:25			
9:30–9:40			
9:45–9:55			
10:00–10:10			
10:15–10:25			
10:30–10:40			
10:45–10:55			
11:00–11:10			
Did you have to provide the student with feedback (corrections, suggestions)? Did he or she display unwanted behaviors (e.g., rolling eyes, making negative comments, huffing and puffing)?			Yes or No
Did the student make at least three positive comments to adult staff today? (e.g, greeting, friendly chat)			Yes or No
For student to complete. Ask the student these questions:	Did I roll my eyes today?	Did I make any negative comments?	Did I huff and puff?
	Yes or No	Yes or No	Yes or No

Figure 4.6.   Mike Slagor's example of a self-management sheet. (Contributed by Mike Slagor.)

1. Select target behavior and define examples and nonexamples of the target behavior.

2. Provide rationale for evaluating target behavior.

3. Provide opportunities to practice behavior.

4. Introduce evaluation system and materials.

5. Model using system while performing behavior.

6. Support student to practice using system using role play.

7. Assess mastery of self-evaluation in role play.

8. Discuss the natural situation when self-evaluation will be used.

9. Provide students with opportunities for independent practice in the natural situation.

10. Assess mastery of self-evaluation in the natural environment.

Research studies documented the impact of self-evaluation procedures alone or in combination with other self-management strategies on academic (Bryan, Burstein, & Bryan, 2001; Farrell & McDougall, 2008; Goddard & Sendi, 2008; Mooney et al., 2005; Wehmeyer, Yeager, Bolding, Agran, & Hughes, 2003), behavioral (DiGangi, Maag, & Rutherford, 1991), and social (Falk, Dunlap, & Kern, 1996) outcomes. For example, Farrell and McDougall implemented an intervention with high school students with learning disabilities, other health impairments, and emotional and behavior disorders to increase math fluency. Students wore a MotivAider while completing math problems, which can be programmed to vibrate at equal intervals. The MotivAider vibrated every 45 seconds, and students circled the math problem they were completing. They then calculated if they were on pace, behind pace, or ahead of pace (based on their performance from the previous day, which the teacher highlighted on their individual worksheets prior to class). Students showed increases in the number of correct problems they completed and the pace they completed problems when wearing the MotivAider and self-evaluating their pace, and they did not depend on teachers to provide this feedback.

Jake's self-management system for the morning has self-evaluation elements embedded in it, as well as self-reinforcement elements (see Figure 4.4). Jake learned to add the number of checkmarks he obtained each week and determined his performance level based on the number of checkmarks—one star, two stars, three stars, or four stars. The different stars corresponded to differing levels of computer and television time on the weekends, a strong reinforcer for Jake. Jake's target was almost always four stars after the first week of using the system. The goal sheet shown in Figure 4.5 also required that students engage in self-evaluation. Each of the students in the class was working on individualized goals, but each had a set criterion they had to meet to consider

> *In order to effectively self-manage their behavior, students also need to understand and properly self-evaluate.*

their goal achieved (e.g., read five pages or one chapter, correctly answer five questions about the text). The number of students who met their goal each day was noted on the SMARTBoard in the classroom. Students then calculated the percentage of students that met their goals on Thursday afternoon to determine if they met the standard (80%) for getting breakfast sandwiches. Students were learning and practicing math skills in addition to learning about self-determination and achieving reading goals.

Self-Reinforcement

Self-reinforcement involves a student first self-assessing a behavior's occurrence. Unique to self-reinforcement is that students then deliver a reinforcer to themselves contingent on the occurrence of the behavior (self-reinforcement alone), after recording the occurrence of the behavior (self-monitoring and self-reinforcement), or after determining that a standard was met for the performance of the behavior (self-evaluation and self-reinforcement). The simplest way to think about self-reinforcement is the student learning to apply a simple contingency to themselves:

If _____, then _____.

The student can fill in the blank after *if* with any behavior, activity or task, and/or any performance expectations, and he or she can fill in the blank after the *then* with any consequence. This can range from

- If *I complete my assignment, then* I will *get myself a snack.*

- If *I complete my assignment with 80% accuracy, then* I will *go to lunch with my friends.*

- If *I earn $200, then* I will *buy a new shirt.*

- If *I complete four interviews and get one job offer, then* I will *buy a new suit.*

It is critical that the behavior, activity, or task is appropriate for the student's level of discriminative ability. Also vital is that the reinforcer is something that the individual can deliver to him- or herself, is motivating for him- or herself, and leads to increases in the desired behavior. Research has shown that when students are in charge of delivering their own reinforcers 1) they do so accurately after appropriate instruction, and 2) their

Teaching Students to Plan, Work, Evaluate, and Adjust

Martin, Mithaug, Cox, et al. (2003) examined the impact of an intervention that taught secondary students with severe emotional and behavior problems to plan, work, evaluate, and adjust their behavior on academic tasks. Martin and colleagues worked with eight students with emotional and behavior disorders and developed self-determination contracts with the students. The contract had four sections—plan, work, evaluate, and adjust.

In the plan section, students identified the time that they would begin their task on a clock by drawing the hands on the clock. They then circled the academic area they would be working on (reading, math, spelling, creative, or social). Next, they designated the number of pages or problems they would complete and drew the time in which the task would be completed on another clock. Finally, they verbally reviewed this plan with their teacher and made adjustments as recommended by the teacher. For the work section, students worked on their targeted activities independently or in small groups and then documented when they actually began their task, how many pages or problems they completed, the number they completed correctly, the points earned, and the end time. In the evaluation phase, the students evaluated the degree to which they began on time, completed the planned number, and achieved performance expectations by comparing their plan and their work data. They then developed a plan to adjust their performance (if necessary) in future work sessions to meet their planned goals. Students earned points, which they recorded in the teacher's grade book after completing all of the sections.

The researchers found that the students were able to implement the plan, work, evaluate, and adjust process to self-direct their completion of academic tasks. After instruction, students showed greater correspondence between their plan for working and the actual work accomplished. The mean increased from 78% correspondence to 93% correspondence over 30 days. They also were much more likely to follow through on necessary adjustments, with the mean increasing from 50% correspondence to 75% correspondence over 30 days. Teachers also reported that they felt that the contracts were effective, and the authors stated that "students enjoyed using them [the contracts] after the initial skepticism of being allowed to plan their own task schedule" (Martin, Mithaug, Cox, et al., 2003, p. 443).

This study suggests that students can learn and benefit from the four self-management strategies discussed in this chapter and become self-regulated learners. It also shows the importance of creating opportunities for these skills to be learned and used. Students are often uncertain of how to self-manage their own behavior and if they will have ongoing opportunities to self-manage. This research and the strategies described in this chapter provide a framework for teaching skills and creating opportunities that allow students to achieve these valued outcomes.

performance is often better when self-reinforcing (Mancina et al., 2000; Newman, Buffington, Hames, 1996). Other researchers, however, highlighted the importance of selecting the appropriate reinforcer. Agran, Blanchard, Wehmeyer, and Hughes (2001) found that teaching students to deliver praise to themselves after completing academic or social skills activities did not have an appreciable impact on behavior, particularly as praise was common across activities and settings and not specific to certain activities for the students. Yet, there was a significant impact on behavior when the reinforcer was changed to a cash reinforcer ($5) for complete accuracy on tasks for a week.

CONSIDERATIONS WHEN APPLYING SELF-MANAGEMENT SYSTEMS

The four self-management strategies can be taught alone or in combination with each other to support students to develop self-determination skills. Although it might make sense to first teach antecedent strategies and then move to consequent strategies or start with consequent strategies and then add in antecedent strategies, the importance of teaching and creating opportunities for students to develop and apply each of these strategies in their lives cannot be underestimated. If students have strategies to manage both the antecedents and consequences of their behavior, then they are able to initiate actions, monitor their actions, evaluate their actions, and choose to reinforce themselves and/or modify their behavior to meet environmental demands. This allows them to move closer to the just-right match between their capacities and the expectations of the environment.

The Teaching Students to Plan, Work, Evaluate, and Adjust research box shares information about a study that used a comprehensive self-management package to teach students with emotional and behavior disorders to plan, work, evaluate, and adjust their performance of academic tasks and work outcomes. Comprehensive self-management interventions, in combination with goal-setting strategies (see Chapter 5) and choice-making strategies (see Chapter 3), provide students with the skills to become self-determined individuals.

5

Promoting Skills Leading to Enhanced Self-Determination Through Goal Setting

We made the Self-Determination Learning Model of Instruction (SDLMI) fit in with what the class was intended to do and meet the individual needs of students like setting goals for grades, organization, and transition goals. The process was good because it broke down the steps of the goal setting into simple parts. Students reached most of their goals.

(Teacher Participant; Shogren, 2010, p. 5)

I learned the process of setting goals, reevaluating my goal, changing my action plan and what it takes to accomplish my goal. I learned about time management. It was more than managing time but also planning the amount of time it takes to go through the process. Before if had a goal, I would think I could do it in a few days. No it takes more. I learned to be wise about allowing enough time. With an assignment I would start planning what I have to do and the time it will take. I had to rely on myself. When it is just me, no one is telling me to do this or that. I internalized it and started using it in everything I do. It got me to consider what needed to be done. Felt like it taught me about my limits and strengths, what I can and cannot do. It gave me confidence and it has become automatic. I see something I want and my mind starts working on it.

(Student Participant; Shogren, 2010, p. 10)

The chapter opening quotes are from a teacher and student who participated in a research study evaluating the impact of the SDLMI on student outcomes (Shogren, Palmer, et al., 2012; Wehmeyer, Shogren et al., 2012). The SDLMI, which is addressed later in this chapter, is a multicomponent intervention that teaches students a self-regulated, problem-solving process that can be used to work toward self-selected goals. These quotes demonstrate the power that teaching students self-determination skills can have and the ease with which this instruction can be implemented throughout the school day.

The SDLMI was developed so that it could be overlaid on any class activities. The teacher whose quote opens this chapter taught a high school resource class. Students were working on diverse, individualized activities related to practicing academic skills and identifying and working toward their postschool goals. This teacher, with support from the research team, set up class time so that students received brief instruction two to three times per week on setting and working toward goals. Students then received individualized instruction using the SDLMI to develop an action plan and evaluate progress toward achieving their goals. The student's quote communicates what he learned through the process. This student, who had learning disabilities and was struggling with managing his time on academic tasks, learned about the importance of setting and accomplishing goals. He also learned important skills that allowed him to make progress toward his goal of passing his English class. He learned how he could rely on himself and use these strategies in many areas of his life to achieve the outcomes he desired.

Students are actively involved in directing their own learning when they take an active role in setting their learning goals and understand, implement, and evaluate the strategies they use to achieve their goals. Chapter 4 described how self-management strategies are also called student-directed learning strategies because students take an active role in prompting, monitoring, evaluating, and reinforcing their behavior. Students have even more strategies to take an active role in their learning and development when they are allowed to set their own goals.

Student-directed learning strategies differ from the more commonly used teacher-directed learning strategies. Teacher-directed learning strategies have dominated special education practice likely because of the strong influence of applied behavior analysis and operant psychology on the field (Wehmeyer et al., 2007). Teacher-directed instruction can benefit students and lead to acquiring many new skills. The transition from school to adult life marks changes not only in students' status, but also changes in expectations and roles. In adult roles, students are expected (and often required) to direct the process of setting and attaining goals. Students will always have a circle of support on which they can rely, but it is important to create many opportunities for student-directed learning. This will prepare students for the expectations of the adult world as well as teach them critical skills that enable them to become self-determined young adults.

This chapter introduces strategies for teaching students to set and attain goals. Goals allow students to identify what they want and to develop a plan for how to go after it. Research has shown that goal setting can have a significant and positive affect on self-determination and transition outcomes. The SDLMI is introduced and using it in the process of goal setting and attainment to enable students to engage in a self-regulated, problem-solving process that allows them to self-direct their attainment of goals is highlighted.

GOAL SETTING AND ATTAINMENT

Self-determination is "volitional actions that enable one to act as the primary causal agent in one's life and to maintain or improve one's quality of life" (Wehmeyer, 2005, p. 117). Self-determination is acting with intent to improve one's quality of life. Goals are a key part of acting with intent because they specify what we want to achieve and provide a framework for achieving it.

Locke and Latham did extensive research on goal setting and consistently found that people perform better when they have goals (Locke & Latham, 1990, 2002). They stated that goals "direct attention, effort, and action toward goal-relevant actions, at the expense of nonrelevant actions" (2006, p. 265). Goals keep us focused on what we are working toward, enabling us to regulate our behavior and direct our attention toward achieving our goals. Researchers in the special education field have confirmed these findings. For example, several studies have found that students make more progress toward academic goals in reading and writing when they have set goals for performance (Figarola et al., 2008; Graham,

In adult roles, students are expected (and often required) to direct the process of setting and attaining goals. Students will always have a circle of support on which they can rely, but it is important to create many opportunities for student-directed learning.

MacArthur, & Schwartz, 1995; Johnson, Graham, & Harris, 1997; Page-Voth & Graham, 1999; Swain, 2005).

Are all goals equally effective? Are there certain features of goals that make us more likely to be successful? Locke and Latham (2002, 2006) identified several features of goals that tend to increase performance. Although their research has been conducted mainly in the fields of business and management, it has been replicated and has applications for our work when we are supporting students to set and work toward goals. One of their consistent findings is that we have to have the "requisite task knowledge and skills" (2006, p. 265) for goals to lead to increased performance. Students who are asked to identify a goal often start off with a very broad goal that they have limited ability to achieve given their current knowledge and skills. For example, a student might say that he or she wants to earn an *A* in a class, but has very limited understanding of what it actually takes to earn an *A*. Or, the student might say he or she wants to be a basketball star, again with no understanding of what it takes to do this. It is important to work with students to break down this large goal into smaller process goals that allow the students to work toward (or revise) their larger goal. For example, a more manageable goal might be to research what it would take to earn an *A* or identify the requirements to become a professional basketball player. The next goal in the goal sequence might be taking action on one of the activities to improve a grade or testing the degree to which a student can meet expectations for a basketball career (e.g., height, shooting percentage), which can then lead to the student thinking about alternative but related careers if he or she cannot meet these expectations.

Another way to think about this is by making a distinction between process goals or outcome or product goals (Graham, MacArthur, Schwartz, & Page-Voth, 1992; Zimmerman & Kitsantas, 1997). Process goals focus on the steps in the process that allow an individual to achieve an outcome or create a product. For example, a goal to learn to read or write a persuasive essay is an outcome or product goal. Process goals facilitate the achievement of outcome-focused goals but tend to be skills and abilities that the student needs to learn and implement in order to achieve the desired outcomes (e.g., identifying letter combinations, learning the components of a sentence). Zimmerman and Kitsantas (1999), researchers who have extensively studied process and outcome goals, found that students who start with outcome goals tend to show lower skill development, lesser belief in their ability to achieve their goals, and limited interest in their goals. For example, they studied writing skill acquisition in high school girls and found that students who focused on process goals (e.g., goals that were related to the steps necessary to rewrite the sentence—circle words, cross out words, combine words into sentence) demonstrated better sentence writing skills as well as more interest in their work and belief that they could learn writing skills than students focused on outcome goals (e.g., rewrite the sentence).

Even though we are focusing on student-directed learning and actively involving students in the process of identifying and working toward their goals, this does not mean that we stop providing instruction, support, and feedback to help students make the most of their learning. We should work with students to help them define process goals for their day-to-day work and remind them of their outcome goals to help facilitate motivation and a long-term perspective.

Locke and Latham (2002) also found that more challenging goals tend to lead to higher levels of performance than easy or vague goals. The goal still has to be something that the students can do (i.e., they have to have the requisite knowledge and skills), but the goal must challenge them. I often think about this in relation to exercise. If I currently can only run for a mile without stopping, a challenge goal might be to train over the next 3 months to run a 5k (3.1 miles). I may be able to achieve this goal with appropriate support (e.g., training schedule, stretching routines, training with friends). But, if I set a goal of running a marathon (26.2 miles) in 3 months, then I am unlikely to have the requisite skills or capacity to reach the goal. My long-term outcome goal may be to run a marathon, but there are process goals (e.g., training for a 5k) that will enable me to more effectively reach my outcome goal. But, if my goal was to simply continue to run for a mile at a time, then it may not be a challenging enough goal. One of the benefits of goals is that they create a discrepancy between what a person is currently doing and what a person wants to be doing in the future. If goals only focus on a current level of performance, then there is not a discrepancy and there can be a lack of drive to adjust behavior to reach the goal. Having a challenging goal to incrementally work toward can foster motivation to achieve something that is personally meaningful.

The issue of meaning or motivation is also important and benefits students who select their own goals. Locke and Latham (2006) found that individuals perform better when they are committed to their goals and when they have a lack of conflict between goals. If an individual is not motivated to achieve a goal, or if he or she is working on goals that pull in two different directions, then that individual is not likely to succeed. It is critical that transition services be based on students' interests and preferences because students are more motivated and engaged in the process of working toward their goals. Researchers have found, however, that there is often a disconnect between interests and preferences and transition goals, particularly for students from diverse backgrounds. Trainor (2005) found that students often express personal goals that were different than the transition-related goals on their IEPs. She suggested the importance of including students in transition-related conversations and creating opportunities for students to reflect on their future goals.

It is important to consider the role of the family in identifying and working toward goals. Families and support systems play a central role in goal setting for many students. Michael's support system has regular meetings called group action planning (GAP) meetings (Blue-Banning, Turnbull, & Pereira, 2000; Turnbull & Turnbull, 1996; see Chapter 8). Developing a vision and goals for an individual with disabilities and identifying the supports needed to achieve those goals is a major purpose of GAP meetings. The vision for Michael that has emerged from the GAP meetings is that he has a rich and activity-filled life. One major goal area that emerged for Michael and his team when planning for the transition from school to adult life was participating in preferred activities, especially after-school activities. The team identified some of Michael's favorite activities, and music was at the top of the list. Michael had access to a thriving music scene in his local community. Transportation, however, was a major barrier. Driving is not possible for Michael, and public transportation was not convenient for getting to the venues that Michael would like to attend, particularly because they were relatively close and the bus routes were neither convenient nor timely. The team brought up biking as a possibility, but issues with balancing on a bike and safety were major concerns. Then someone thought of a great alterative—an adult tricycle. A local bike shop customizes adult tricycles, and Michael has ridden customized tandem bicycles all throughout his childhood and adolescence, so he and his team set a process goal of learning to ride the adult tricycle. This was designed to eventually lead to an outcome goal of using the adult tricycle to gain access to music events in the local community. Michael is currently working on riding the adult tricycle around his

> **TIP**
>
> *Students are more motivated and engaged in the process of working toward their goals when transition services are based on students' interests and preferences.*

neighborhood, and will keep building more challenging goals with his support team until he is gaining access to music events throughout his community.

Finally, the importance of feedback cannot be overstated. It will be important to keep track of how often Michael rides, how far, and how many events he attends. All of this information will let his team know if Michael is making progress on his goal, if he has achieved his goal, or if he needs to revise his goal. For example, Michael and the team may try the adult tricycle and then decide something else may be better (e.g., getting rides with friends). Michael could then revise his goal and continue to make progress toward his outcome goal of attending musical activities in the community. The self-management strategies discussed in Chapter 4 provide a means for enabling students to be actively involved in monitoring and evaluating their progress toward their goals. The following sections discuss how to build student-directed data collection and feedback into the goal-setting process.

Teaching Goal Setting and Attainment

Researchers have identified four steps in the goal setting process.

1. Identifying a goal

2. Clearly and concretely defining a goal

3. Specifying the actions necessary to achieve the desired outcome

4. Evaluating progress and adjusting plan or goal as needed (Wehmeyer et al., 2007)

There are numerous ways to identify a goal. Michael's support team plays a critical role in identifying meaningful goals and enabling him to go after those goals. It can be useful to identify goals and allow students to choose the goal on which they want to work, especially in academic areas. Figure 5.1 is an example of a PowerPoint presentation used in the SDLMI project described at the beginning of the chapter. Students were working on writing 11-minute essays, a skill they needed for a state assessment that all students were required to take. The teacher identified three goals that all of the students in the class needed to target. Students then selected one goal to work on each week. The PowerPoint shows a mini-lesson the teacher did with the class to review goals, self-monitor, and provide feedback and reinforcement.

Other students may select their own goals based on their personal experiences and dreams for the future. Jake, the other student featured throughout this book, set a goal to become a keynote speaker when he identified career and personal development goals. Jake had seen a young woman with autism give a keynote at an autism conference he attended and became excited about the possibilities of learning to tell his story. But, Jake had never given a professional presentation. So, his support team worked with him to identify process goals that would move him closer to his outcome goal. The initial process goal was to develop a presentation that he could give about himself and about autism. Next, he had to give this presentation, starting first with family and friends and then finding opportunities to speak at the local university and at parent conferences. Jake identified his outcome goal and developed process goals with the support of his team, which allowed him to move closer to his outcome goal. Jake has now given more than 20 presentations at professional and parent conferences and to classes at his local university. He also achieved his long-term goal giving a keynote presentation titled "Aim High," to a professional conference with more than 500 attendees. His presentation was even translated into Spanish.

The next step is having the student write, type, or dictate the goal. You should work with the student to revise the goal as needed by using all of your knowledge of writing

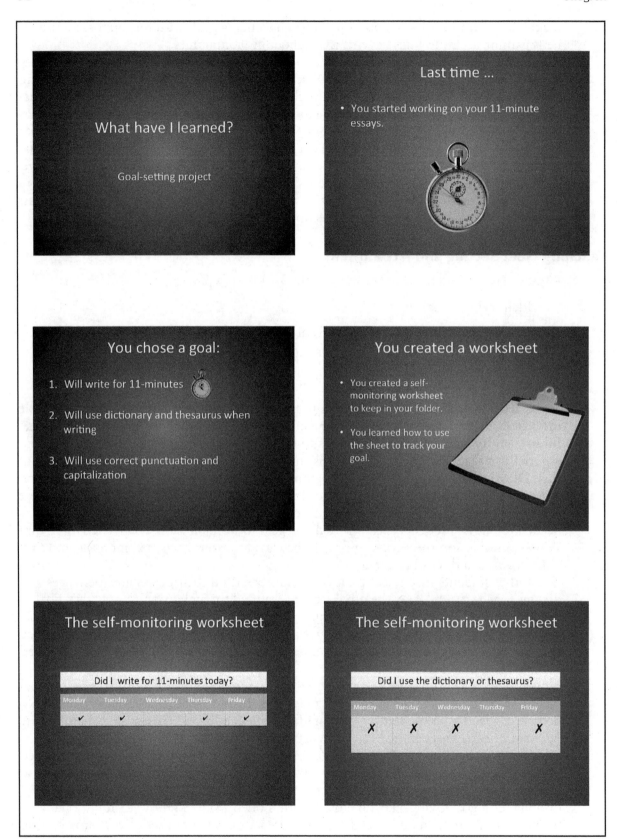

Figure 5.1. Goal-setting PowerPoint from SDLMI project.

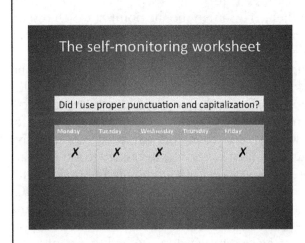

The self-monitoring worksheet

Did I use proper punctuation and capitalization?

Monday	Tuesday	Wednesday	Thursday	Friday
X	X	X		X

Rewards

- Class award: Breakfast party!!!

- Individual awards: surprise!

Class Goal

- Did the class meet the goal?

- According to our plan, does the class get a breakfast party?

Individual Goal

- Did you meet your goal?
- According to our plan, do you get an award?

Tuesday we will...

- Create a new action plan for our goals.
- See you then!

effective goals and sharing. Students need to learn to write clear, specific, measurable goals that specify a time line for attaining them. This might be the point in which discussions about process versus outcome goals emerge as you support students to learn to break their outcome or product goals into smaller, attainable goals.

Action planning can begin after students have a clear, specific, measurable, and attainable goal. Action planning involves specifying the strategies and resources needed to make progress as well as the schedule for progress and how progress will be measured. The strategies and resources needed to make progress may involve a diverse array of supports. Students may need to learn new skills, and educators' knowledge of effective instructional strategies can be useful. Systematic instruction was necessary to aid Michael as he learned to ride the adult tricycle. Prompts and supports were faded over time with Michael moving from riding with a partner on a tandem bicycle, to riding independently in the alley behind his house (accompanied on foot by a support person), to riding around the block, and then (hopefully) to music venues. Students may also need support to learn and implement self-management strategies to develop a schedule for progress and how progress will be measured. Jake had to learn to develop a time line for creating and practicing presentations before he delivers them. Jake has learned that he needs several weeks to create the presentation and several opportunities to practice the presentation before he feels comfortable delivering it. He had to develop a time line based on the dates of his presentations and a system for monitoring his progress to make sure he was on track. Finally, students will need to engage in self-evaluation. Students need to determine if they achieved their goal and evaluate the reasons why if they did not achieve it and the factors that might need to change. For example, Jake was approached after he gave a presentation and invited to give another presentation to a different professional group in a few months. The woman that invited him gave him a card and asked him to call her to let her know the amount he would charge for the presentation. This was the first time that Jake had been offered a fee for presenting and he was uncertain about how to handle this. He was also uncertain about calling and engaging in conversation about the presentation. Jake put off calling the woman because of his uncertainty, and another speaker was identified. Jake and his mother discussed what should happen differently in the future (e.g., Jake requesting support in making the telephone call, identifying a price) and discussed a process goal of managing anxiety around scheduling presentations and dealing with financial issues.

Impact of Goal Setting on Outcomes

Learning to set and pursue goals can make a real difference in the lives of students with disabilities. Simply having a goal can lead to increased performance, and combining the identification of a goal with evaluation of progress and other self-management strategies can be powerful for students. Copeland, Hughes, Agran, Wehmeyer, and Fowler (2002) taught four high school students with intellectual disabilities in general education classes to self-monitor their classroom performance, set performance goals, and evaluate their progress on goals. The researchers also modified worksheets that students without disabilities were completing in the class and measured the students' completion of the modified worksheets as well as use of self-monitoring and goal-evaluation strategies. They found that the students increased their completion of class worksheets and grades after they were taught to set goals, monitor their performance, and evaluate their progress. They were also able to learn to self-monitor and self-evaluate progress, enabling students to more effectively participate in inclusive environments and general education activities with their peers. The Reviews of Research on the Relationship Between Goal Setting and

Reviews of Research on the Relationship Between Goal Setting and Valued Outcomes

Copeland and Hughes (2002) reviewed research on the impact of goal-setting interventions on the task performance of people with intellectual disability. They identified 10 studies that included 284 individuals with intellectual disability ranging from 9 to 54 years old. They found that the majority of tasks included in the studies were work related, specifically assembly and sorting tasks. The goals were typically related to performance criterion (e.g., completing a certain number of work tasks), and only 35% of studies included goals selected by the students/adults, 41% of studies targeted researcher selected goals, and 29% used "jointly selected goal levels" (p. 49). The majority of studies provided training and support for participants to remember their goals (e.g., daily review of goals, goals written near work area, feedback on performance toward a goal). They found that having goals in place led to increases in performance rate or quality across studies. They did not find any differences between researcher-selected and participant-selected goals, although they suggested this might have to do with a lack of focus on long-term or outcome goals when individuals were involved in selecting their own goals. They emphasized a need for future research that examines goal setting in additional domains and settings with this population. A small body of research has emerged since this review was published that looked at the impact of goal setting in academic and social domains for individuals with intellectual disability (Copeland et al., 2002; Hughes, Copeland, et al., 2002), suggesting similar positive effects.

Several researchers have explored the impact of goal setting on academic outcomes for students with learning disabilities. Konrad and colleagues (2007) systematically reviewed self-determination interventions for students with learning disabilities in academic domains and identified 12 self-determination studies (out of 31) that included goal setting as part of the intervention. They found that goal-setting interventions were commonly combined with self-management interventions and that combined interventions had the largest impact on behavior. Rogers and Graham (2008) examined writing intervention research and identified strategies that were commonly used to improve writing skills. Goal setting was one of these strategies. They identified seven studies that examined the impact of goal-setting interventions. The interventions ranged from teachers encouraging students to do better to students actively setting goals and monitoring progress toward goals. They found that goal setting had a large to moderate effect on writing productivity in students in grades 2–5 and 8–12.

These reviews suggested that setting goals has a significant positive impact on student behavior. Simply having a goal can increase performance, and combining goal setting with other student-directed learning strategies can lead to significant, positive results. Although there is evidence for the benefit of goal setting for students with high- and low-incidence disabilities, more research is needed to examine the impact of goal setting on academic domains for students with low-incidence disabilities and transition-related domains for students with high-incidence disabilities.

Valued Outcomes research box summarizes several reviews of the research on goal setting, suggesting its benefits across disability populations and content areas.

SELF-DETERMINED LEARNING MODEL OF INSTRUCTION

The SDLMI incorporates multiple student-directed learning strategies to form a teaching model. Teaching models provide a "plan or pattern that can be used to shape curriculums (long term courses of study), to design instructional materials, and to guide instruction in the classroom and other settings" (Joyce & Weil, 1980, p. 1). Teachers can incorporate the SDLMI into any curricula or instructional activity they are working on in the class-room. They simply organize the instruction to include goal setting linked to the desired outcomes and directly involve students in setting and working toward the goals. The SDLMI has a growing body of research supporting its efficacy in promoting student self-determination and achieving academic and transition goals. This research is summarized in the Research Studies on the SDLMI research box.

Research Studies on the
Self-Determined Learning Model of Instruction

The Self-Determination, School Outcomes, and Adult Outcomes research box highlighted two studies demonstrating the impact of the SDLMI on self-determination, goal attainment, and access to the general education curriculum (Shogren et al., 2012; Wehmeyer, Shogren et al., 2012). But, these are not the only studies that have looked at the impact of the SDLMI. The initial research study on the SDLMI included 40 high school students with intellectual disability, learning disabilities, and emotional and behavior disorders (Wehmeyer, Palmer, et al., 2000). Students showed an average of 80% progress on their learning goals and increased self-determination after instruction with the SDLMI.

Researchers have implemented the SDLMI with students with severe intellectual disabilities (Agran, Blanchard, & Wehmeyer, 2000; McGlashing-Johnson, Agran, Sitlington, Cavin, & Wehmeyer, 2003), modifying the questions in ways that enabled students to learn the process of self-regulating their behavior toward self-selected goals. For example, McGlashing-Johnson and colleagues used interviews and picture cues to enable students to respond to the questions included in the SDLMI. The students set goals related to completing tasks and navigating around the community. Interestingly, three of the four students selected goals that were not referenced in their current IEP goals. The researchers created and taught students to use self-monitoring materials and engaged students through interviews and pictures in the evaluation process. All students showed improvement in their targeted tasks, and these improvements were maintained over time.

Mazzotti, Wood, Test, and Fowler (2012) developed a computer-assisted version of the SDLMI. Three students with behavior problems were taught to navigate through the computer program and independently complete the phases of the SDLMI. They found that students could learn and implement the SDLMI when it was delivered through computer-assisted instruction, and students had significant gains in their knowledge of self-regulated problem-solving skills as well as significant reductions in their disruptive behavior in the classroom.

Benitez, Lattimore, and Wehmeyer (2005) modified the SDLMI to focus on career and vocational goals with students with emotional and behavior disorders. The Self-Determined Career Development Model (SDCDM) follows the same format as the SDLMI, but includes student questions specific to career development activities (e.g., What career and job do I want? What actions can I take to reach my career or employment goal?). The researchers implemented the SDCDM with six adolescents with emotional and behavior disorders and found that students were able to learn the self-regulated problem-solving process and showed improvement in their self-selected career development goals.

These studies show that diverse student populations can learn a self-regulated problem-solving process in multiple instructional formats with diverse goals when provided with instruction and opportunities to apply these skills to goals that have meaning for them.

The model has three phases:

1. Set a goal

2. Take action

3. Adjust goal or plan

These phases should sound similar because they are the steps of the goal-setting process. The SDLMI teaches students how to engage in goal setting, action planning, and evaluating and to do this in a self-directed manner. Each of the three phases poses a problem for the student to solve. The problem to solve in Phase 1 is, "What is my goal?" (see Figure 5.2). The problem to solve in Phase 2 is, "What is my plan?" The problem to solve in Phase 3 is, "What have I learned?" There are four student questions for each phase or problem that students learn, use, and make their own to solve the problem. The questions guide the students through a self-regulated problem-solving process. Although the four questions slightly differ across phases, they are asking students to 1) identify the problem, 2) identify potential solutions, 3) identify potential barriers, and 4) identify outcomes of each solution. Students learn a systematic process to reduce the discrepancy between where they are and where they want to be by learning and repeatedly applying these questions when working on goals. Furthermore, the model creates a natural feedback loop because Phase 3 involves evaluation. If students achieve their goal, then they return to Phase 1 to set a new goal. If students do not achieve their goal, then they return to Phase 2 to revise their action plan. The SDLMI provides a mechanism to explicitly teach students with disabilities how to set goals, solve problems, and direct their own behavior, enabling them to become self-regulated learners.

Each phase in the model is linked with educational supports (see Figure 5.2), which are the skills that enable students to self-regulate their behavior. If students do not yet have these skills, then it is important that instruction in these skills is provided so that students can effectively engage with the model. For example, the fourth in the PowerPoint mini-lesson in Figure 5.1 mentions that students created and were taught to use self-monitoring sheets. This mini-lesson was delivered before students engaged in Phase 2 of the SDLMI to ensure they had necessary self-monitoring skills so they could take action.

Each student question is linked to teacher objectives, which provide a "road map" for teachers defining the expected outcomes for the student answering the question. If students are not meeting these objectives, then it is often necessary to revisit the educational supports to make sure that students have the self-determination skills needed to engage in the goal setting, action planning, and evaluating. The Using the SDLMI in Practice research box discusses how John Kelly, a former special education teacher and current Assistant Professor of Special Education, implemented the SDLMI with students with emotional and behavior disorders.

The SDLMI provides a mechanism to explicitly teach students with disabilities how to set goals, solve problems, and direct their own behavior, enabling them to become self-regulated learners.

The research and personal stories of teachers and students shared in this chapter clearly show the power of goal setting and student-directed learning for improving student outcomes. The potential to embed opportunities for students to learn and practice goal-setting skills across instructional activities exists with teaching models such as the SDLMI. Teaching students self-determination skills does not have to be a separate, stand-alone activity. These activities can be embedded through the school day and beyond with creativity and openness to active student involvement.

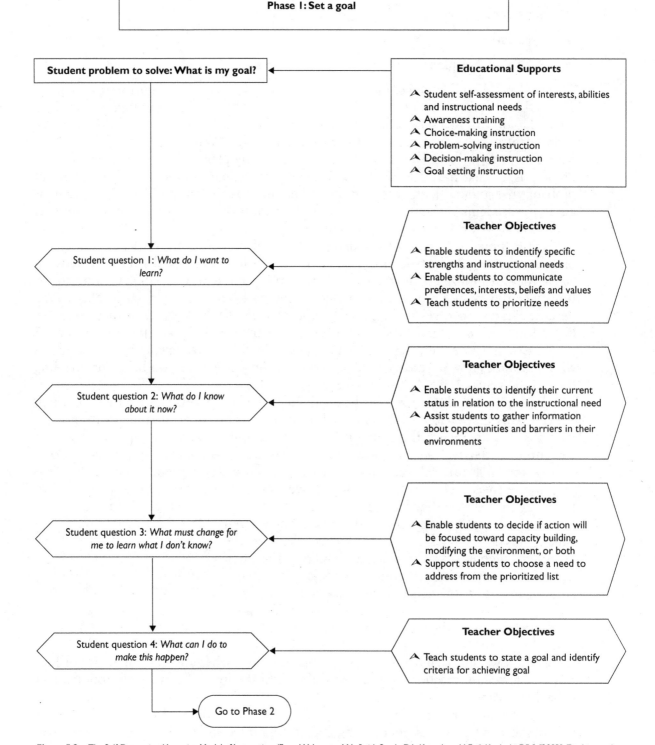

Figure 5.2. The Self-Determined Learning Model of Instruction. (From Wehmeyer, M.L. [with Sands, D.J., Knowlton, H.E., & Kozleski, E.B.]. [2002]. *Teaching students with mental retardation: Promoting access to the general curriculum* [pp. 246–248]. Baltimore, MD: Paul H. Brookes Publishing Co.; reprinted by permission.)

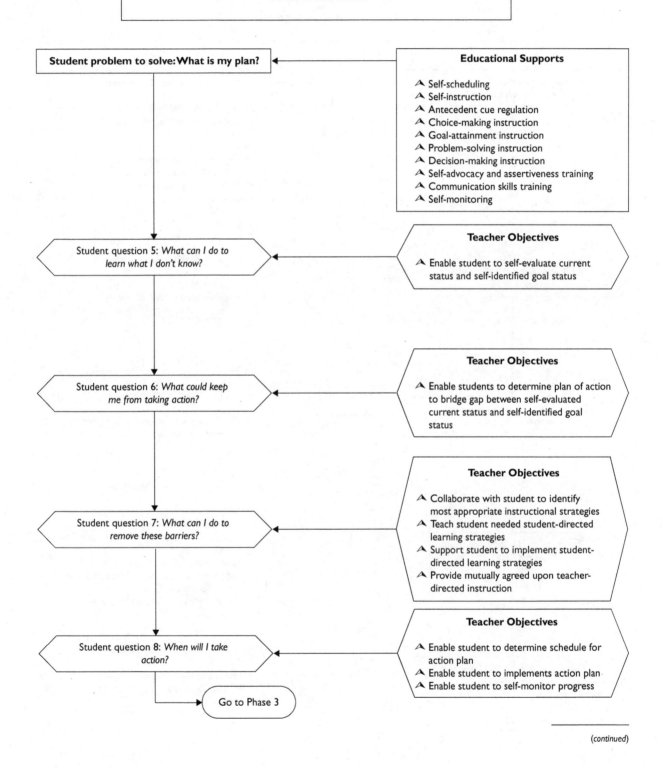

Phase 2: Take action

Student problem to solve: What is my plan?

Educational Supports

- Self-scheduling
- Self-instruction
- Antecedent cue regulation
- Choice-making instruction
- Goal-attainment instruction
- Problem-solving instruction
- Decision-making instruction
- Self-advocacy and assertiveness training
- Communication skills training
- Self-monitoring

Student question 5: *What can I do to learn what I don't know?*

Teacher Objectives

- Enable student to self-evaluate current status and self-identified goal status

Student question 6: *What could keep me from taking action?*

Teacher Objectives

- Enable students to determine plan of action to bridge gap between self-evaluated current status and self-identified goal status

Student question 7: *What can I do to remove these barriers?*

Teacher Objectives

- Collaborate with student to identify most appropriate instructional strategies
- Teach student needed student-directed learning strategies
- Support student to implement student-directed learning strategies
- Provide mutually agreed upon teacher-directed instruction

Student question 8: *When will I take action?*

Teacher Objectives

- Enable student to determine schedule for action plan
- Enable student to implements action plan
- Enable student to self-monitor progress

Go to Phase 3

(continued)

72

Shogren

Figure 5.2. *(continued)*

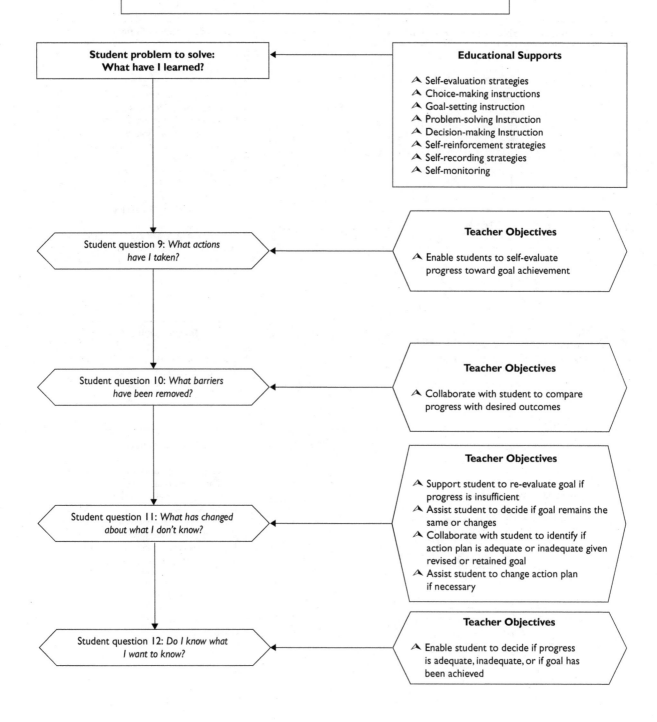

Using the
SDLMI in Practice

I faced a formidable task in a large high school located in a mid-size suburban school district in the Southwest. I had four male students with emotional and behavior disorders who were at risk of school failure, presumably due to challenging behaviors expressed in the classroom. Charles, Jack, and George were 16 years old and in 10th grade, and David was 14 years old and in the 9th grade. Charles and George also had specific learning disabilities, whereas Jack was also diagnosed with a cognitive disorder— processing speed discrepancy. All four students received academic and behavior support for one period in a segregated classroom, and each had an individualized behavior intervention plan that was rarely implemented in their general education classrooms. Each student appeared to have fairly stable relationships with other students but not their teachers. Each student's general education teachers reported severe academic problems due to their challenging behaviors in their classroom, despite an IEP that included access to specialized behavior instruction and accommodations. Behaviors included sleeping in class, daydreaming, talking without permission, texting, and talking out to the teacher and other students, which disrupted the learning environment.

I endeavored to independently teach each student self-determination skills because all four students appeared to be having difficulty regulating their school environments. Over a 6-week period between February and March, the four students received from six to ten 90-minute sessions of direct instruction in self-determination using the self-regulated, goal-setting, and problem-solving approach of the SDLMI. SDLMI is a research-based instructional model based on the theoretical principles of self-determination. I used a person-centered planning approach to guide my support for each student's engagement in SDLMI in a core general education classroom. Each student's focus was on increasing the on-task behavior they chose to emulate in the classroom. SDLMI instruction is composed of three problem-solving instructional phases. Each phase presents a problem in the form of a question to be solved by the student: What is my goal? What is my plan? What have I learned? Each of the three phases contained four supporting questions for a total of 12 questions. After I explicitly taught and modeled every step, each student utilized the 12 questions in a self-directed problem-solving sequence to set his own behavior goal, develop and implement an action plan to attain the behavior goal, and execute self-directed learning strategies (e.g., self-monitoring, self-evaluation, self-management) that allowed him to evaluate his progress toward his individual goal. Figure 5.3 shows one of the student's self-monitoring sheets.

All four students achieved significant gains in their on-task behaviors and subsequent reductions in off-task behaviors following introduction of SDLMI instruction. In addition, they were able to maintain and generalize their behavior to other classrooms and settings. Their inclusion teachers reported changes in attitudes, work completion, active participation, and improved attendance and grades. All students were excited about reaching their behavior goals and were ready to move on to another goal. Each student considered self-determination important to his improvement in the classroom, would use the process in the future, and would recommend it to others.

(continued)

Charles' Self-Monitoring Sheet

Date: _____ Class: _____

Goal: I will focus more in class to improve my performance as a student in order to make better grades so I
       can remain on the wrestling team, graduate, and go to college with a wrestling scholarship.

Action plan: 1) Check daily agenda with teacher.
              2) Get materials needed (e.g., pencil, timer, self-monitoring sheet).
              3) Enter assignments into planner's calendar and log.
              4) Place notes, reviews, and graded work behind divider in planner.
              5) Review goals, action plan, and on-task list and begin scoring.

Score on-task behaviors	9:10	9:20	9:30	9:40	9:50	10:00
1. Self-monitor on-task behaviors	On/Off	On/Off	On/Off	On/Off	On/Off	On/Off
2. Pay attention to the speaker	On/Off	On/Off	On/Off	On/Off	On/Off	On/Off
3. Work on assigned tasks	On/Off	On/Off	On/Off	On/Off	On/Off	On/Off
4. Use appropriate materials	On/Off	On/Off	On/Off	On/Off	On/Off	On/Off
5. Speak out appropriately on topic	On/Off	On/Off	On/Off	On/Off	On/Off	On/Off

Figure 5.3.   Self-monitoring sheet from John Kelly's work with students with emotional and behavior disorders. (Contributed by John Kelly.)

Contributed by John Kelly.

6

Promoting Skills Leading to Enhanced Self-Determination Through Self-Advocacy

I think I found my voice when I went to my first self-advocacy meeting and people were talking about dreams and hopes. I got to thinking about my dreams and hopes.

(Shogren and Broussard, 2011, p. 91)

I began to attend IEP meetings in the tenth grade, but the teachers did not ask me what I wanted. My dad asked me at home, and then he and my mom spoke for me in the meetings. At the end of the tenth grade, my guidance counselor, Mrs. Suter, asked me what courses I wanted to take the next year. I picked my classes. Some of the classes got changed in the IEP meeting, but they asked me first. I liked that. At the end of the eleventh grade, Mrs. Suter asked me what classes I wanted to take in the twelfth grade. I picked my classes. I got to take all of them that time. I felt great.

(Pauley, 1998, p. 125)

Self-advocacy is another skill associated with self-determined behavior. Field wrote that self-advocacy "refers to taking action on one's own behalf; acts of self-advocacy lead to greater self-determination" (1996, p. 42). Self-advocacy is all about understanding yourself and developing the skills to stand up and speak out for yourself. Self-advocates have the skills to take on leadership roles and go after the things they want in life. Students can use self-advocacy skills to advocate for their right to make choices, manage their own learning and behavior, and set goals.

The term *self-advocate* is often used within the disability field to refer to people with disabilities who are taking an active role in advocating for themselves and for the community of people with disabilities. This term emerged from the self-advocacy movement (Wehmeyer, Bersani, & Gagne, 2000), which was modeled after the civil rights movements of the 1950s and 1960s, including the African American and women's rights movements. The self-advocacy movement focused on establishing civil rights and creating opportunities for people with disabilities so they could be in charge of their own lives. The movement led to establishing self-advocacy organizations that were developed and run by people with intellectual and developmental disabilities. People First of Oregon was the first group and was established in 1974. There are more than 800 active self-advocacy groups across the country (Caldwell, 2010) in addition to Self-Advocates Becoming Empowered (SABE; http://www.sabeusa.org/), a national organization. Self-advocacy groups provide learning opportunities, social support, and community for people with disabilities, particularly regarding disability rights issues. Although SABE focuses on issues related to intellectual and developmental disabilities, other organizations focus on issues faced by other disability groups, such as the Autistic Self-Advocacy Network (http://autisticadvocacy.org/).

The chapter opening quote demonstrates the affect that self-advocacy organizations can have on the lives of people with disabilities and the power that comes from learning to advocate and having role models with disabilities. This quote was from a young adult who participated in a research study on the meaning of self-determination in the lives of people with disabilities (Shogren & Broussard, 2011) and reported that self-advocacy groups had been a major part of developing his self-determination. He emphasized that opportunities to interact with other people with disabilities and to advocate for disability rights allowed him to get to know himself better, expand his hopes and dreams, and learn to go after them.

"Nothing about us without us" is a quote often used by self-advocacy groups (http://autisticadvocacy.org/). It highlights the emphasis in the self-advocacy movement on actively involving people with disabilities in the organizations that affect their lives and providing a forum for advocating for individual and group rights. Although self-advocacy groups often target adults with disabilities, the importance of self-advocacy skills to positive transition outcomes has been repeatedly acknowledged in the literature (Izzo & Lamb, 2003; Thoma & Getzel, 2005). Several researchers have emphasized how self-advocacy groups can mentor and support students with disabilities as they are preparing for transition (Caldwell, 2010; Shogren & Broussard, 2011). Promoting the development of self-advocacy skills in youth who are transition age teaches them the skills that they will need when moving from the entitlement-driven education system to the eligibility-driven adult service system (Shogren & Plotner, 2012). Establishing needed supports and services can be a complex and difficult process in an eligibility-driven system. Young adults have to take an active role in requesting accommodations in postsecondary education and employment settings and in establishing eligibility for necessary services and supports (e.g., vocational rehabilitation, financial and insurance related supports, housing and community living supports).

Multiple opportunities are available for students to take advantage of during the transition process to develop their self-advocacy skills. Supporting students to participate in their IEP meetings is one mechanism to promote leadership and advocacy for students with disabilities. This provides a context for students to learn about and express themselves, as well as an opportunity to participate in developing their educational program. The second chapter opening quote is from Cecelia Pauley, an adult with a disability reflecting on her involvement in her IEP meetings when she was in school. She talks about how she did not have a role in her IEP meetings early in her high school career. Her quote shows that the meetings did not have meaning for her when she was not actively involved in some way. Cecelia felt more empowered and as though she was deciding the things happening in her life as she became a part of the team and was able to express her opinion and advocate for the things that mattered to her, first through her parents and then on her own with the support of her parents.

The Individuals with Disabilities Education Act Amendments (IDEA) of 1997 (PL 105-17) first required that students with disabilities be invited to attend their IEP meetings when transition-related issues were being discussed. Since this requirement was put in place, data suggest that a large number of students, such as Cecelia, are attending their IEP meetings and participating in transition planning in some way. Data from the National Longitudinal Transition Study–2 (http://www.nlts2.org), which collected data on a nationally representative sample of students with disabilities to examine their secondary school experiences and postschool outcomes, suggested that the majority of students do participate in some way in their transition planning. For example, educators reported that only 2% of students ages 17–18 did not attend transition planning meetings or participate in the transition planning process (Cameto, Levine, & Wagner, 2004).

A difference exists, however, between being an active, self-determined participant in the IEP and transition planning process and a passive participant who just sits at meetings and does not actively engage in setting goals and making action plans. Researchers found that if students attend meetings without instruction on how to participate or knowledge about what their role is in the meeting, then it can be detrimental to students' perceptions of themselves and their education (Lehmann, Bassett, & Sands, 1999; Powers, Turner, Matuszweski, Wilson, & Loesch, 1999). Unfortunately, data suggest that passive participation is the case for many students. Martin, Van Dycke, Greene, et al. (2006) observed more than 100 IEP meetings to examine who participates and how they participate. They recorded who was talking in every 10-second interval during the meeting. Students only talked 3% of the time.

> **TIP**
>
> *Promoting the development of self-advocacy skills in youth who are transition age teaches them the skills that they will need when moving from the entitlement-driven education system to the eligibility-driven adult service system.*

Martin, Van Dycke, Greene, et al. also looked at 12 "essential IEP meeting leadership skills" (p. 191) that can be taught to students to enable them to actively participate and even lead their own IEP meetings. These skills are listed in Table 6.1 and provide natural entry points for students to participate in the meeting and develop their self-advocacy skills. Martin, Van Dycke, Greene, et al. found that students did not engage in the majority of these activities during the meeting. Six percent or less of students engaged in the majority of the IEP meeting leadership skills. Almost 50% of students did state their interests during the meeting, 20% expressed their options and goals, and 27% expressed their skills and limits. So, students can take on these roles with opportunities and instruction. IEP meetings provide excellent opportunities for students to describe their interests and preferences (verbally or in other accessible ways), take ownership over their goals, and learn and practice leadership and advocacy skills as shown in Cecelia's quote.

This chapter discusses strategies to teach and create opportunities for developing self-advocacy skills. Taking a leadership role at IEP meetings, participating in self-advocacy

Table 6.1. IEP meeting leadership skills from the Self-Directed IEP process

Introduce myself
Introduce team members
State the purpose of meeting
Review past goals and progress on goals
Ask for feedback
Ask questions if I do not understand
Deal with differences of opinion
State needed supports
Express my interests
Express my skills and limitations
Expression options and goals
Close the meeting by thanking everyone

Source: Martin et al, 1996; Martin et al., 2006.

activities, and having opportunities to learn about and speak up for their needs are all ways to support students to develop the skills needed to advocate in their life.

TEACHING SELF-ADVOCACY SKILLS

Test, Fowler, Wood, Brewer, and Eddy (2005) reviewed the literature on self-advocacy and developed a conceptual framework for thinking about the components that define self-advocacy. They based their conceptual framework on more than 20 definitions of self-advocacy found in the literature, the intervention components included in multiple research studies examining the impact of self-advocacy, and input from 30 researchers, teachers, parents, and people with disabilities. They identified four components that can be the basis of teaching self-advocacy skills:

1. Knowledge of self

2. Knowledge of rights

3. Communication of one's knowledge of self and rights

4. Leadership

Knowledge of Self

Knowledge of self and knowledge of rights are called the "foundations of self-advocacy" (Test, Fowler, Wood, et al., 2005, p. 45). It is impossible to effectively communicate or lead unless you know yourself, your interests, and your rights. Knowing yourself is all about understanding your strengths, preferences, and interests as well as understanding your needed supports. The strategies described in Chapter 3 to assess preferences and teach choice making can be key parts of supporting students to gain knowledge of themselves. Other strategies for teaching self-awareness and knowledge exist. For example, the Self-Advocacy Strategy, an instructional strategy developed to teach students the skills to participate in meetings, teaches students five steps called I PLAN to help them understand their strengths, needs, and goals (Van Reusen, Bos, Schumaker, & Deshler, 1994). The five steps are 1) *I*nventory strengths, needs, goals, and choices; 2) *P*rovide your inventory; 3) *L*isten and respond; 4) *A*sk questions; and 5) *N*ame your goals. During the inventory step, students complete a personal inventory in which they list their strengths, areas to improve, learning preferences, and goals. In the following steps, students learn how to effectively share this information with others. Researchers have documented that students with learning disabilities and emotional and behavior disorders can learn this process of inventorying their strengths, needs, goals, and choices to more effectively participate in their IEP meetings (Test & Neale, 2004; Van Reusen & Bos, 1994).

Students learning about and understanding their disabilities is another aspect of developing self-knowledge. For example, Campbell-Whatley (2008) developed a 13-week curriculum to teach students with learning disabilities and mild intellectual disability about their disabilities. Lessons focused on what it means to have a disability, successful people with disabilities, understanding special education programs, and understanding strengths and weaknesses. Students showed improvements in their self-concept and increased understanding of their disability and associated strengths and weaknesses after the curriculum was implemented. Jake, one of the students featured throughout this book, developed a presentation that enabled him to build his self-awareness. Jake learned in a workshop at a self-advocacy conference for youth with disabilities to create a PowerPoint that shared information about his strengths and talents, his autism and how it affected him, his interests, and things that work well for him in learning and life (see Figure 6.1).

Introducing Me

By
Jake

Strengths and Talents

Everyone has strengths and talents.

My strengths and talents are things I can do well and enjoy doing:

1. Foreign languages
2. Music
3. Remembering details
4. Perfect pitch
5. Calendar calculation

Autism is Another Thing About Me

- Another thing about me is that I have Autism. Most children do not have Autism, but some do. I am one of the children who has Autism.

- There are children and adults all over the world who have Autism. I might not know any other people who have Autism, but maybe someday I will meet others.

- People with Autism are different from each other. Some talk a little and some talk a lot!

- I have a special kind of Autism called high-functioning Autism or Asperger Syndrome. Sometimes it is called PDD or PDDNOS. It can be called Autism Spectrum Disorder. All of these terms are related to Autism.

What is Autism?

- Autism is invisible. No one can see Autism. It is one of the things that make me who I am.

- Autism affects the way my brain works. The brain is like a computer which is always on and keeps people living and learning. Autism causes my brain to sometimes work differently than other people's brains.

- Having a brain with Autism is like having a computer with an Autism Operating System (AOS), while most other people have a Plain Operating System (POS).

- Autism makes me experience the world in a certain way. Sometimes it's the same as most people, but sometimes I experience the world differently.

Why Do I Have Autism?

No one knows why I have Autism. Scientists are not sure what causes Autism in particular people. They are trying to find out why some children have Autism and others do not. Autism is still a mystery. But they do know *some* things about it.

Why Do I Have Autism? cont'd

Scientists know that

– Autism is not a disease, and it does not mean that I am sick.

– "Autism is not contagious" - Jessica "Jazz" Summers, Sept. 7, 2007.

– It does not mean that I am bad or wrong, or that I am better than other children.

– It's nobody's fault that I have Autism.

– Autism is called *neurological* because it involves my brain.

– Sometimes it appears to be genetic. Cousins, uncles, aunts, brothers, sisters, or other family members might also have Autism.

Figure 6.1. Jake's PowerPoint presentation. (Reprinted with permission from Jake's family.)

(continued)

Figure 6.1.   *(continued)*

Special Interests

- Airplanes, cockpits, highways, the internet, music, travel and football.

- I like to talk about, research or sometimes draw what my interests are.

- Some children with Autism have the same special interests for a long time.

Details

- Sometimes people say I have a good memory.

- The kinds of things children with Autism notice and remember are called details.

- Details can be colors, letters, numbers, shapes, places, names, signs, smells, sounds, dates, times, phone numbers and many other things.

Details (cont.)

I usually remember details that are interesting to me, or that are related to my special interests. Some details I notice and remember are:

1. Information about maps

2. Information about United States Presidents

3. Information about Airlines/ Airports

Styles Of Learning

Everyone learns. Sometimes learning is easy and sometimes learning is difficult. Children learn in different ways. Everyone has his or her own style of learning.

·I like it when:
- I can watch what people are doing.
- There are pictures I can see.
- There are words I can read.
- Someone reads to me.
- It's my special interest.
- People talk a lot.
- If I feel motivated.

Routines and Familiarity

Children with Autism like routines and familiarity. A routine is when I do the same things in the same ways. Familiarity means being used to something.

Routines make me feel good because I know what to expect. I like to know what is going to happen and when it will happen. I usually feel better when things are familiar to me.

Routines and Familiarity, cont'd

·I like these things to *stay the same*:
- Where I usually go every day
- What I like to do every day at the same time
- Who I usually see on a particular day of the week
- When we eat dinner
- The date of departure to and return from my cousins stays the same
- The time that something is scheduled to start or to end

Jake expanded this presentation and used it multiple times when speaking in university courses, to parent groups, and to other professional audiences working to achieve his goal of becoming a keynote speaker (see Chapter 5). Jake has also been able to use information from the presentation on autism to educate others about his needs, including the staff at the community college he attends.

Knowledge of Rights

In addition to understanding oneself, it is also important for students to understand their rights. This includes "knowing one's rights as a citizen, as an individual with a disability, and as a student receiving services under federal law" (Test, Fowler, Wood, et al., 2005, p. 50). The right to reasonable accommodations is one important area for students to learn about. Students with disabilities are often very unclear about their rights and responsibilities when they make the transition from high school to postsecondary education (Field, Sarver, & Shaw, 2003; Janiga & Costenbader, 2002). Students tend to be unclear about what reasonable accommodations are and what protections there are for students with disabilities under the Americans with Disabilities Act (ADA) of 1990 (PL 101-336) and Section 504 of the Rehabilitation Act of 1973 (PL 93-112). Numerous studies have taught college students how to request accommodations and advocate for themselves in postsecondary environments (Walker & Test, 2011; White & Vo, 2006). Other studies have taught adults with disabilities how to request reasonable accommodations in job settings (Rumrill, 1999). Teaching these skills while students are still in school has the potential to improve transition outcomes.

Wood, Kelley, Test, and Fowler (2010) developed an intervention to teach high school students with disabilities their rights and responsibilities in postsecondary settings under the ADA. The researchers used a document from the U.S. Department of Education called "Students with Disabilities Preparing for Postsecondary Education: Know Your Rights and Responsibilities" (available at http://www2.ed.gov/about/offices/list/ocr/transition.html) as the basis for their intervention. They compared the impact of 1) having students interact with the document with audio support for reading the text and 2) having students read the document with audio support plus explicit instruction on the skills (e.g., having students respond to questions about accommodations and rights). Students developed more knowledge of rights and responsibilities when explicit instruction was provided and generalized their learning to new situations. The authors held a mock interview with the students structured around interacting with someone from a disability services office, and students were able to use their knowledge gained through instruction to more effectively discuss their needed accommodations. This suggests the importance of explicit instruction on rights and responsibilities to an adult with a disability.

Communication

After developing the foundation for understanding yourself and your rights, students have to learn how to effectively communicate this knowledge of themselves and their rights to others. Effective communication is complex and requires students to demonstrate numerous different skills. In addition, effective communication about oneself and one's rights may require specific communication skills related to requesting accommodations and needed supports. Researchers have identified key elements that should be a part of communication training when the focus in on supporting self-advocacy, including body language, listening skills, recruiting help, and assertiveness training (Test, Fowler, Wood, et al., 2005).

Several researchers suggested assertiveness training is key to self-advocacy because of the nature of communicating knowledge of yourself and your rights. Weston and Went identified four elements of assertiveness:

1. Knowing what you want

2. The confidence and ability to express your wants, needs, and opinions openly and honestly

3. The skill to negotiate with others

4. A respect for the rights of others (1999, p. 110)

The strategies previously described can enable students to better understand what they want. Opportunities to explore wants and needs can assist students in developing the confidence to express them. Researchers have suggested a variety of strategies to teach students to negotiate and demonstrate respect for others. For example, researchers created scenarios in which students need to express their goals and request supports to achieve those goals. They first role-played the situations with students and then tested the degree to which students generalized the skills modeled to real situations (Balcazar, Fawcett, & Seekins, 1991; Weston & Went, 1999). They found that role-playing instruction was an effective strategy for teaching communication skills, but real-world opportunities to practice the skills were also important. Creating such opportunities is possible throughout the instructional day. Students can be involved in setting up a class schedule, working out their needed supports with a resource room teacher or other support provider, and participating in IEP and transition meetings. Figure 6.2 highlights a strategy that can be used to integrate students with disabilities into the process of understanding and requesting accommodations in high school. Michel Stringer, a high school special education teacher, created this accommodation card. After instruction in a resource setting on understanding yourself, your disability, your rights and responsibilities, and assertive communication, students were given the responsibility of talking to all of their general education teachers about their accommodations and getting each teacher to sign off on the student using the requested accommodations in class. Students also had a laminated card that they carried with them listing their accommodations on one side and giving them tips to remind them how to use their accommodations on the other side.

Students will likely differ in the support they need to assertively communicate personal knowledge of themselves and their rights. The accommodation letter and card shown in Figure 6.2 will be appropriate for some students, such as Jake. Other students may communicate in different ways and may need different supports to communicate their knowledge of themselves. Michael, the other student featured throughout this book, communicates differently, primarily through technology and behavior as highlighted in earlier chapters. For example, Chapter 3 showed how Michael communicated his preferences and choices through technology by picking between different pictures on his computer. Michael's support team is also exploring the creation of video portfolios depicting Michael completing work-related tasks that he can then use to assertively communicate his skills as he is seeking employment opportunities. Although this differs from the forms of communication that Jake and other students might use, Michael is still acting as a self-advocate by assertively communicating his knowledge of himself with technology supports.

Leadership

Leadership is the last component of self-advocacy identified by Test, Fowler, Wood, et al. (2005). Leadership is all about learning the roles of a group and learning how to function

Dear Teachers,

This letter is to inform you that I, _____, have worked with my case manager to develop reasonable accommodations that I am allowed to receive within the classroom. I am aware that in order for me to receive these accommodations I am responsible for approaching you and requesting those accommodations in advance.

Please review the accommodations listed at the bottom of this page and sign below identifying that you have viewed this letter. A copy of this letter will be provided for you to reference. If you have any questions, please feel free to contact my case manager, _____.

Thank you,

List of reasonable classroom accommodations

1. _____   5. _____
2. _____   6. _____
3. _____   7. _____
4. _____   8. _____

Teacher's signature_____

1st Hour _____   5th Hour _____
2nd Hour _____   6th Hour _____
3rd Hour _____   7th Hour _____
4th Hour _____

Front

Name: _____

My reasonable accommodations are

  1.

  2.

  3.

  4.

  5.

  6.

  7.

  8.

Back

Steps to accessing reasonable accommodations

1. Talk with the teacher, show them this card, remind them of my reasonable accommodation

2. Use reasonable accommodation in class the way I am supposed to use it

3. Talk to my case manager if I have a question.

Figure 6.2.   Michel Stringer's accommodation letter and card. (Reprinted with permission from Michel Stringer.)

in a group. Leadership is often associated with students leading their IEP meetings, which is discussed in the following section. Although this is a great opportunity for students to learn and practice leadership skills, it is important to remember that there are also many other opportunities for leadership during the instructional day and beyond. Students can be involved in setting up their class schedule, taking on a leadership role in group activities, and participating in extracurricular activities. Youth Leadership Forums (YLF; http://www.aylf.net/index.html) are one effort that has focused on developing youth leadership skills outside of the school day. YLF focuses on teaching leadership skills, promoting career exploration, teaching about civil rights, and handling discrimination (Wehmeyer, Gragoudas, & Shogren, 2006). YLF are typically intensive training programs held over the summer, with ongoing support and communication throughout the school year.

Involvement in Transition and Educational Planning   Taking an active role in transition and educational planning is another way for students to practice their self-advocacy skills, including communication and leadership skills. Martin, Huber Marshall, and Sale (2004) conducted a 3-year study of IEP meetings and found that the condition of the

Sue Walter's Experiences with Student-Led IEP Meetings

I worked diligently to prepare my daughter, Jennifer, for an IEP meeting at the high school that would also include her first transition plan. We talked about why it was important, who would be at the meeting, and what we would be discussing. I knew how important is was for Jennifer to know what to expect so that she could meaningfully participate because I am a professional in the field, serving as a statewide transition consultant and working with districts across the state. Jennifer did not quite make it through the doorway before she started to cry and insist that she did not want to stay for this meeting, in spite of what I considered a thorough preparation. Looking back, I hate to admit it, but I was rather upset and just a little embarrassed. I felt like I had prepared Jennifer and I asked myself, "What didn't I do right?" I was talking to Jennifer later that same day at home and trying to explain my disappointment. My son, a couple of years older than Jennifer, was snacking in the kitchen listening and soon gave me a reality check. He said, "You're upset at her for not wanting to be in a room with all of those adults, including the principal, where all they did was talk about what was wrong with her? I'd never forgive you, Mom, if you put me in a situation like that!" His perspective really made me step back and think about this from a teenager's point of view. We tried to understand and respect Jennifer's anxiety as we moved forward. It was certainly a great benefit and good luck that I was involved in a state systems change grant focused on transition, with a strong emphasis on promoting student involvement in IEP meetings. I had access to training, resources, and experts in the field that provided me with a lot of ideas for supporting students with disabilities to be more actively engaged in their IEP decisions.

We started to use some of the materials from this grant with Jennifer. There was a person-centered transition planning workbook that helped Jennifer think about what worked and did not work for her, what she wanted to accomplish and learn while still in high school, what she wanted to do after high school, and who she wanted to participate in her IEP/transition planning meeting. The results of this workbook helped the team, including Jennifer and myself, prepare for a more student-centered, positive IEP meeting. We also tried to tune into and respect Jennifer's anxieties about different areas of life; the IEP meeting being an anxiety-inducer because it was intimidating and unfamiliar. All of the team's adults agreed to give Jennifer more choice in how she would be involved at the next IEP meeting. She decided to stay in the hallway outside the room where the team met with the door open. At first we were not sure if she was paying attention; she drove her power chair back and forth in front of the open door. But, we heard Jennifer yell, "No way," from the hallway when we were talking about a particular class we thought she should take. She was still able to express her ideas even though she was not in the room.

Jennifer moved forward from there. She sat in the doorway the next year. She joined the circle that the IEP team was sitting in the following year. Everyone on the team accepted her on her terms and supported her to participate in ways that were comfortable for her. We were teaching students 10 steps to lead their own IEP meeting as part of the systems change grant. Jennifer never completed all of the steps because of her support needs and anxiety. But she did about three of them by her final IEP meeting. It was so exciting; she welcomed everyone and actively contributed throughout the meeting.

An observable transformation occurred in the adult participants as each year passed. There were more than a dozen people in the room in some meetings, including representatives from the local community college, the local adult services provider, and all the school team members. As we continued to employ self-directed strategies, each and every one of them began to look at Jennifer when they were talking, and they directed their questions to her (instead of focusing on me for input); they essentially made her a true member of the team. I think this changing dynamic helped Jennifer feel more confident. I do not think Jennifer would have been as comfortable and able to participate without these subtle changes and without a flexible team spirit. So many of the team members commented on how exciting the meeting was and how much more meaningful the IEP and transition planning process was for everyone.

The confidence that Jennifer developed from participating in her meetings has played a big role in Jennifer's postschool success. She was really anxious and was thinking about backing out when she first started at the local community college, but she went and experienced that high that we all do upon succeeding at something scary or difficult. She was crying out, "I did it, Mom, I did it," when she was rolling up the sidewalk after her first day. I think all of these experiences have made her more self-determined and helped her develop confidence that has allowed her to be part of the community and navigate difficult situations. She learned how to respectfully communicate with others, while also advocating for her needs. She also learned how to communicate when people struggle to understand her. Jennifer now has connections throughout our community and is pursuing her dream of being an artist. She is participating in art fairs and just had an art show in the community. She is well known at her church and in local shops all around the community. All of the activities around participating in the IEP helped Jennifer have the confidence to express herself and, I believe, laid a foundation for her ongoing development as a self-determined adult.

The systems change project and Jennifer's experiences have shaped the professionals that worked with her, her school, and all the people that have heard me present on these experiences at transition conferences, workshops, and in-service trainings. Hearing how this can actually work with an individual with significant support needs shows the power of this approach for the individual and for the team. Teachers in Jennifer's school (and schools throughout the state) have continued using these materials with other students; they have even been adapted for students with significant learning and communication barriers. Jennifer's experiences positively affected her, but have also rippled forward to affect other students and professionals throughout the state. I believe that the seemingly simple tools used for person-centered planning and support for self-direction hold a transformative power that moves young adults with disabilities onto a pathway where small successes build to success in adult life—a place where all of us want to be.

Contributed by Sue Walter.

Research on Student Involvement in IEP Meetings

Test and colleagues (2004) conducted a systematic review of the literature published on student involvement in IEP meetings. They identified 16 articles that implemented an intervention to teach students skills necessary to participating in their IEP meetings. These studies included approximately 300 students. Nine studies examined a curriculum designed to increase student participation in their IEP meetings, including several of those described in the resource list at the end of this book. Six studies looked at the impact of person-centered planning strategies on student involvement in their IEP meetings (see Chapter 8). One study looked at a combination of a curriculum and a person-centered planning strategy.

The students included in the studies had a wide range of disabilities, including learning disabilities, intellectual disability, developmental disabilities, behavior disorders, other health impairments, and traumatic brain injury. Instruction occurred in a classroom setting, typically a resource or self-contained classroom for students with disabilities, for the nine studies that evaluated the implementation of a curriculum. The instruction was delivered in small groups in eight studies and in one-to-one, individualized instruction in one study. The instructional time ranged from 2–3 hours to 36 hours, with an average of 13.2 hours. Instruction typically involved verbal rehearsal, role play, and prompts. The intervention typically occurred in the community when person-centered planning was the focus of the study. Several studies that used person-centered planning included both direct instruction for the student in the targeted skills as well as a facilitator who supported the student to use these skills during the IEP meeting. This suggests that a facilitator may be important in creating the conditions at an IEP meeting where a student can use his or her self-advocacy skills.

Findings across studies suggest that students can learn and apply the necessary skills to participate in their IEP meetings and simultaneously show increases in self-determination. Although diverse disability groups were represented in the sample, the majority did have a label of learning disability. This is consistent with other reviews of the self-determination literature that suggested that research on self-advocacy interventions is most common with students with learning disabilities (Algozzine et al., 2001). Further research is needed on strategies to promote student involvement for students with other disabilities labels and, in particular, for students who may use different means of communication to express their interests, preferences, and goals. In addition, diverse curricula were examined in the nine studies that included a formal curriculum to teach these skills. Several of the curricula only had one study evaluating their effectiveness and were not readily available for purchase or use.

Additional research on curricula to involve students in their IEP meetings has been done since Test, Fowler, Brewer, and Wood (2005). Two important studies implemented randomized control trial designs, which randomly assigned students to a treatment group that received the intervention or a control group that did not. These designs are important to establishing the efficacy of the intervention. The Self-Directed IEP (Martin, et al., 1996) curriculum was evaluated in a randomized control trial by Martin, Van Dycke, Christensen, et al. (2006). They looked at the impact of the Self-Directed IEP curriculum on the meeting behaviors, including the percentage of time students talked, and the leadership behaviors (see Table 6.1) of students with disabilities. They found that students went from talking in 3% of intervals to talking in 13% of 10-intervals, and students demonstrated many more leadership behaviors after intervention with the self-directed IEP. Another randomized control trial study examined the impact of the *Whose Future Is It Anyway?* curriculum and found that intervention with the curriculum led to increases in students' self-determination (Wehmeyer, Palmer, Lee, Williams-Diehm, & Shogren, 2011). These and various other curricula described at the end of this book provide a diverse set of resources that can be matched to the unique needs of each student, teacher, and school to promote self-advocacy and student involvement in IEP meetings.

Research on the Impact of Self-Advocacy Interventions for Students with Disabilities

Test, Fowler, Brewer, et al. (2005) reviewed the published literature in the area of self-advocacy interventions between 1972 and 2004. They identified 25 intervention studies and 175 position papers, nonintervention studies, books, and curricula. They focused on the 25 intervention studies and analyzed the research to determine the characteristics of self-advocacy interventions and their impact. The 25 studies included 626 students with disabilities. The participants ranged in age from 12–69, but the majority were between the ages of 13–21. The majority of participants had a learning disability (273 students) or an intellectual disability (243 students), but other sensory, physical, and behavioral disabilities were also represented in the articles.

The majority of interventions were delivered in a school classroom, typically a self-contained or resource classroom. Six of the studies focused on teaching assertiveness skills using role play and visual prompts. Two studies focused on teaching rights, one study taught students a series of steps to follow to request accommodations, and another focused on skills for recruiting help. Eight studies focused on teaching students to participate in their IEP meeting using video, lecture, simulated IEP meetings, and workbook tasks. The remaining studies focused on teaching multiple self-advocacy and self-determination skills, using researcher-developed materials and curricula. For example, one study had units on living with a disability, role models with disabilities, and needed skills for successful transition.

Researchers found that students learned self-advocacy skills as a result of instruction and were able to generalize these skills to new situations. Some researchers observed students in planning meetings and found they were able to use the self-advocacy skills they were taught. Other researchers followed students after intervention ended and found that students continued to use their skills up to a year after intervention ended.

The research provides support for the impact of self-advocacy instruction on students' self-advocacy and self-determination skills. Thinking back to the four elements of self-advocacy identified by Test, Fowler, Wood, et al. (2005), however, the knowledge of self and communication domains were primarily addressed in this research base. Some studies also provided instruction in knowledge of rights, but leadership, aside from participation in the IEP meeting, was not taught or assessed. Delivering instruction and creating opportunities in all of these domains is important to promote self-advocacy and valued outcomes for students with disabilities.

meetings changed when students attended. There was an increase in parent involvement and in the likelihood that a student's strengths, needs, and interests would be discussed. Students can do more than just attend meetings. Students can learn to use self-advocacy skills to be involved in their transition and educational planning. Students can be included by expressing their preferences and interests, generating their own IEP goals and objectives, and monitoring their progress on goals and objectives. Students can also take on an active role during the meeting itself. Table 6.1 shows an array of behaviors that students can use during their IEP meetings to express their communication and leadership skills. Some students may target performing one or two of these behaviors, whereas others may take on a leadership role during their entire meeting, engaging in all of these behaviors. Students can do this orally or through pictures, videos, and technology. The Sue Walter's Experiences with Student-Led IEP Meetings research box provides an example from Sue Walter, a statewide transition consultant, on how her daughter Jennifer took an active role in her IEP meeting.

Numerous instructional strategies and curricula have been developed to teach students specific skills related to taking a leadership role in their educational planning. The Research on Student Involvement in IEP Meetings research box summarizes findings from research on promoting student involvement in IEP meetings. The resource list at the end of the book also provides an overview of several curricula that are readily available to use to teach the skills necessary to promote student involvement.

IMPACT OF SELF-ADVOCACY ON OUTCOMES

Self-advocacy skills are critically important to enabling students to navigate the adult world, given the fact that disability-related discrimination is still present and that students with disabilities struggle to achieve the outcomes they desire (Wagner, Newman, Cameto, Garza, & Levine, 2005). Self-advocacy involves a diverse array of skills and abilities and is vital to the development and expression of student self-determination. Researchers have consistently demonstrated that students with diverse disability labels can learn self-advocacy skills and effectively use these skills to advocate for what they want and need in many domains of life. The Research on the Impact of Self-Advocacy Interventions for Students with Disabilities research box summarizes a review of the literature on the characteristics and impact of self-advocacy instruction on students with disabilities.

Adults with disabilities confirm that self-advocacy is critical to their success and to their ability to express and use their other self-determination skills (Carter, Swedeen, Walter, Moss, & Hsin, 2011; Shogren & Broussard, 2011; Thoma & Getzel, 2005). For example, Thoma and Getzel interviewed college students with disabilities about the role of self-determination in success at college. Students said, "No one understood my disability and I was told that I could not attend college. I had to explain it to others and ask for accommodations" (p. 237). Shogren and Broussard interviewed self-advocates about the role of self-determination in their life, and self-advocates repeatedly discussed how they had to advocate, particularly in employment settings, because people were "looking at my disability and not the person I am" (p. 91).

Self-advocacy skills are critical for successfully expressing and obtaining what one needs and wants.

Providing students with disabilities with instruction in the skills discussed in this and previous chapters has the potential to enable students to become self-determining young adults. Each of the skill domains–choice, self-management, goal setting, and self-advocacy–involve unique implications for instruction, but together lay the foundation for students to achieve the outcomes they want in life.

7

Creating Opportunities for Self-Determination

She needs to learn [to solve problems] because we are not always going to be around her, to fix things, to guide her all the time. So she needs to learn.

(Shogren, 2012, p. 173)

You have to go do something or you won't be nothing at all.

(Shogren and Broussard, 2011, p. 90)

Chapters 3–6 explored specific skills associated with self-determination—choice making, self-management strategies, goal setting, and self-advocacy—that can be the targets of instructional activities embedded throughout a student's instructional program. The word *opportunity* was repeatedly used throughout these chapters. Chapter 1 introduced the functional theory of self-determination, and the importance of teaching skills, creating opportunities, and building supports for students to become causal agents—or people that make things happen to improve their quality of life—was emphasized.

Systematically planning for the creation of opportunities for student self-determination is necessary for the development of self-determination. Teaching and mastering skills is important, but creating repeated opportunities for students to practice these skills so that they develop the attitudes that define self-determination is just as important. Think about this for yourself. If you learn to do something but never apply it, then will you feel confident, comfortable, and empowered to use the skill in your day-to-day life? People often say, "It's just like riding a bike," to refer to a skill that is learned and retained. If we learned to ride a bike once, then we can usually jump back on a bike and remember how to pedal and steer, even if we have not ridden a bike in 10 years. Does this mean that you would be comfortable going on a long-distance ride? Biking on a road with multiple lanes of traffic? Keeping up with friends who ride every week? Just because we have mastered a skill does not mean we will use the skill in a functional way across diverse situations if we do not have repeated practice on an ongoing basis. The same is true for self-determination. We can learn self-determination skills, but we will not be able act as causal agents over our lives unless we repeatedly use these skills. Being a causal agent is all about acting with intent across multiple domains that define quality of life. That is why opportunities are so important to developing self-determination. Students need to become empowered users of choice-making, goal-setting, self-management, and self-advocacy skills so that they are able to apply these skills with confidence to whatever situations life throws at them.

The chapter opening quotes demonstrate that families and individuals with disabilities see the importance of opportunities to develop self-determination. The first quote is from a mother of a daughter who is transition age and has an intellectual disability that was interviewed as part of a research project exploring how Hispanic mothers perceived self-determination (Shogren, 2012). Her family placed a great deal of emphasis on self-determination, especially on problem solving and goal setting. Knowing that their daughter would be able to communicate her needs and handle challenges that came her way, even if they were not able to support her, was something that was critically important to them when thinking about adulthood. The second quote is from an individual with an intellectual disability and epitomizes the importance of opportunities. This young man was talking about going after job opportunities and how he would not be able to grow into the person that he wanted to be and to go after the things that he wanted in life if he did not use his self-determination skills when opportunities arose to go after jobs. These quotes and the stories that are shared throughout this chapter tell us that self-determination is about much more than discrete skills, it is about using these skills in a meaningful, flexible, and empowered way to go after things in life.

This chapter introduces the importance of opportunities to developing attitudes that support self-determination. It focuses on strategies to assess the learning environment and identify and implement opportunities for students to practice self-determination skills. The relationship of opportunities and attitudes to positive outcomes is detailed.

ATTITUDES ASSOCIATED WITH SELF-DETERMINED BEHAVIOR

The environments in which students with disabilities live, learn, work and play exert a significant influence on the development of self-determination. Environments that are full of opportunities for practicing the skills listed in Table 1.1 and described in Chapters 3–6 lead to students developing the attitudes associated with self-determination—an internal locus of control, self-efficacy, and positive outcome expectancies—which are defined and described in the following sections. As these attitudes develop, students become psychologically empowered, which is an essential characteristic of self-determination. Environments are not always full of opportunities to practice the skills listed in Table 1.1, however. Students with disabilities often have restricted opportunities for choice, are passive participants in IEP and transition planning meetings, and have goals set for them rather than being involved in the process of setting their own goals. It can be challenging to think about embedding self-determination throughout an instructional day when there are so many instructional considerations. Yet, self-determination can make things more meaningful for everyone.

Students develop attitudes that lead to psychological empowerment when we create repeated opportunities for self-determined behavior. The following sections describe these attitudes and why they are important to the outcomes that students with disabilities experience.

Locus of Control

People typically talk about locus of control on a continuum that ranges from a highly internal to a highly external locus of control orientation. People with an internal locus of control orientation perceive their actions as influencing the outcomes they experience, whereas people with an external locus of control orientation perceive their actions as having little or no influence on the outcomes they experience (Nowicki & Strickland,

1973; Rotter, 1966). Researchers found that younger children tend to demonstrate more external orientations, but orientations tend to become more internalized as children and youth age (Wehmeyer, 1994b). This occurs as children and youth have opportunities to see the relationship between their actions and the consequences they experience. This is why repeated opportunities are so important to developing internal locus of control orientations. Youth will not come to see their actions as influencing their outcomes without opportunities to see the consequences of one's actions (good and bad).

Students develop attitudes that lead to psychological empowerment when we create repeated opportunities for self-determined behavior.

Research has linked internal locus of control orientations with many positive outcomes, including positive academic outcomes (Huebner, Ash, & Laughlin, 2001; Wehmeyer & Kelchner, 1996) and adult outcomes (Wehmeyer, 1993, 1994a; Wehmeyer, Kelchner, & Richards, 1996). Researchers found, however, that students with disabilities tend to have more external locus of control orientations than their peers without disabilities. A study examined the locus of control orientations of students ages 8–18 with learning disabilities, intellectual disability, and no disabilities (Shogren, Bovaird, Palmer, & Wehmeyer, 2010). The researchers found that students with learning disabilities developed more internal perceptions as they aged, but they still had more negative orientations than their peers without disabilities. Students with intellectual disability had more negative orientations than their peers with both learning and no disabilities and did not develop more adaptive perceptions as they aged. One of the possible explanations for these findings discussed by the researchers is that students with disabilities do not have enough exposure to experiences that allow them to develop an understanding of the relationship between their actions and the outcomes they experience, which is why creating opportunities for self-determination skills is so important.

Self-Efficacy and Positive Outcome Expectancies

Self-efficacy and positive outcome expectancies are another attitude associated with self-determination. Albert Bandura, a major researcher in this area, wrote that self-efficacy is "not a measure of the skills one has but a belief about what one can do under different sets of conditions with whatever skills one possesses" (1997, p. 37). Specifically, self-efficacy is a "belief in one's capabilities to organize and execute the course of action required to produce given attainments" (1997, p. 3). Related to this, outcome expectancies are "a judgment of the likely consequence such performance will produce" (1997, p. 21). Self-efficacy essentially represents a belief in the ability to set goals and develop action plans to achieve those goals. Outcome expectancies relate to the belief that the expected outcome will result. Bandura and other researchers noted that these beliefs are critical to the motivation to apply the skills that were learned. Skills will not be used unless environments create opportunities to learn that outcomes will be achieved if skills are applied. If this belief does not emerge, then students will have little motivation to persist in the face of challenges. If students develop the belief that other people (e.g., teachers, peers, family) or other circumstances (e.g., disability) are what lead to outcomes, and not their own behavior, then students are likely to learn to defer to others and/or believe that their behavior cannot influence their circumstances.

If students learn self-determination skills and have meaningful opportunities and supports to apply these skills, then they can grow to feel empowered and able to act in a way that leads to desired outcomes. This does not mean that students need to be successful all the time, however. Sometimes students need to have opportunities to fail and be supported to learn the process of understanding why things did not work and how to identify a different goal or action plan to make things work. These experiences lead to a sense of self-efficacy.

Self-efficacy and positive outcome expectancies are associated with positive outcomes. Researchers have consistently found that children and youth without disabilities who believe that they can regulate their own learning (e.g., set goals, develop action plans, problem-solve when difficulties arise) perform better academically independent of skill level (Schunk & Zimmerman, 2007; Zimmerman, 2000; Zimmerman & Kitsantas, 2005). This suggests that one's beliefs about how well one can perform are as important as one's skill level, and creating opportunities for these beliefs to develop is critically important when supporting students with disabilities. Bandura (1997) suggested four ways that support the development of self-efficacy and positive outcome expectancies in youth, including 1) mastery experience, 2) vicarious learning, 3) verbal persuasion, and 4) physiological cues. Students must have repeated opportunities to perform similar tasks to promote mastery experiences, internalizing the belief that their behavior influences the outcomes they experience. They may not be successful all the time, but having multiple opportunities for success leads to feelings of self-efficacy. Vicarious learning involves observing others completing tasks and learning about the relationship between action and attainment. This suggests the importance of teachers and other students modeling the completion of tasks and verbalizing the relationship between their actions and outcomes. Verbal persuasion is specific feedback from others, focused on reinforcing the relationship between actions and outcomes (e.g., telling a student that you are proud that he or she engaged in specific actions and achieved specific outcomes). Physiological cues relate to feelings of anxiety or calmness students may feel before and during task completion. New tasks are likely to lead to higher levels of anxiety, but the cues will change as the task is mastered and as the student sees others perform the task and receive feedback. Teaching students about these feelings and changes in their behavior can help them see the relationship between their feelings and their actions.

All of these strategies provide insight into how to structure opportunities and feedback to support students to develop self-efficacy and positive outcome expectancies. Implementing these strategies are important for youth with disabilities because researchers have found that youth with disabilities tend to have more negative perceptions of their self-efficacy than youth without disabilities (Gans, Kenny, & Ghany, 2003). Researchers also found, however, that the self-efficacy and outcome expectancies of students with disabilities improve when utilizing the four strategies previously mentioned. For example, Feldman, Kim, and Elliott (2011) found that matching students with appropriate accommodations (e.g., extended time, reading questions out loud, dictating responses) during high-stakes testing influences academic self-efficacy. Students with disabilities started with lower perceptions of their efficacy in passing high-stakes tests, but they rated their self-efficacy higher after completing the test when they were provided with appropriate accommodations. Achieving the right match between the accommodations provided and the needs of the students is a critical issue. Researchers also found that teaching students strategies for reading comprehension and providing them with opportunities to use these strategies over time leads to changes in perceptions of self-efficacy (Nelson & Manset-Williamson, 2006). The Research on Student and Teacher Perceptions of Self-Efficacy research box highlights a study on the perspectives of students with learning disabilities and their teachers regarding self-efficacy. This study suggested that teachers need to be careful not to attribute learning challenges to the student's disability and, instead, focus on how to support the student to be successful. Attributing challenges that students face to their disability rather than attributing them to a lack of skill or opportunity can lead to students not learning that there is a connection between their actions and the outcomes they experience.

Research on Student and Teacher Perceptions of Self-Efficacy

Klassen and Lynch (2007) interviewed seven special education teachers and 28 secondary students with learning disabilities using focus groups and individual interviews. A semistructured script was used to elicit opinions about self-efficacy held by students and teachers. The researchers asked interviewees about their beliefs and also provided them with academic scenarios in which they asked about the educators' confidence levels and the general confidence levels of the students with learning disabilities. The researchers analyzed the data by developing codes based on key themes across all of the interviews. They found that both students and teachers felt that self-efficacy exerted a significant influence on academic performance. Teachers felt that self-efficacy had to be developed over time and that they had to be careful not to hamper its development.

Students felt that verbal persuasion was important to developing self-efficacy. For example, one student said that "if the teacher is like, 'I know you can do better, you just have to try harder, and like not get lazy,' then I know I could do better" (Klassen & Lynch, 2007, p. 498). But, teachers minimized the role of verbal persuasion, commenting that it was not useful in building self-efficacy. This suggests that teachers and students have different views on positive feedback, and students may value it more than teachers realize.

Students and teachers also differed in their views on student confidence. Students tended to feel that they were relatively accurate in their judgment of their performance, whereas teachers tended to feel that students were overconfident. Teachers did feel that students were less confident around their peers without disabilities, however. Students also said they acted overconfident because they were trying to protect themselves, not always because they were actually overconfident. This suggests that students seek out mastery experiences and positive feedback on their mastery experiences and often may not get enough. Consequently, this may mean they engage in solitary behaviors to try to make themselves feel better. For example, students felt that vicarious experiences could actually be detrimental when they observed others being successful, but were never successful themselves. This suggests that vicarious experience alone is not enough to build self-efficacy, and mastery experiences and verbal persuasion are important parts to developing self-efficacy.

Finally, there was a disconnect between how students and teachers viewed academic failure. Teachers tended to attribute failure to student impairments, suggesting that external or uncontrollable factors such as a disability label more directly affected student outcomes, not students' actual behavior. This view can negatively affect self-efficacy. Students, however, tended to attribute their failures to a lack of effort, an internal state. This suggests that teachers may be inadvertently suggesting to students that they cannot exert influence over outcomes through their actions because of their disability. This highlighted the importance of having high expectations for all students and recognizing that disability is not necessarily the causal factor in outcomes that students with disabilities experience.

This research suggests the importance of open communication between students and teachers, repeated opportunities for success and positive verbal feedback, avoiding attributing outcomes to disability labels, and high expectations.

Why Do Attitudes Matter?

Even if you know how to do something, if you do not believe your actions will lead to the outcomes you seek, then you eventually learn not to expend the time and energy to engage in those actions. You become disempowered. Everyone has probably experienced this at some point in life. Perhaps you were trying to stay connected with a friend, you reached out to them multiple times, but they had too many other things going on to call you back and you eventually stopped trying to reach out and connect. As a result, you never achieved the outcome of maintaining the friendship. Or, perhaps it happened with a restaurant. You really wanted to like the food and have a good dining experience, but you went several times and the food was bad. You even talked to the manager, but nothing got better. The circumstances were outside of your control. Sometimes circumstances will be outside of our control. But, often, they are not, and finding ways to navigate around the obstacles is a key part of being self-determined. Perhaps it is finding an activity you and your friend can do together (e.g., an exercise class, lunch in between classes or activities) or finding a restaurant with the same type of food whose service meets your expectations. These actions will still get you the outcome you want and lead to you feeling empowered.

Facing challenging situations can often lead to questioning ourselves and feeling uncertain. People who generally feel that they have an internal locus of control, self-efficacy, and positive outcome expectancies can navigate those challenging situations. Jake, one of the students featured throughout this book, said that he sometimes asks himself, "Am I fact or fiction?" (Jake, personal communication, July 17, 2012). He means that he sometimes struggles to believe that he is an effective self-advocate when situations are challenging. For example, he struggled during his first semester at community college with navigating requesting accommodations from the office for students with disabilities and coordinating with the vocational rehabilitation office to get his tuition bill paid. His mom, Jeanine, reminded him that he did not have to be perfect 100% of the time and that he, like anyone else, will have a "bumpy flight." Jake does a presentation now that is called "Aim High" in which he talks about how his disability does not define him or anyone else with a disability and that we all have to have opportunities to succeed, fail, and learn.

Jake also emphasizes the importance of positive feedback. Jake reminds himself of the positive feedback (e.g., verbal persuasion) he has received from his support system when he asks himself the questions about being fact or fiction. Jake often refers to receiving a prestigious self-advocacy award when he was still a senior in high school. Jake describes this as a "crowning achievement." He says it "validated me as a self-advocate and helps me keep going" (Jake, personal communication, July 17, 2012). He says that he often looks back to this accomplishment (which still sits in his living room) as a reminder that he is "fact." This also led to other opportunities, such as serving as a self-advocate on the Board of Directors of the organization that presented him the award. All of these experiences led to Jake feeling that he is empowered and is a causal agent over his life. This highlights the importance of promoting the attitudes associated with self-determination as well as specific self-determination skills.

ASSESSING OPPORTUNITIES FOR SELF-DETERMINATION

What do we know about the opportunities provided to students with disabilities for self-determination and how these opportunities are perceived by youth with disabilities? We know that opportunities for self-determination have historically been restricted for youth with disabilities for reasons described in this and other chapters. Research also suggests there may be disconnects between how youth with disabilities perceive opportunities and how teachers perceive opportunities. The What Does the Research Say About Opportunities for Self-Determination? research box highlights what researchers have learned about opportunities for self-determination and how these opportunities are perceived by youth, teachers, and others who support youth. Understanding these disconnects can be a critical part of working to explore new opportunities to promote self-determination.

What Does the Research Say About Opportunities for Self-Determination?

Carter and colleagues (Carter, Lane, Pierson, & Glaeser, 2006; Carter, Owens, Trainor, Sun, & Swedeen, 2009; Carter, Trainor, Owens, Swedeen, & Sun, 2010) conducted several studies examining the self-determination capacities of and opportunities for students with diverse disability labels. They used the AIR Self-Determination Scale (Wolman et al., 1994; see Chapter 2) to assess students' capacities and opportunities for self-determination. The researchers found that students with emotional and behavior disorders were judged by parents and teachers to have a lower capacity for self-determination than students with learning disabilities (Carter et al., 2006). Parents and teachers also reported that students with emotional and behavior disorders had less confidence in their ability to engage in self-determined behaviors.

Adolescents with emotional and behavior disorders rated themselves as having fewer opportunities for self-determination at home and at school when compared with students with learning disabilities. Furthermore, students rated themselves as having fewer opportunities than their teachers and parents. But, parents tended to rate students as having fewer opportunities at school than at home, and teachers tended to report students as having fewer opportunities at home than at school. These findings suggest that students, teachers, and parents have different perceptions about the available opportunities for self-determination, and developing a shared understanding of self-determination opportunities at home and at school among youth, parents, and teachers has the potential to facilitate better collaboration. This also may potentially lead to better opportunities that are matched to students' interests, preferences, and abilities.

Other researchers also found a disconnect between parent and teacher perceptions. Grigal, Neubert, Moon, and Graham (2003) surveyed parents and special and general education teachers of students with disabilities and found that 98% of parents felt that self-determination instruction was important for their children, but only 78% of parents felt that opportunities were being provided at school. Teachers only "slightly agreed" (p. 107) that students with disabilities were being provided with opportunities for self-determination at school, but special education teachers were more likely to suggest that opportunities were being provided. The researchers suggested that this may result from teachers being uncertain about how to provide self-determination opportunities, a finding supported by previous research that suggests teachers do not feel that they have received adequate training to promote self-determination (Mason, Field, & Sawilowsky, 2004; Wehmeyer, Agran, & Hughes, 2000).

Carter and colleagues (2009) also explored the perception of capacities and opportunities for self-determination among teachers and parents of youth with severe intellectual and developmental disabilities. Both teachers and parents reported that youth had limited ability, knowledge, and confidence in their self-determination. Teachers reported that students were more able to express their needs, interests, and abilities than set and develop action plans toward goals—perhaps because of the focus on strengths, preferences, and interests in transition services. Teachers and parents also felt that opportunities for self-determination were available at home and at school, but there was no assessment of the quality of these opportunities and the degree to which they were matched with the needs of students (e.g., more support for goal setting because this was a skill that needed further development). Researchers also found a relationship between problem behaviors, self-determination skills, and opportunities. They suggested that communication limitations may lead to students with severe disabilities using problem behaviors to communicate and attempt to express their preferences.

This research highlights the relationship between capacity and opportunity for self-determination as well as the need to individualize interventions to support needs. It also suggests that talking to students and parents about instructional opportunities for self-determination is necessary to match self-determination instruction and opportunities to the values, strengths, interests, and preferences of students and their families.

Jeanine, Jake's mom, says she is "always scanning for opportunities for self-determination" (Jeanine, personal communication, July 17, 2012), and those opportunities have changed over time (see Chapter 1). Jeanine served as Jake's advocate when he could not speak for himself, making sure his preferences were respected and that people understood his behavior. She created vicarious learning opportunities for Jake. She then became more of a collaborator and a facilitator, working with and supporting Jake to identify opportunities for him to engage in advocacy. She enabled Jake to have mastery experiences and provided verbal persuasion to encourage him to go after opportunities. She has stepped back even more now that Jake has started college. Jake now independently initiates and follows through on self-advocacy activities, but still with the support and encouragement of his family. Michael's, the other student featured throughout this book, parents also advocate, facilitate, collaborate, and support him. His parents have often had to advocate for him because he is nonverbal, but Michael's preferences have always guided their advocacy. Building a system of support that understands and learns from Michael's behavior to find technology that enables Michael to express his strengths, interests, and preferences has created more opportunities for causal agency.

The Assessing Opportunities for Self-Determination form (see Figure 7.1) provides a framework for assessing the environment to identify what opportunities for self-determination are currently being provided, how those opportunities could be enhanced, and how to include youth with disabilities in the process of identifying new opportunities. The environmental inventory process can also be useful when trying to assess the environment and identify activities in which self-determination can be embedded (see Chapter 2; Categorical Core Vocabulary Selection form [see Figure 2.6]).

CREATING REPEATED OPPORTUNITIES FOR SELF-DETERMINATION

Multiple strategies and situations in which self-determination can be taught are described in the first six chapters. Almost any academic, vocational, or transition-related task provides natural opportunities for using goal-setting, problem-solving, choice-making, self-management or self-advocacy, and leadership skills. It is also important to explore opportunities in extracurricular activities, community activities, and disability-related activities. Carter and colleagues (2011) interviewed young adults with disabilities about developing leadership skills, and one of the clear and consistent findings was that opportunities across all domains of life were important to developing skills associated with leadership and self-determination.

Focus on planning with high expectations and with the future in mind when planning for repeated opportunities for self-determination. Self-advocates with disabilities have consistently identified the negative effect that low expectations have had on their self-determination (Caldwell, 2010, 2011; Shogren & Broussard, 2011). The attitudes of others, especially the belief that people with disabilities cannot obtain a specific type of job, go to college, or participate in inclusive community activities, is identified as a major limiting factor. Refraining from assuming that students with disabilities cannot do things and focusing on allowing students to explore different outcomes, providing support for access, and looking at setbacks as opportunities to identify a new or different goal or revise one's action plan is critical to supporting the development of the attitudes associated with self-determination.

For example, postsecondary education for students with intellectual disability was not a commonly discussed option in the past. A growing array of postsecondary options are available to young adults with intellectual disability on college campuses, however, as a result of many professionals, parents, and individuals with disabilities having high expectations (Hart, Grigal, & Weir, 2010). The opportunities for further development of self-determination skills abound. Tony Plotner, Assistant Professor of Special Education and Director of an inclusive

Assessing Opportunities
for Self-Determination

Instructions: Carefully think about the following activity domains—academic, vocational, transition, extracurricular, community, and disability related.

	Choice making	Self-management	Goal setting	Self-advocacy
Think about the opportunities that students currently have to practice self-determination skills. Circle the top three in each box.	Academic Vocational Transition Extracurricular Community Disability related	Academic Vocational Transition Extracurricular Community Disability related	Academic Vocational Transition Extracurricular Community Disability related	Academic Vocational Transition Extracurricular Community Disability related
Brainstorm ways to further enhance these opportunities, especially in areas that were not circled in the previous step. List your top three ideas to enhance opportunities in each box.	1. 2. 3.	1. 2. 3.	1. 2. 3.	1. 2. 3.
Consult with other teachers and members of the support team. Fill in with whom you consulted, the current opportunities identified, and the ideas generated to enhance opportunities.	Teachers consulted with: Current opportunities: New opportunities:	Parents consulted with: Current opportunities: New opportunities:	Other support team members consulted: Current opportunities New opportunities:	Other support team members consulted: Current opportunities New opportunities:
Have students and parents complete the first three steps as well. You can print out those rows and send the form home to parents. You can also have a conversation with youth about their experiences. You can also use the tools introduced in other chapters in combination with this assessment of opportunities.				

Figure 7.1. Assessing opportunities for self-determination.

(continued)

	Choice making	Self-management	Goal setting	Self-advocacy
Compare your ideas with those of students, parents, and other teachers and members of the support team. Identify commonalities and differences.	Commonalities: Differences:	Commonalities: Differences:	Commonalities: Differences:	Commonalities: Differences:
Develop a list of the top ideas for enhancing self-determination opportunities. Discuss this list with youth and parents.	List top ideas:	List top ideas:	List top ideas:	List top ideas:
Identify the top three ideas. Develop an action plan for integrating these new opportunities into a student's life.	1. 2. 3. Action plan:	1. 2. 3. Action plan:	1. 2. 3. Action plan:	1. 2. 3. Action plan:
Include teaching and practice opportunities in your action plan.	Teaching opportunities: Practice opportunities:	Teaching opportunities: Practice opportunities:	Teaching opportunities: Practice opportunities:	Teaching opportunities: Practice opportunities:
Determine how mastery experiences, vicarious learning, verbal persuasion, and physiological cues will be used to support students to develop attitudes associated with self-determination.	Mastery experiences: Vicarious learning: Verbal persuasion: Physiological cues:	Mastery experiences: Vicarious learning: Verbal persuasion: Physiological cues:	Mastery experiences: Vicarious learning: Verbal persuasion: Physiological cues:	Mastery experiences: Vicarious learning: Verbal persuasion: Physiological cues:

postsecondary education program for individuals with intellectual disability, highlights how students with intellectual disabilities can continue to develop their self-determination skills in postsecondary education environments in the Postsecondary Education for Students with Disabilities research box. His example also highlights the diverse ways that peers and

Postsecondary Education for Students with Disabilities

Quinn's New Chapter in Life: College

Quinn moved into her dorm 1 year ago, ready for the next chapter in her life—college (an inclusive postsecondary education program for students with intellectual disability). She was eager to make lifelong friends and learn about what she wanted to do for a career. Quinn had several goals that she had started working on in high school to make herself more self-determined, including managing stressful situations, setting goals, advocating for herself, and making her own decisions. Quinn's postsecondary education plan included many supports aimed at facilitating self-determination, building on what she had learned in school. The postsecondary environment created many new opportunities for Quinn to learn about and practice her self-determination skills.

Peer Mentor

Having a peer mentor is one of the most effective supports for Quinn. Peer mentors provide social and student life support and go through a rigorous training program on how to facilitate social relationships as well as self-determined behavior. Lindsey, Quinn's peer mentor, met with Quinn three times per week to go over her schedule, set goals for the week, and utilize self-management strategies to deal with stressful situations. Lindsey also helped Quinn identify causes of her stress, which included dealing with change, difficulty communicating needs and wants, feeling overwhelmed, and feeling pressure. Lindsey would help Quinn model and practice a variety of coping strategies to use in times of stress, such as taking a break, listening to music, exercising, and using a reflective journal. In addition, Quinn has made major strides in connecting her knowledge of her disability with academic success with support from Lindsey by appropriately coordinating meetings with the disability student support office and requesting supports from her professors.

Living Learning Communities

University living learning communities give students a unique, inclusive residential learning experience that connects classroom learning with residential life. Quinn has been able to broaden her perspectives and understanding of the campus, the community, and the world around her by being actively involved in a living learning community and through student, faculty, and staff partnerships and educational and cultural programs. The "Y-drill" was one of the activities that made an impact on Quinn. "Your decision" or "Why" drill is an activity that encourages all students to make their own decision when presented with a hypothetical situation. They must then reveal their decision to the group and explain their reasoning. The objective of this drill is to show the students that emerging leaders must make their own decisions based on their personal values. This approach has complemented her classroom experience and has given Quinn many opportunities to grow and examine her potential to lead as a student on campus and beyond. All of the students in the postsecondary education program, as well as traditional students, participate in the Emerging Leaders Living Learning Community (ELLLC). This is dedicated to enacting positive change in which students desire to embark on or extend their leadership journey. Quinn has become more confident and self-aware in her short time in college and plans on being a mentor and ELLLC facilitator in her sophomore year.

Contributed by Tony Plotner.

members of the school community (secondary and postsecondary) can create opportunities for self-determination. High expectations and creating opportunities for students to gain access to and experience these environments is critical to success.

The goal of transition services is to engage in planning that is linked to the strengths, preferences, and interests of youth that enables them to move into postschool activities with the best foundation for success. Students need to have opportunities to practice their self-determination skills in day-to-day academic, vocational, and transition-related activities as well as to think about applying those self-determination skills in the context of future activities. For example, Mazzotti, Test, Wood, and Richter (2012) developed an innovative computer-assisted instruction program using PowerPoint and SNAGIT to teach students with disabilities about postschool options while also supporting the development of self-determination skills and creating opportunities for students to use those skills. The program provided students with disabilities information about postschool possibilities in three areas—postsecondary education, employment, and independent living. The students specifically learned about different options in each of these areas and about the specific choices available. These options and choices were individualized to the students' community using community mapping and interviewing members of the school team. Students gained knowledge and skills in each of the three areas and showed an increased ability to express their preferences after they participated in the instruction. Educating students about these options and choices early on and giving them repeated opportunities to learn and practice promotes psychological empowerment and self-determination. This is laying the foundation for the ongoing development of self-determination after high school.

Creating conditions in which students can take risks, challenge themselves with high expectations, and have opportunities to succeed and fail (with supports) are critically important to planning with the future in mind. For example, Michael's family has had to creatively think about postsecondary living opportunities for him. They wanted Michael to be able to be more independent as an adult, but also recognized that he would need ongoing support and that they wanted to be actively involved in providing that support. Michael's family identified a creative situation that worked for them. The box shows what his mom stated when preparing for Michael's transition.

Michael's family moved about an hour away from where they had previously lived. They found a two-story house in the heart of a medium-sized city with public

Many years ago, my husband and I realized that Michael was easily distracted and did not like interruptions. He did his activities in an area in our old home that was very open. It had big windows, open stairway access with an open stairwell, and it was a crossroad to all the rooms downstairs. We noticed that he would stop working on an activity when he heard us nearby. Sometimes when we entered his space, he would try to communicate that he wanted us to leave his area (either by pushing us out or by trying to say "go away please"). Because we work from home, we knew this might become a bigger problem when he exited the school system.

When we decided that we had to move in order to give Michael the vocational, social, and community opportunities he needed, we very carefully chose a house that would allow him to have a separate but accessible living arrangement. This was one of the best decisions we made. It has greatly contributed to his overall independence and my husband and I no longer have to sneak around in our own home. In fact, we sometimes have to plan times to go downstairs to see him.

transportation and many opportunities within a mile or two. The house was previously designed to accommodate almost completely separate living quarters on the bottom story, so they enhanced it by adding a kitchen, pantry, bar-style eating area, and washer and dryer. Michael's own kitchen and dining area that accommodates his preferred food items and meal choices was extremely incentivizing because his daily schedule has always centered around food (it has always been an extremely strong reinforcement; he has been on the Atkins diet for the past 3 years, and his daily schedule involves snacks every 2 hours). Michael now had an apartment that was directly underneath the main part of the house but had its own entry/exit, living room, bedroom, bathroom, and kitchen. This allows Michael to operate independently of the main household, and vice versa, while still making it convenient to interact.

CONSIDERING CULTURE WHEN CREATING OPPORTUNITIES FOR SELF-DETERMINATION

It is critically important to make sure we are actively thinking about the values that guide the students and families with whom we work when thinking about opportunities for self-determination, especially when we are planning with the future in mind. Trainor (2005) found a disconnect between the values of diverse students with disabilities and goals for their futures on their IEPs. For example, not every individual or family may seek independent living immediately after school. There are a variety of living conditions and experiences, and developing an understanding of what works best for each adolescent and his or her family will be important to the process of developing goals. Kalyanpur and Harry (2012) suggested using a posture of cultural reciprocity when we are working with youth and families who may have differing values or visions for the future to ensure that the youth's strengths, interests, and preferences remain at the center of their goals, plan for instruction, and provided supports. The posture of cultural reciprocity involves four steps.

1. Identify the cultural values embedded in your recommendations/ideas for goals.

2. Explore the degree to which the family shares the same values or how their values differ from yours.

3. Acknowledge and give respect to any cultural differences identified.

4. Collaborate to identify the most appropriate way to adapt recommendations (Kalyanpur & Harry, 2012).

For example, a common professional recommendation might be that transition goals be developed for independent living, specifically goals around the youth moving out of the family home and into a supported or independent living environment after leaving school. A family may not share the same value for this outcome that the professional does, however. They may wish for the youth to stay home through college as is the case for Jake and his family, or they may wish to explore an arrangement such as creating an apartment within a family home as is the case for Michael and his family. The professional needs to communicate with the family that professional practice suggests that independent living may be beneficial and then provide education on why this is a common professional recommendation. Then, the person needs to develop a plan that works for the family. For example, instead of immediately focusing on independent living, perhaps focus on developing

There are a variety of living conditions and experiences, and goals should be developed based on an understanding of what works best for each adolescent and his or her family.

a plan for improving skills that will lead to success in any home environment. Then, create a transition plan that accommodates, for example, a situation in which the family home becomes unavailable for some reason. The benefit of this approach and actively communicating with families in this way is that it empowers everyone; promotes self-awareness for youth, families, and professionals; and leads to the development of goals that are meaningful, personal, and feasible with a realistic and appropriate action plan.

8

Creating Systems of Supports for Self-Determination

She has grown up with a strong extended family . . . She has developed independence and set goals, but . . . when she sets goals, you see a little bit of her cousins, her grandma and grandpa and all of that like a network. Not to fall into that, but to know that you can count on them for advice, for guidance, for support.

(Shogren, 2012, p. 177)

Self-determination is speaking up for our rights and responsibilities and empowering ourselves to stand up for what we believe in. This means being able to choose where we work, live, and our friends; to educate ourselves and others, to work as a team to obtain common goals; and to develop the skills that enable us to fight for our beliefs, to advocate for our needs, and to obtain the level of independence that we desire.

(Self Advocates Becoming Empowered, 1996, p. 1)

The saying, "It takes a village," often refers to the importance of a system of support in raising a child. The saying can also be applied to supporting the development of self-determination. A system of support that facilitates teaching skills and creating opportunities is critical to developing self-determination. Supports that enable students to learn and practice self-determination skills are as important as teaching skills and creating opportunities for self-determination. Different students will need different types of supports. For example, all students will benefit from effective teaching strategies, such as those in Chapters 3–6. But, different students might need different types of support to apply what they have learned to their lives.

Jake and Michael, the two students featured throughout this book, have benefited from direct instruction to learn self-determination skills, but have needed different supports. Technology-related supports have been critical to Michael's expression of self-determination (see Figures 3.1 and 4.1). Written scripts and monitoring systems have been more effective for Jake (see Figures 4.2 and 4.4). Michael and Jake have also required different intensities of supports. Michael and Jake have become more independent as they have gotten older, but each requires different ongoing support to be self-determining. Jake now requires more emotional support to navigate through the challenges of adulthood. For example, he frequently discusses decisions that he has to make with his mother and other key people in his life, but then independently executes the decisions. Michael expresses his preferences but then relies on other members of his support team to take action regarding these preferences because of the intensity of his support needs. Group action planning (GAP), a form of person-centered planning, is a key way that this occurs for Michael. Each student will have an individual pattern of support needs based on his or her unique pattern of strengths, needs, abilities, and preferences. It is critical to understand this pattern of support needs and to consider this in selecting the best ways to support students to develop self-determination.

The development of self-determination does not occur in a vacuum, as Jake's and Michael's stories and the chapter's opening quotes demonstrate. The first quote is from a mother who participated in an interview project on Hispanic mothers' perceptions of self-determination (Shogren, 2012). She emphasized that her daughter had learned about goal setting from her family and this vicarious learning influenced how her daughter learned and practiced setting goals. Her daughter still relies on her family for advice and guidance, even though she has had mastery experiences with goal setting. SABE's (1996) definition of self-determination highlights how self-advocates view self-determination as being empowered, engaging in advocacy, and going after the life that one wants. SABE also emphasized the importance of working as a team, advocating for collective goals, and essentially supporting each other to achieve a common cause.

Students with disabilities need supports to learn and practice the skills leading to enhanced self-determination. This chapter elaborates on the process of developing a comprehensive system of support for students with disabilities that facilitates developing self-determination. Researchers have suggested that a comprehensive system of support is a key variable associated with positive transition outcomes (Thompson, Wehmeyer, & Hughes, 2010). This chapter discusses the role of person-centered support teams in supporting self-determination. Examples from person-centered support teams and systems of supports are used to illustrate these points.

SUPPORTS AND SUPPORT NEEDS

What are supports, and what defines a system of support for a student with a disability? Researchers define *supports* as "resources and strategies that aim to promote the development, education, interests and personal well-being of a person and that enhance individual functioning" (Schalock et al., 2010, p. 105). Supports can take a variety of forms, including teaching strategies, environmental modifications, technology, peer supports, emotional support, and any other resource or strategy that helps individuals with disabilities develop their full potential. We all have a need for support in some domain of our life. Each of us is likely dependent on technology-related supports to manage some parts of our lives (e.g., telephone, calendaring system) or on our friends to encourage us to get up in the morning and meet them at an exercise class. These supports enable us to be self-determining (i.e., people who act with intent to achieve the things we want in life). Teaching strategies for choice making, self-management, goal setting, and self-advocacy are supports that lead to developing self-determination skills and achieving desired life outcomes in the same way that people and technology are also supports that lead to these outcomes.

Every person has an individual profile of support needs. *Support needs* are defined as "the pattern and intensity of support necessary for a person to participate in activities linked with normative human functioning" (Thompson et al., 2009, p. 135). Students with disabilities tend to have a greater need for support than students without disabilities. Exploring each student's unique support needs is important to developing a comprehensive system of support. Understanding a student's overall support needs can also inform us about the supports that might be most useful when teaching or creating opportunities for self-determination. This understanding guides the development of a comprehensive system of support, which is "the planned and integrated use of individualized support strategies and resources that encompass the multiple aspects of human performance in multiple settings" (Schalock et al., 2010, p. 224).

Our current understanding of *disability* defines it as an interaction between personal competencies and environmental demands, rather than as a deficit that resides within a person (Schalock et al., 2010). The specific support needs that each student with a disability has emerge from the interaction of their personal competencies and environmental demands. Students with disabilities often experience a mismatch between the environments that they live, learn, work and play within, and their personal competencies. This mismatch creates a need for individualized supports. Assessing support needs and then planning, implementing, and evaluating a comprehensive system of support for students with disabilities can lead to improved outcomes. Schalock et al. wrote,

> Educators adopting a support needs orientation . . . devote time and energy to developing and implementing systems of supports that bridge the gap between a child's level of personal competence and the demands of school environments. (2012, p. 40)

Understanding support needs can help us understand the best strategies to use when supporting students' self-determination, given each student's personal competencies and the demands of his or her environments. And, support needs can change over time. For example, Jake needed different supports when he was younger to ensure that his interests, preferences, and abilities were understood. Jake commonly used problem behavior as a form of communication when he was in elementary school. At one point, the school's autism/behavioral support specialist was called because Jake was having significant problems in computer class. The computer teacher was having students work on their typing skills by having them type *cat, dog,* and *fish* multiple times. Jake had significant behavior problems when he was asked to do this exercise, and the teacher could not figure out what was going on. The autism/behavioral support specialist came to the class, observed Jake, and asked the teacher to let the class have "free typing" time to see what Jake would do. Jake first typed *cat dog fish* but then went on to type *once apon a time in a far away land a yong* (see Figure 8.1). These were lines from the movie *Beauty and the Beast,* which Jake was frequently watching at this time. Jake's problem behavior had been an expression of his frustration with repeatedly typing *cat, dog,* and *fish* and a request to do something else. Although Jake's typing had some spelling errors, he was showing his team that he had competencies beyond what he was being asked to do in class. An arrangement was worked out in which Jake had to complete the required assignment (e.g., typing specific words that had been selected to teach letter and typing combinations) and then had time to type whatever he wanted. The autism/behavioral support specialist also began to work one-to-one with Jake to teach him strategies to understand his feelings and communicate these feelings using words, rather than his behavior. The support he received from the autism/behavioral support specialist was critical to his success and to his self-determination in his computer class.

The autism/behavioral support specialist became a key, lifelong member of Jake's system of support. She worked with Jake through elementary and secondary school and remains in touch with Jake even as he has made the transition to community college, texting to keep in touch and provide support and feedback as Jake navigates adulthood. She actually encouraged Jake to take part in the workshop in which he developed his PowerPoint presentation (see Chapter 6) that enabled him to communicate about his autism and begin to give presentations as he worked toward his goal of being a keynote speaker. Jeanine, Jake's mom, describes the autism/behavioral support specialist

jake kc 2-6-98

cat dog fish

once apon a time in a far away land

a yong prince lived in a shiney

casle he transform the enchantress

into a beast

Figure 8.1. Jake's early expression of self-determination. (Reprinted with permission from Jake's family.)

as "going above and beyond" and that she "did not work by the clock." The autism/ behavioral support specialist did in-home training with Jake for several years and shared many meals with the family, developing a strong relationship with the whole family and capitalizing on natural opportunities such as dinnertime to support Jake to develop and express his preferences. Jeanine says that this member of Jake's support team helped her to "see the possibilities for Jake's future" (Jeanine, personal communication, July 16, 2012). She feels that Jake could have been overlooked or excluded from many of the opportunities he experienced if the autism/behavioral support specialist had not provided so many supports and recruited other supports (e.g., occupational therapists, speech-language therapists) for Jake and for the entire family. These supports enabled Jake to develop many of the skills that have been discussed in this book and have contributed to his success as a young adult. Supports provide a bridge between what is and what can be, and this is why supports are so important in education planning and planning to promote self-determination.

BUILDING A SYSTEM OF SUPPORT

Thompson and colleagues (2009) suggested a five-component process for building a system of support: (a) identify desired life experiences and goals, (b) assess support needs, (c) develop and implement the individualized plan, (d) monitor progress, and (e) evaluate. Authors suggested the relevance of this process to educational planning (Schalock et al., 2010, 2012; Thompson, Wehmeyer, & Hughes, 2010). Furthermore, building a system of support provides natural opportunities for actively involving students with disabilities, providing natural opportunities for developing and enhancing self-determination skills.

Identify Desired Life Experiences and Goals

The goal of building a system of support is to move beyond using a disability label as the primary tool in attempting to determine the most appropriate supports and services for students with disabilities. We should instead focus on the strengths of individuals and how we can build a comprehensive system of support to address each person's unique support needs. Supports in an educational setting may alter elements of the curriculum, classroom, lesson, or activity so that the targeted person is educated with his or her peers without disabilities. It may also involve creating new experiences, modifying the environment, or incorporating self-determination skill instruction. All of this will be based on the desired goals of the individual, the mismatch between the environment in which these desired goals can occur and the individual's personal competencies, and the resulting need for support. This starts with identifying desired life experiences and goals (Thompson et al., 2009). This fits naturally with transition services and promoting student self-determination, as IDEA 2004 specifies that transition planning should be based on the individual child's needs, taking into account the child's strengths, preferences, and interests.

What are the best practices in identifying the desired life experiences and goals of an individual? Strategies to assess preferences and teach students to set goals and make choices are described throughout this book. Thinking about future goals does not occur in a vacuum, however. Each of us can significantly benefit from having a group of people around us that helps identify a vision for the future and goals to achieve that vision. Person-centered planning has emerged as a strategy that is commonly used in the disability field to bring together a team of people to identify the vision for the future. The following section provides more information on person-centered planning.

Person-Centered Planning Person-centered planning emerged in the mid-1980s as an approach to design supports and services for individuals with disabilities using the strengths, perspectives, and goals of the person with a disability as the starting point (Holburn, 2002; Michaels & Ferrara, 2006). The ultimate goal of person-centered planning is to bring together people with disabilities, their families, and other important people in their lives to develop a shared vision for the future. The strengths, preferences, and interests of the individual form the basis for this process.

Anyone can significantly benefit from having a support team to help them identify a vision for the future and goals to achieve that vision.

A variety of person-centered planning approaches have been identified in the literature, including GAP (Turnbull & Turnbull, 1996), Making Action Plans (MAPS; Forest & Pearpoint, 1992), Personal Futures Planning (PFP; Mount, 1991) and Planning Alternative Tomorrows with Hope (PATH; Pierpoint, O'Brien, & Forest, 1995). Each approach uses a slightly different process of identifying the vision for the future and developing a plan for making that vision happen. For example, GAP has five components.

1. Inviting support
2. Creating connections
3. Envisioning great expectation
4. Solving problems
5. Celebrating success (Turnbull & Turnbull, n.d.).

The first step includes identifying key people to involve, especially when thinking about transition. This will vary for each individual, but thinking about family, friends, educators, support providers, and community connectors (e.g., local business owners, church members) is a great place to start. A diversity of perspectives and connections is crucial to creating diverse opportunities for support. Each of these perspectives can help identify various possibilities to support the individual with a disability achieve his or her goals for the future. It is also necessary to identify an effective facilitator to coordinate the meeting and lead the team through the GAP process. The facilitator should be a person with

> Strong communication skills who can support others to feel connected to the group and to take specific action steps in supporting the individual to "get a life." You might choose a facilitator who is another family member, a family friend, or a professional. (Turnbull & Turnbull, n.d., p. 6)

Turnbull and Turnbull (n.d.) also suggested that GAP meetings focus on creating social and emotional connections. They recommended holding meetings in homes, not professional settings, with food and opportunities for socializing. They also recommended using stories to communicate hopes and dreams for the future rather than relying on formal reports. The focus of sharing great expectations is on identifying the vision for the future and recognizing that this vision will likely evolve over time, which is why ongoing GAP meetings are necessary to continue to expand the vision. Strengths of the individual should be emphasized and used in developing the vision. One of the benefits of this approach is that it allows individuals with disabilities and their families to hear and focus on positives, which is often a different approach than typical, professional meetings. The team also needs to recognize that problems will emerge over time, especially as steps are taken to achieve the evolving vision. Problem solving and identifying creative solutions will be a key role for team members. The team may change over time, both as the vision changes and as problems emerge and are solved. Strategies that provide a structured framework for using a problem-solving process to identify a goal, develop an action plan, and evaluate progress can be a useful part of the GAP process and a way to involve both the team and the individual with a disability (see Chapter 5).

Finally, Turnbull and Turnbull (n.d.) emphasized the importance of celebrating success. They encouraged the GAP team to find opportunities for celebrating within and outside of meetings. Having birthday parties, potluck dinners, and other informal activities to celebrate key steps in achieving the vision can be critically important to create connections and can be an opportunity to invite new and diverse sources of support. These diverse sources of support can be involved in not only identifying and implementing action steps to enable individuals with disabilities to be self-determining, but also generating ideas about effective supports (e.g., technology, teaching strategies) that can be useful across home, school, and community environments.

Michael has a long-standing person-centered support team that holds monthly GAP meetings. Christy Nittrouer, Michael's sister, shares her perspective on how person-centered planning has had an impact on her family in the Michael's Person-Centered Support Team research box. She specifically describes the roles that educators have played in Michael's GAP team and how Michael's GAP differs from other meetings in which her family has been involved. Educators can serve multiple roles in GAP teams, as Christy describes. Teachers working with students with disabilities can educate the GAP team about school programs and look for opportunities to coordinate home and school supports. Educators can still play a role in person-centered support teams after students move to different classrooms and teachers. They can continue to share their expertise and knowledge of the student with whom they have worked, leveraging their connections, and working to promote positive transition outcomes for students as a member of the support team.

Michael's Person-Centered Support Team

My parents have hosted monthly Group Action Planning (GAP) meetings for the past 2 years for my brother Michael. The power of these meetings to keep me and a diverse support team connected to Michael and the vision for his future has been amazing. I live more than 1,000 miles away from Michael because I am going to graduate school. Remaining involved and integrated in his system of support has been a consistent challenge because I am so far away. I'm no longer involved in the day-to-day support that Michael's team provides, but I'm the executor for his special needs trust and guardian for him if anything happens to my parents. I need and want to stay connected. I've been able to participate in GAP meetings via Skype and review meeting notes, which keeps me involved and informed. Seeing the team that Michael has and seeing how they come together to support him in so many ways is comforting, especially being so far away.

My mom, Kay, said the following when I talked to her about the difference between GAP and other planning activities she has been involved with, including IEP meetings.

> The teacher would come over to our house about once every month or two and she had a list of items she felt we needed to collaborate on. I, too, would make a list and we would try to cover those items. Eventually, we found ourselves needing additional help, particularly in the areas of communication and occupational therapy. Once or twice a semester, the teacher would set up a home meeting with the speech pathologist and occupational therapist on Michael's IEP team. Eventually, we had two meetings a semester with this core group and we worked on home program goals, like dressing, shaving, and laundry skills. But, our thinking was limited to our experiences and revolved around what the four of us thought Michael was capable of. Jobs were chosen based on what his teacher and I thought he could do and the life skills curriculum he was learning at school. We did know that we should try to turn his obsessions (basketball, music, scribbling) into something productive. We also knew that job trials were the way to do this. But our thinking was somewhat limited. These meetings were not as collaborative or nearly as creative as our GAP meetings, partly because the overall direction and goals were so narrow. In person-centered planning we focus on the big picture, the vision for how to achieve self-determination, maximum independence, and overall happiness. This guided us in our specific goals and objectives. But in the traditional meetings, we did not emphasize this and there was less buy-in, from everyone. For example, my husband never attended these sessions. I would just fill him in after the meetings. And, we never really had a diverse team that supported Michael outside of those meetings, outside of the professionals completing their specific job duties and responsibilities.

The variety of people involved is one of the biggest values from GAP meetings, aside from my dad attending every single meeting. It is not only professionals who come to the meetings, but also family members, work colleagues, support providers, Best Buddy members, current and previous school teachers and aides, and even local artists and musicians that our family has met. All of these people collaborate to decide how best to design Michael's daily life to enhance his self-determination, happiness, and quality of life.

Although our family has facilitated these meetings, Michael's teachers have played a key role in the GAP team. One of Michael's regular GAP team members is a school teacher who has known Michael and I since we were in middle school, and another has known both of us since high school. This highlights the importance of longevity with regard to the relationships in Michael's (and my family's) life and how the connections, desire to be involved, and knowledge can be leveraged in creative ways to enhance Michael's life, even when an immediate role expires. I think there typically is not another role for a teacher to step

(continued)

into when he or she is no longer in a formal teaching role. GAP has allowed our family to create new roles for Michael's former teachers and allowed them to still be meaningfully involved in diverse ways.

Four school teachers come to mind when thinking about those who have participated in and had a large impact on my brother's GAP meetings. The first is Michael's middle and high school vocational and autism program teacher. She led Michael's original at-home training team, helped secure Michael's first job, and worked with him on many job skills. She is now a regular attendee at GAP meetings, shares ideas based on her knowledge and experiences, leverages her connections for Michael, and takes on action items on his agenda when she has time. The second teacher is Michael's high school teacher. She was instrumental in supporting my family when they moved and Michael had to get used to a new home and community. She brought him to the new house and community every Friday for 4 months before the actual move and helped Michael meet with future team members to ease his transition anxiety. She attended GAP meetings for another year to provide insight on his transition goals and help his new team set up his school program based on her knowledge of Michael's interests, preferences, and abilities. One of Michael's aides who worked with him in the school program for individuals over 18 years old is still involved. He is an artist and has been working with Michael to turn his scribbling obsession into painting. He is also a musician (Michael loves music) and was Michael's job coach for all of his volunteer jobs. He shares unique insights about art, music, and Michael's success (and struggles) in the work world at GAP meetings. Finally, Michael's teacher in the school program for individuals over 18 years old was instrumental in sharing with the GAP team the activities that Michael was working on at school, how job coaching was structured for him, and helped accommodate Michael's transportation needs. He enabled us to coordinate work on transition goals between home, school, and the community, which has been key to Michael's success. We were able to have members of Michael's home support team observe him at morning jobs affiliated with school so that job coaching and instruction at home and school were seamless.

All of these school-based attendees of my brother's GAP meetings have a wealth of community knowledge and new ideas. They always contribute to the team's problem solving and come up with creative job ideas. Each of them brings a unique perspective to the table, and everyone is important to keeping the colleagues who directly work with Michael in the loop.

It is extremely important that I (and my new husband) remain involved in these GAP meetings and up to date on the latest, pressing issues because of the creative discussion that occurs at GAP meetings and their role in laying the foundation for my brother's future. Frequent and detailed communication, family succession planning, and clear expectations for the enviable life my family sees in my brother's future are vital to fulfilling our roles as future guardians. School-based participants have been a vital part of this planning and communication, especially throughout my brother's transition out of the school system. A system of support does not have to be limited by time or space. Everyone in my brother's life has a presence that can be leveraged to positively affect his future.

Contributed by Christy Nittrouer.

Educators can serve as facilitators of person-centered support teams in some circumstances. For example, Flannery and colleagues (2000) trained 183 educators to facilitate Personal Futures Planning (PFP). Educators received information on PFP and other person-centered planning tools, observed a PFP meeting for a student, conducted a PFP during a role-play exercise, and were encouraged to use PFP during the transition planning process. The researchers found that the training led to a higher number of nonpaid individuals providing support and participating on the support team and higher satisfaction with the planning process by educators and students/parents. Educators do not necessarily have to serve in a facilitator role. Family members may choose to facilitate teams or may identify other community members to serve in that role.

Researchers suggested that person-centered planning is a natural fit with transition planning. Using a person-centered approach can facilitate more effective collaboration between the individual with a disability, his or her family and other important people, and educators and adult service providers. Person-centered planning differs from more traditional planning meetings because of a focus on

(a) who controls the process, (b) who is present at the planning, (c) the time taken to listen to and build from accomplishments, strengths, and vision, (d) the process for identifying what is important about the form and outcomes of supports, and (e) development of a plan of action that results in real change in the life of the focus person. (Flannery et al., 2000, pp. 123–124)

The Research on the Impact of Person-Centered Planning research box summarizes reviews of the literature exploring the impact of person-centered planning.

Key Members of Person-Centered Support Teams During Transition   Include people from diverse backgrounds who can help with planning all aspects of adult life when building person-centered support teams. Identifying the different areas that supports will be needed for adult life is critical to inviting creative, connected people that can identify supports in diverse areas. Turnbull and colleagues (1996) suggested several domains that students with disabilities should consider when making the transition from school to the adult world, including employment, living arrangements, mode of transportation, managing of finances, social activities, and ongoing education. Nontraditional invitees may include bus or cab company personnel, landlords, athletic club members, accountants, and any others that the team can identify as able to make meaningful contributions to the desired life of the individual with a disability. Each of these voices can move the team beyond traditional or familiar ways of thinking and identify creative solutions to promote desired outcomes. As the team grows and changes so will the connections. The team constantly will be growing, contracting, and shifting as the person with a disability moves forward in different domains of life.

Key Roles of the Person-Centered Support Team in Identifying Opportunities for Self-Determination   Keeping the team focused on the vision for the individual with a disability and keeping the individual with a disability as the leader in this process is a central issue in person-centered planning. The individual with a disability can play a key role in identifying members of the team, based on his or her preferences and interests. He or she can also play a role in planning and organizing meetings and identifying and implementing action plans to achieve goals set by the person-centered planning team. All of the skills described in Chapter 6 on self-advocacy can also be applied to promoting student involvement in person-centered planning meetings. Person-centered planning teams can also be part of the process of identifying meaningful goals for students and then play a key role in supporting students to pursue those goals (see Chapter 5).

Assess Support Needs

After a vision for the future is established through person-centered planning and/or other methods, a direct assessment of student support needs needs to be completed. Determining support needs can involve many of the procedures already discussed. For example, we

Research on the Impact
of Person-Centered Planning

Claes, Van Hove, Vandevelde, van Loon, and Schalock (2010) reviewed all published research on person-centered planning. They identified 15 studies that empirically analyzed the impact person-centered planning had on the outcomes of individuals with disabilities. The studies included children, adolescents, and adults with disabilities. A handful of studies focused on youth with disabilities who were transition age. For example, Miner and Bates (1997) worked with 22 students with disabilities and their families in the transition planning process. Students and families were randomly assigned to participate in transition planning using Personal Futures Planning (PFP) or in a traditional transition planning process. They found that parents tended to speak more at meetings and feel that more change had occurred in these planning meetings for adulthood when PFP was used. Claes and colleagues found across 15 studies that using a person-centered planning process tended to increase the number of people in social networks and promote closer contact with family and friends and greater engagement in group activities. Using person-centered planning also tended to lead to more of the individual's preferences being incorporated in written goals. Some studies were inconclusive in their results on this front, however; researchers suggested this ambiguity could be because of limited sample sizes and indicated a need for more research to examine the effects of person-centered planning on outcomes.

Everson and Zhang (2000) conducted a qualitative study to examine the perspectives of facilitators and members of person-centered support teams. Nine individuals that were family members and service providers who had gone through training on PFP participated in focus groups. They represented person-centered planning teams that had been successful in scheduling initial and ongoing meetings, although the teams had struggled at different points in the process. The purpose of the focus group interviews was to identify inhibitors and supports of effective person-centered planning teams. Some individuals felt that the initial meetings were a struggle because it took time to become comfortable and confident as a team. All of the team members felt that person-centered planning teams became stronger with time and ongoing meetings. Figuring out how to support the target person with a disability to express what he or she wanted, finding a common time for everyone to meet, keeping team members engaged and committed over time, and identifying creative ways to achieve a vision were some of the main struggles reported by team members. Finding community members who were open and aware of disability-related issues and willing to commit to participate was also identified as an inhibitor. Keeping the meetings positive, hosting social events, and staying focused on the future vision were factors that promoted success. All of the focus group participants thought the outcomes of the person-centered planning process were positive, despite the challenges, and continuing to build a system of support was going to be beneficial for the person with a disability, especially as more people got involved.

This research suggests that person-centered planning can have significant, positive benefits for individuals with disabilities, their family, the professionals that support them, and even the community at large. Using person-centered support teams can be a way to keep focus on the vision for the future held by students with disabilities and support them to become self-determining.

can use environmental inventories to assess the activities that occur in the environments to determine environmental demands and what support students need to meet those demands (e.g., teaching, technology, peer support; see Chapter 2).

Assessing support needs is different from assessing preferences or current skills. Understanding support needs tells us about the pattern and intensity of supports needed to function in regular environments, and this goes beyond just understanding what the individual wants to get out of life or what the individual can currently do. It tells us more about what might be needed to get there. Therefore, assessing support needs differs from more traditional assessments, such as assessing adaptive behavior. These assessments focus on identifying skills that an individual has (and has not) learned, whereas support needs assessments focus on the supports the individual needs to participate in desired life activities (Schalock et al., 2010). Only one standardized assessment currently exists for assessing support needs because assessing support needs is relatively new to the disability field, the Supports Intensity Scale (SIS; Thompson et al., 2004). The Supports Intensity Scale research box provides more information.

Developing, Implementing, Monitoring, and Evaluating Support Plans

Developing, implementing, monitoring, and evaluating a plan for providing those supports is the next part of the process. Support plans focus on identifying how supports will be provided to address the mismatch between personal competencies and environmental demands. Does this mean that there are no achievement-oriented goals? No, of course not. Learning new things and developing new skills is a part of life for everyone. Developing new skills is critical to developing self-determination. The supports model suggests the importance of also planning, implementing, monitoring, and evaluating supports and the degree to which they enable people with disabilities to achieve desired life outcomes. Finding ways to blend achievement-oriented goals with the supports needed to achieve them has the potential to lead to success for everyone involved. For example, Michael's GAP team developed a communication support plan (see Figure 8.2). It highlights skills that Michael is working on learning and practicing, but also highlights how his GAP team will support these skills (e.g., creating opportunities, using specific teaching strategies). Blending these two elements provides a framework to move beyond skill development alone to create a system of support that facilitates learning, opportunities, and supports that enable an individual with a disability to be self-determining and achieve the outcomes that he or she values in life.

The Supports Intensity Scale

The Supports Intensity Scale (SIS; Thompson et al., 2004) was developed by a team of experts to provide a standardized means of assessing support needs for individuals with intellectual disability. The SIS examines the support needs of individuals with disabilities across seven life activity areas: home living, community living, lifelong learning, employment, health and safety, social activities, and protection and advocacy activities. The SIS is completed as an interview, and respondents are those that know the person with a disability well. Respondents provide information on the type of support, frequency of support, and daily support time for each of the items. Raters also complete information on exceptional supports needed to address medical conditions or prevent challenging behavior.

The information generated on the SIS can be used to identify overall support needs as well as specific domains that may benefit from supports planning. This information can assist the person-centered support team in developing an individualized supports plan to facilitate self-determination and desired life outcomes. Further information about the SIS is available at http://www.siswebsite.org/.

Michael's Communication Support Plan (Draft)

Recommendations

For Michael

Establish a core vocabulary of intelligible spoken words
Develop ability to answer questions
Increase use of social language
Independently follow a sequence of directions
Reduce dependence on verbal prompts

For Family and Care Providers

Accept any means of intelligible communication
Use natural language when giving directions
Program AAC device to promote social interaction
Develop interactive routines that incorporate turn-taking
Use consistent prompting techniques

Specific Communication Goals

Long-term goal: Increase social language skills
Objective: Greet others independently
Objective: Show items/share information with others with minimal prompting
Objective: Imitate actions of others

Long-term goal: Increase expressive language skills
Objective: Request items and activities using spoken, signed, or aided communication
Objective: Label emotions of others and self

Long-term goal: Increase receptive language skills
Objective: Respond to naturally spoken, single-step direction without gestural cues
Objective: Answer questions about personal information

Plan of action: To be developed

Figure 8.2.   Sample support plan from Michael's group action planning team. (Reprinted with permission from Michael's family.)

ROLE OF SYSTEMS OF SUPPORTS IN PROMOTING SELF-DETERMINATION

Leaders in the field of transition agree that promoting student self-determination is a valued outcome of transition services (Alwell & Cobb, 2006; Wehman, 2013). The process of planning for transition is all about involving the student with a disability, teaching him or her skills, creating opportunities, and supporting him or her to become a self-determining young adult. Numerous instructional strategies and curricula have been developed since the mid-1990s to teach skills associated with self-determined behavior (Algozzine et al., 2001; Cobb et al., 2009), many of which are highlighted in this book. Promoting self-determination involves three elements—teaching skills, creating opportunities, and providing needed supports (Wehmeyer, 2003b). Developing a system of support is a critical part of the process to promote self-determination and other valued transition outcomes. Using person-centered planning and a supports orientation has the potential to facilitate the development of self-determination by actively involving the student with a disability in the process of building a system of support and then leveraging this system of support to further enhance self-determination skills and opportunities. The system of support can identify other supports (e.g., teaching strategies, technology, emotional support) that facilitate the development of self-determination and enable students to achieve their vision for the future.

9

Systems Change to Promote Self-Determination

I think that self-determination should be used so differently from independence in schools! But it is not!
(Shogren, 2012, p. 173)

Working on self-determination has opened my eyes that I could do it, but I think I've opened a lot of eyes too.
(Jake, personal communication, July 17, 2012)

We have learned about how self-determination enables individuals to act as causal agents over their lives—a person that acts with intent to make things happen to achieve desired quality of life outcomes. We have also learned about the importance of 1) teaching skills, 2) creating opportunities, and 3) building a system of support. Integrating these three elements is necessary to support students to be self-determining.

We have also learned, however, about barriers to self-determination, such as restricted opportunities to make choices and set goals and a lack of knowledge within education and disability service systems on how to teach skills and create opportunities for self-determination. For example, the chapter's opening quote is from a mother who participated in a study exploring Hispanic mother's perceptions of self-determination (Shogren, 2012). This mother felt that the teachers and the schools she interacted with often mistakenly equated self-determination with independence. She felt this alienated her and other parents that focused on interdependence for their children and reduced the opportunities her son had for transition services based on his interests, preferences, and abilities. For example, she highlighted how educators were focused on teaching her son the skills needed to live independently, but her family planned for her son to reside with them throughout his life. The family had a long history of multiple generations of family members living together and wanted to maintain this. She felt that schools could have presented goals in a way that made them meaningful for her son, such as setting goals for employment, navigating around the community, and identifying ongoing learning opportunities while also recognizing that he did not need to learn about how to navigate around different kitchens or learn about different living arrangements because that was already being addressed by the family. The whole point of developing goals based on each person's interests, preferences, and abilities is to make sure they lead to self-determination.

This chapter describes barriers and facilitators of self-determination at the school and community level. Examples from research and practice on creating schools and communities that are supportive of self-determination are provided, and integrating self-determination within other school reform efforts is discussed. Jake's, one of the students featured throughout this book, eyes were open to all of the possibilities within his reach when he worked to develop self-determination skills. He feels that it also opened the eyes of other people he has encountered, enabling them to understand that people with disabilities can set and achieve goals and make things happen in their lives—a key ingredient to lasting changes in attitudes and systems. Jake's mom, Jeanine, elaborated that Jake was included in general education classes early on and he was very successful with his system of support, including the autism/behavioral support specialist described in Chapter 8, despite some initial struggles. Jeanine feels that Jake's experiences opened doors for other families and has even created opportunities for students with more intensive support needs to be included in their school district. She also highlights how it is always so powerful for parents and professionals to hear Jake present at conferences. He is often approached after his presentation and asked, "What can I do to help my child/student achieve a life like yours?" Questions such as this are a first step in creating a network of teachers, parents, and school team members that have the tools and the attitudes to support students to achieve their outcomes.

CHARACTERISTICS OF SCHOOLS AND COMMUNITIES THAT SUPPORT STUDENT SELF-DETERMINATION

Teachers and other members of the system of support must have the capacity to facilitate 1) teaching skills, 2) creating opportunities, and 3) building systems of supports for schools and communities to support self-determination. The following sections describe several factors that can support or inhibit creating schools and communities that support self-determination.

Family and Professional Knowledge and Self-Determination

Several researchers identified family and professional knowledge as a necessary element of building systems capacity for self-determination (Field & Hoffman, 2002b; Karvonen, Test, Wood, Browder, & Algozzine, 2004). For example, Field and Hoffman suggested quality indicators for school environments that support self-determination, and the first indicator is "knowledge, skills, and attitudes for self-determination are addressed in the curriculum, in family support programs, and in staff development" (p. 114).

The need for staff development to enable educators to support self-determination has been highlighted in multiple studies of teachers' perceptions of their knowledge of how to teach self-determination skills (Mason et al., 2004; Thoma, Nathanson, Baker, & Tamura, 2002; Wehmeyer, Agran, & Hughes, 2000). For example, Mason and colleagues studied 523 special education teachers across the United States and found only 22% indicated they felt very prepared to teach self-determination skills, although secondary teachers felt more prepared than elementary teachers. Karvonen and colleagues (2004) suggested that a critical feature of schools that are supportive of self-determination is that teachers should be provided with instruction on how to teach self-determination in personnel preparation programs as well as through ongoing in-service and professional development activities. The Research on Infusing Self-Determination into Teacher Preparation Programs research box discusses the integration of self-determination instruction into personnel preparation programs (Thoma, Baker, & Saddler, 2002). Using active learning strategies during pre- and in-service training is a key factor in developing teacher skills.

Research on Infusing Self-Determination into Teacher Preparation Programs

Thoma, Baker, and Saddler (2002) surveyed special education faculty at universities throughout the United States to develop an understanding of how faculty members were preparing special educators to teach the skills associated with self-determination. Forty-one faculty responded, and only 22 reported they taught self-determination in their courses. Thoma, Baker, and Saddler conducted follow-up interviews with those that included instruction in self-determination in their courses and found that the self-determination content was typically embedded in classes on disability-specific strategies, transition strategies, and secondary special education methods. All of the courses in which the content was taught were required in graduate or undergraduate degree programs. Instructors were most likely to focus on teaching strategies for choice making, decision making, and self-advocacy and used a variety of different instructional strategies, including traditional lectures and class discussion as well as writing transition IEP plans, writing reflection journals, and role-playing.

Thoma, Baker, and Saddler (2002) described a course they developed to teach key skills related to transition and self-determination because of the limited number of courses on instructing teachers about self-determination and the need to understand the factors that promote effective learning for pre- and in-service teachers. They highlighted the importance of empowering teachers and giving them skills to promote reflection, active participation, and feedback. They incorporated several strategies to provide direct experience with self-determination instruction and assessment in the class. For example, they had teachers keep a reflective journal, personally complete self-determination assessments, create a resource file on community resources, complete a survey, systematically examine their cultural beliefs about self-determination, and role-play student-led transition meetings. Pre- and in-service teachers who took the course had positive feedback and felt that the course made them more sensitive to the importance of actively involving students with disabilities in their education.

All of these strategies have relevance for pre- and in-service education on self-determination. Instruction that promotes teacher empowerment and self-determination through active learning has the potential to enable teachers to have the ability to teach skills, create opportunities, and build systems of support for self-determination.

Teachers should be active participants when learning about self-determination. Many of the skills that we teach students may also be beneficial for us.

Field and Hoffman (2002a) emphasized the importance of teacher self-determination, suggesting that teachers have to be self-determined in order to effectively promote self-determination through modeling, role-playing, and adapting the curriculum to individualize self-determination instruction for each of their students. They suggested five elements of teacher self-determination:

1. Know themselves and their students

2. Value themselves

3. Put their knowledge and beliefs into a plan

4. Put their plan into action

5. Evaluate their implementation efforts (p. 93)

They highlighted that teachers who have self-awareness, self-management skills, and goal-setting experience are able to use these skills and attitudes in their classroom to effectively model self-determination and can use self-determination instruction as an opportunity to co-learn with students by going through the same goal-setting process that students go through.

Family knowledge and beliefs about self-determination and ways to support its development in the home is similarly important to creating environments that are supportive of self-determination (Zhang, 2005). Families can benefit from information on how to think about self-determination in home environments (Brotherson, Cook, Cuncoran, Lahr, & Weymeyer, 1995; Field & Hoffman, 1999) and from the coordination of self-determination activities across home and school environments. This provides a natural opportunity to use the strategies described in Table 2.1 on communicating with families about self-determination and the posture of cultural reciprocity. Families and professionals can be partners in promoting self-determination in transition planning by sharing information across home and school environments. Abery and colleagues (1994) developed a curriculum that can be used to share information with families about self-determination, and other researchers (Doss & Hatcher, 1996; Field & Hoffman, 1999; Turnbull & Turnbull, 1997) have identified strategies ranging from involving families in promoting self-determination and participating in workshops with their children on self-determination to teaching families how to model self-determined behavior for their children. Jake's mom, Jeanine, emphasized the key role that Jake's autism/behavioral support specialist played in teaching her to have high expectations for Jake and introducing her to self-management strategies that enabled Jake to develop his self-determination skills (see Chapters 3 and 8). Christy, Michael's sister, highlighted how the involvement of educators in Michael's GAP team enabled his entire system of support to coordinate across home, school, and the community, allowing Michael to have the consistent support he needed to be self-determining (see Chapter 8).

School Culture

Researchers highlighted, however, that it can be a challenge for teachers to be self-determined and find ways promote self-determination without leadership and support within school systems. Eisenman and Chamberlin (2001) evaluated seven schools that were implementing self-determination activities to identify issues that were effective in promoting systems change to infuse self-determination into the curriculum. They found that teachers struggled with having time to plan, develop, or implement instructional activities focused on self-determination, even if they thought self-determination was important. The teachers saw power in teaching self-determination, but found that integrating self-determination was not as high of a priority as other instructional activities within their schools. Instead, self-determination was often an "add on" that tended to be "short, one-shot workshop-like activities with limited impact on students" (Eiseman & Chamberlin, 2001, p. 144). Developing administrative support and promoting a culture in schools that supports self-determination is critical to addressing these issues and is discussed in the following sections.

Broad Commitment   Karvonen et al. identified six school programs that were engaged in "exemplary" (2004, p. 26) practices regarding promoting student self-determination. They then conducted in-depth case studies at these six sites. One of their key findings was that a broad commitment to self-determination instruction across the school was needed to lead to change in the time, resources, tools, and support for promoting self-determination.

Karvonen et al. (2004) highlighted the importance of an "impetus person" (p. 34) in beginning the process of promoting self-determination in a school program. This person tended to take the lead and coached other professionals, including general and special education teachers, related services professionals, and administrators on self-determination. Many of the impetus people in the Karvonen et al. (2004) study had connections to local universities and special education teacher training programs, suggesting that access to research-based resources and teacher preparation programs may be a factor that is supportive of self-determination instruction.

Karvonen et al. (2004) as well as other researchers (Eisenman & Chamberlin, 2001; Field & Hoffman, 2002a), however, mentioned that there is often limited sustainability of efforts to promote self-determination, even with a strong impetus person, unless cultural change and administrative support are achieved. In fact, a lack of administrative support was one of the most consistently identified barriers to promoting self-determination (Karvonen et al., 2004). A lack of administrative support leads to a lack of time, resources, or tools to develop instructional materials for self-determination and a plan for creating opportunities throughout the curriculum for self-determination (Eiseman & Chamberlin, 2001).

Administrative support, however, is not the only commitment that is needed. Other professionals in the school also have to be committed to promoting self-determination. This often requires change in the attitudes of multiple teachers and related services providers. The possibilities of self-determination do not become clear to many people until they see the power the approach can have for people with disabilities. Sue Walter emphasized the affect that her daughter Jennifer's participation in the IEP meeting had not only on Jennifer, but also on all of the adults that participated in the meeting (see Chapter 6). Inviting other teachers, professionals, and administrators to observe self-directed instruction, student participation in IEP meetings, and documentation of the benefits of self-determination on student outcomes has the power to lead to attitudinal changes and greater buy-in from administrators and other professionals. For example, Branding, Bates, and Miner (2009) created videos of student-directed IEP meetings and externally directed IEP meetings and had 95 special education and rehabilitation professionals watch the two videos to explore the effect it had on their perceptions of student self-determination. They found that the professionals viewed the students as more capable when watching the self-directed IEP videos, and they had a better understanding of the students' abilities. Creating opportunities for professionals to observe these types of behaviors and outcomes can be a key element to creating a school culture that supports self-determination. Sharon Slover describes how she works to empower teachers and students by mentoring and modeling the process of implementing person-centered planning in the Perspectives on Empowering Teachers research box. Her approach uses active learning and empowers teachers to be self-determining. Also, using the framework for thinking about adopting evidence-based practices can provide a means for exploring and initiating the implementation of evidence-based self-determination instructional strategies while being respectful of family, school, and community culture (see Chapter 1).

Self-Determination for All Students Emphasizing that self-determination is advantageous for students with a wide range of support needs is another factor described in the literature that can facilitate understanding the benefits of self-determination. The strategies provided throughout this book show that students can use and apply self-determination skills in diverse ways. In addition, self-determination can be taught in any type of instructional setting and across instructional settings. For example, Heather Haynes described how choice making can be used in a general education math class and a recovery math class in Chapter 3. An array of research suggests that self-determination strategies can

Perspectives on
Empowering Teachers

Not everyone is fortunate enough to have the guidance of a mentor and role model. It was my goal to develop leaders and share the knowledge, expertise, and ability to move mountains in the field of transition.

It is important to empower others, teaching them to believe in their own abilities. As I reflect back on the years I have spent with others, it is the passion that comes to the forefront. It is important to pass on the passion that revolves around believing in others and believing in students. I demonstrate this by conducting person-centered plans with students, adult agency personnel, and team members. One of the first times I experienced the power behind the process was with a student on the autism spectrum disorder and his team. The team was hitting a wall in terms of planning the next steps. I became the mentor and role model through this process.

It has often been said that seeing is believing, and this is exactly what happened that day. I was able to model how to move a whole team toward meeting the needs of a student through person-centered planning. As I moved through the process and called for others to join me, the team was able to see how empowering it is to think differently and map out a student's life.

After I conducted a mapping, I immediately began handing over control and empowering others to take this process and continue to provide this to other families and teams in need. I was the individual taking notes while someone else was conducting the mapping. Then, I moved to a participant level, empowering others to run the entire mapping. It is amazing to observe the empowerment process. I empower teachers, who now empower students. Believing in others is necessary. Encouraging others to trust themselves and have faith in their own judgments and abilities is a must.

Contributed by Sharon Slover.

support students to gain access to the general education curriculum, which has the potential to raise expectations for students with disabilities across settings (Wehmeyer, Field, Doren, Jones, & Mason, 2004).

Several researchers also suggested that self-determination does not have to be a disability-specific issue (Field et al., 1998b; Shogren, Lopez, Wehmeyer, Little, & Pressgrove, 2006). Making effective choices, self-managing learning and behavior, setting goals, and self-advocating are all great skills for students without disabilities as well. Eisenman and Chamberlin wrote the following in their analysis of school programs implementing self-determination instruction: Teachers "believed they would be most successful in their efforts to implement self-determination activities if others in their school also perceived student self-determination as a primary goal of education" (2001, p. 143).

Initial Resistance   Having a professional that serves as an impetus person for bringing attention to self-determination within a school, developing administrator buy-in, and promoting attitudinal changes are all important aspects of developing self-determined schools, teachers, and students. It is necessary, however, to remember that systems change takes time, and as Karvonen et al. (2004) suggested that there may be initial resistance. For example, Karvonen et al. found many of the impetus people in the exemplary schools struggled in developing broad commitment. They tended to find limited administrative support, especially at first or if the benefits of self-determination focused instruction were not clear. One impetus person said, "I think [building administrators] trust my judgment, but they don't push anyone else to have to do it" (p. 36). In the Experiences as an Impetus Person research box, Anne Clark describes the resistance she encountered in working to create attitudinal changes and administrator buy-in as she worked to promote systems change to initiate student-led IEP meetings in her school. It took time, patience, and recognizing the importance of building relationships. Fortunately, it paid off in the end.

Self-determination is a developmental process for students. It does not suddenly emerge. It takes multiple teaching strategies, opportunities, and supports across a person's life span. Students may even show initial resistance to learning about their disability, talking about goals for the future, and taking responsibility for their learning, especially if this is the first time they are doing it. They may also feel intimidated or nervous. Wehmeyer et al. (2012) found it took 2 years of instruction to see significant, positive gains in students' scores on The Arc's Self-Determination Scale, although the researchers did see increased progress on goals and access to the general education curriculum during this 2-year period (Shogren, Palmer et al., 2012). Recognizing that change takes time and resistance may occur on multiple fronts is an important part of systems change activities. Patience and focus on the end goal is necessary to drive systems change. The Questions for an "Impetus Person" to Think About form (see Figure 9.1) provides questions that can be used by an impetus person to assess areas within his or her school and community that can be targeted to promote systems change related to self-determination.

SELF-DETERMINATION AND ONGOING RESTRUCTURING EFFORTS

The multiple demands on teachers' time can be a limiting factor when thinking about developing and implementing instruction to promote self-determination. It is hard to argue that self-determination is not important when reading research on the outcomes of teaching self-determination. Infusing efforts to promote self-determination into other school reform and restructuring efforts is one way that researchers and practitioners are increasingly thinking about promoting self-determination. The SDLMI can be overlaid on any instructional activities to teach students how to set goals for any curriculum domain on which they are working (see Chapter 5). Also, choice making can be infused throughout the instructional day (see Chapter 3). Multiple opportunities can be embedded into other efforts within school programs to promote student success. Promoting access to the general education curriculum for students with severe disabilities has received significant attention in the disability field, and researchers found that promoting self-determination affects students' access to the general education curriculum (Palmer, Wehmeyer, Gipson, & Agran, 2004; Shogren et al., 2012).

Many schools are focused on building positive behavior interventions and supports that provide schoolwide behavioral supports and expectations (Sailor, Dunlop, Sugai, & Horner, 2009; Sugai & Horner, 2010). Teaching self-determination skills can be a natural part of that process. Self-determination is all about supporting students to develop strategies to use their behavior in effective ways that allow them to get the things they want and need *Teaching self-determination skills can be a natural part of many processes and programs.* out of life. Developing ways for students to communicate their wants and needs in a just-right way can be a great way to promote positive behavior (Carr et al., 2002; see Chapter 4). For example, Wehmeyer, Baker, Blumberg, and Harrison (2004) developed an innovative assessment called the Person Guided Functional Assessment, based on the

Questions for an "Impetus Person" to Think About

Instructions

The following questions provide a starting point for assessing the school culture and knowledge related to self-determination. Answer the questions and note which ones were answered with a "no." Select one or two of these areas and use this as a starting point for introducing the concept of self-determination to school culture. Progress will likely be slow, but addressing these areas can build a culture that is supportive of self-determination over time.

1. Can the majority of members of the special education teaching staff provide a definition of self-determination?

2. Can the majority of members of the general education teaching staff provide a definition of self-determination?

3. Is instruction on promoting self-determination integrated into professional development activities for general and/or special educators?

4. Is self-determination recognized as a key outcome of transition services?

5. Are systematic practices in place for documenting that student's interests, preferences, and abilities are guiding the transition planning process?

6. Are any of the skills associated with self-determination targeted in the general education curriculum? Does this provide an entry point for students with disabilities?

7. Do administrators know the definition of self-determination?

8. Have administrators observed student-led IEP meetings or observed self-determination instruction?

9. Are there opportunities for communication and collaboration between home and school on self-determination?

10. Are there opportunities for students with disabilities to participate in and provide feedback on systems change activities?

Figure 9.1. Questions for an "impetus person" to think about when working to begin systems change to promote self-determination.

Experiences as
an Impetus Person

System change and changing school attitudes and culture are two ideas that I have thought about a lot in the last year and a half. This year has been a challenge. I started off the year excited to get students actively involved in their IEP meetings. It makes sense to me to involve the person you are talking about in the process. It definitely calls for more time preparing instruction to teach the student how to get involved, but it also should make the student's goals more meaningful because he or she helped create them. Involving students keeps them more motivated if they know what they are working toward and why, and it focuses the team on the individual rather than getting caught up in past practice and paperwork. I was more than willing to do the work up front and put the time in with my students to prepare them for the meeting, so I could not understand why there was resistance from other professionals regarding students participating in their meetings. I realized over time that I was asking people to make a significant cultural shift. They had never had students actively participate in IEP meetings and did not know what to expect.

I am also amazed at how long it can take a system to change. I thought change would be relatively easy in a small school (there are only about 40 staff at my school). I thought I could create some handouts and share findings from research about the benefits of including students in the IEP process and that would lead to other people being immediately excited about it too. I found that people did not want anything additional to read. Most people did not even want to do a seven-question survey with Likert Scale questions to express how they felt about students participating in their meetings. Having personal conversations and making verbal connections with other staff members about the positive effect for teachers and students is what seemed to make a big difference. Staff wanted to express their concerns and have them addressed. They worried that these meetings would take more time or that certain things could not be verbalized in front of students. I tried to address their concerns with the information I had read in the literature and share my personal feelings on why it was so important to get students involved in the process. It was hard to quell their fears because I did not really know what would happen. I could not be sure that the meetings would not take a lot longer or that students would not get upset about things we talked about. It was tough trying to advocate for a change that I had only read about and thought was a good idea.

I had a student present to her IEP team in September after a lot of preparation and work. The student was able to present her strengths, areas of need, goals, and accommodations using a PowerPoint presentation I had helped her create. I had spent a lot of time practicing and preparing with her for the meeting. The student was intimidated by having so many people to talk in front of, however, and I was a little bit disappointed that she forgot to do and say quite a few of the things that we had practiced. But, the response from the IEP team members was fantastic; people could not believe the PowerPoint she had put together and the fact that she was even able to answer some questions about her goals. This student met two of her eight goals within 2 months (and I would be the first to admit that I usually write pretty ambitious goals). She was motivated by knowing her goal and graphing her progress and was proud to report to her mom and teachers as she got closer to reaching her goals.

I was glad to get such positive feedback from the team about this first meeting. But, many concerns were voiced as we began discussing another meeting I wanted a student to attend. This was a bit confusing to me because I felt like we had made encouraging strides forward only to go right back to where we started. Luckily, this student's parents were on board, so there was a real push to have her lead her meeting. Consequently, the other members of the team seemed to come around a bit sooner this time. One of the biggest lessons I have learned is that making systems change is personal for the person trying

(continued)

to change things and the people being asked to change. I thought it would be more matter of fact and professional, but there are a lot of feelings and opinions involved.

I have also learned that it is important to have patience, recognize there may be a lot of resistance to change, and have people (even if they are outside of the school) to communicate with about what I am trying to do as I am doing it. Taking classes at the university and having access to professionals and peers who were working on similar issues was really powerful for me and helped keep me on track. This persistence has led to positive outcomes. We are working with even more students next year to lead their IEP meetings, and a few more teachers are getting excited about this and interested in being involved. Plus, some of the administrators are starting to buy-in to the benefits, so I am hopeful this might be something that can become a part of our school's culture.

Contributed by Anne Clark.

Functional Assessment Interview (O'Neill, Horner, Albin, Storey, & Sprague, 1997), that actively involves students with disabilities in the process of understanding the function of their behavior.

These examples highlight how self-determination can be integrated throughout school programs and culture to actively engage all students, teachers, and schools in the process of becoming self-determined. Systems change to promote self-determination can occur within any of the domains described in Chapter 7. Students with disabilities can be actively involved in this process, creating even more opportunities for practicing self-determination skills. For example, Jake was invited to serve on a stakeholders' committee for a statewide autism conference because he was an experienced presenter on autism. He made a wish list that described the topics he thinks are important for youth with autism to learn (see Figure 9.2). The conference previously focused only on family and professional issues. Jake used his advocacy skills to make family members and professionals more aware of the need for youth with autism to be educated about the things that affect their lives. His work led to a block of self-advocacy sessions being offered at the next statewide autism conference, providing educational opportunities for the first time for youth with autism, not just their parents and professionals.

Mike, Michael's father, has also worked to promote systems change in domains that affect his son's life with the interests, preferences, and abilities of Michael at the forefront. For example, Mike served on the school board and advocated for reform in the special education program because of multiple frustrations of parents (and teachers) with regard to the services that were being provided. The issues were finally recognized by the school administration after several attempts to develop administration buy-in and with time and persistence, a parent liaison was appointed to host parent meetings that were attended by administrators. This led to better understanding by the administration regarding the needs of students with disabilities and the beginning of systems change within the district focused on accountability for the outcomes of students with disabilities.

CONCLUSION

Self-determination is a key part of everyone's life. Making choices and decisions, managing learning and behavior, setting goals, and advocating for what we want and need in life allows us to be the people that make things happen in our lives. Everyone may

---

State Autism Conference Stakeholders' Meeting

1. Self-advocacy skills
   - Asking for help when you need it
   - Explaining your disability
   - Knowing your modifications and how to ask for them when you need them

2. Managing challenging teachers
   - Dealing with tough teachers (teachers that are not really experienced with autism issues)

3. Understanding my disability
   - Understanding which behaviors are happening
   - How it may affect your self-esteem

4. Organization
   - Managing your time
   - Keeping your schoolwork (notebooks and binders) clean and organized

5. Social interaction
   - Proper ways to communicate with friends or anyone you do not know really well

6. Participation in IEP meetings
   - Being able to attend meetings
   - Understanding what is going on

Figure 9.2. Jake's wish list for the statewide autism conference. (Reprinted with permission from Jake's family.)

define what they want out of life differently, but everyone has the right to have the skills, opportunities, and supports to go after what they want. This book provides strategies to 1) teach skills, 2) create opportunities, and 3) build systems of support that enable youth to develop into self-determined adults. The power of educators and school systems to influence self-determination is immense, and young people are able to achieve outcomes such as those of Jake and Michael when attention is directed to self-determination as a key educational outcome.

References

Abery, B.H., Eggebeen, A., Rudrud, L., Arndt, K., Tetu, L., Barosko, J., . . . Peterson, K. (1994). *Self-Determination for youth with disabilities: A family education curriculum.* Minneapolis: Institute on Community Integration, University of Minnesota.

Abery, B., & Stancliffe, R. (2003). An ecological theory of self-determination: Theoretical foundations. In M.L. Wehmeyer, B. Abery, D. Mithaug, & R. Stancliffe (Eds.), *Theory in self-determination: Foundations for educational practice* (pp. 25-42). Springfield, IL: Charles C. Thomas Publishing Co.

Agran, M., Blanchard, C., & Wehmeyer, M.L. (2000). Promoting transition goals and self-determination through student self-directed learning: The Self-Determined Learning Model of Instruction. *Education and Training in Mental Retardation and Developmental Disabilities, 35*(4), 351–364.

Agran, M., Blanchard, C., Wehmeyer, M.L., & Hughes, C. (2001). Teaching students to self-regulate their behavior: The differential effects of student- vs. teacher-delivered reinforcement. *Research in Developmental Disabilities, 22*(4), 319–332.

Agran, M., King-Sears, M., Wehmeyer, M.L., & Copeland, S.R. (2003). *Teachers' guides to inclusive practices: Student-directed learning strategies.* Baltimore, MD: Paul H. Brookes Publishing Co.

Agran, M., & Krupp, M. (2011). Providing choice making in employment programs: The beginning or end of self-determination? *Education and Training in Autism and Developmental Disabilities, 46*, 565–575.

Agran, M., Snow, K., & Swaner, J. (1999). Teacher perceptions of self-determination: Benefits, characteristics, strategies. *Education and Training in Mental Retardation and Developmental Disabilities, 34*, 293–301.

Algozzine, B., Browder, D., Karvonen, M., Test, D.W., & Wood, W.M. (2001). Effects of interventions to promote self-determination for individuals with disabilities. *Review of Educational Research, 71*, 219–277. doi: 10.3102/00346543071002219

Alwell, M., & Cobb, B. (2006). A map of the intervention literature in secondary special education transition. *Career Development for Exceptional Individuals, 29*, 3–27.

Americans with Disabilities Act (ADA) of 1990, PL 101-336, 42 U.S.C. §§ 12101 *et seq.*

APA Presidential Task Force on Evidence-Based Practice. (2006). Evidence-based practice in psychology. *American Psychologist, 61*, 271–285.

Balcazar, F.E., Fawcett, S.B., & Seekins, T. (1991). Teaching people with disabilities to recruit help to attain personal goals. *Rehabilitation Psychology, 36*(1), 31–42. doi: 10.1037/h0079072

Bandura, A. (1997). *Self-efficacy: The exercise of control.* New York, NY: W.H. Freeman.

Benitez, D.T., Lattimore, J., & Wehmeyer, M.L. (2005). Promoting the involvement of students with emotional and behavioral disorders in career and vocational planning and decision-making: The self-determined career development model. *Behavioral Disorders, 30*(4), 431–447.

Blackorby, J., & Wagner, M. (1996). Longitudinal post-school outcomes of youth with disabilities: Findings from the National Longitudinal Transition Study. *Exceptional Children, 62*(5), 399–413.

Blue-Banning, M.J., Turnbull, A.P., & Pereira, L. (2000). Group action planning as a support strategy for Hispanic families: Parent and professional perspectives. *Mental Retardation, 38*(3), 262–275.

Branding, D., Bates, P., & Miner, C. (2009). Perceptions of self-determination by special education and rehabilitation practitioners based on viewing a self-directed IEP versus an external-directed IEP meeting. *Research in Developmental Disabilities, 30*(4), 755–762. doi:10.1016/j.ridd.2008.10.006

Brotherson, M.J., Cook, C.C., Cunconan-Lahr, R., & Wehmeyer, M.L. (1995). Policy supporting self-determination in the environments of children with disabilities. *Education and Training in Mental Retardation and Developmental Disabilities, 30*(1), 3–14.

Bryan, T., Burstein, K., & Bryan, J. (2001). Students with learning disabilities: Homework problems and promising practices. *Educational Psychologist, 36*(3), 167–180. doi: 10.1207/s15326985ep3603_3

Caldwell, J. (2010). Leadership development of individuals with developmental disabilities in the self-advocacy

movement. *Journal of Intellectual Disability Research,
54*(11), 1004–1014.

Caldwell, J. (2011). Disability identity of leaders in the self-
advocacy movement. *Intellectual and Developmental Disabilities, 49*(5), 315–326.

Cameto, R., Levine, P., & Wagner, M. (2004). *Transition
planning for students with disabilities: A special topic report of
findings from the National Longitudinal Transition Study–2.*
Retrieved from www.nlts2.org/reports/2004_11/nlts2
_report_2004_11_complete.pdf

Campbell-Whatley, G.D. (2008). Teaching students about
their disabilities: Increasing self-determination skills and
self-concept. *International Journal of Special Education,
23*(2), 137–144.

Cannella, H.I., O'Reilly, M.F., & Lancioni, G.E. (2005).
Choice and preference assessment research with people
with severe to profound developmental disabilities: A
review of the literature. *Research in Developmental Disabilities, 26*, 1–15.

Carr, E.G., Dunlap, G., Horner, R.H., Koegel, R.L., Turnbull, A.P., Sailor, W., . . . Fox, L. (2002). Positive behavior
support: Evolution of an applied science. *Journal of Positive Behavior Interventions, 4*(1), 4–16, 20.

Carter, E.W., Lane, K.L., Pierson, M.R., & Glaeser, B.
(2006). Self-determination skills and opportunities of
transition-age youth with emotional disturbance and
learning disabilities. *Exceptional Children, 72*, 333–346.

Carter, E.W., Owens, L., Trainor, A., Sun, Y., & Swedeen,
B. (2009). Self-determination skills and opportunities of
adolescents with severe intellectual and developmental
disabilities. *American Journal on Intellectual and Developmental Disabilities, 114*(3), 179–192.

Carter, E.W., Swedeen, B., Walter, M.J., Moss, C.K., &
Hsin, C.T. (2011). Perspectives of young adults with dis-
abilities on leadership. *Career Development for Exceptional
Individuals, 34*(1), 57–67.

Carter, E.W., Trainor, A., Owens, L., Sweden, B., & Sun, Y.
(2010). Self-determination prospects of youth with high-
incidence disabilities: Divergent perspectives and related
factors. *Journal of Emotional and Behavioral Disorders, 18*,
67–81. doi:10.1177/1063426609332605

Cihak, D.F., Wright, R., & Ayres, K.M. (2010). Use of self-
modeling static-picture prompts via a handheld computer
to facilitate self-monitoring in the general education
classroom. *Education and Training in Autism and Developmental Disabilities, 45*(1), 136–149.

Claes, C., Van Hove, G., Vandevelde, S., van Loon, J., &
Schalock, R.L. (2010). Person-centered planning: Analysis of research and effectiveness. *Intellectual and Developmental Disabilities, 48*, 432–453.

Cobb, R.B., Lehmann, J., Newman-Gonchar, R., &
Alwell, M. (2009). Self-determination for students with
disabilities: A narrative metasynthesis. *Career Development for Exceptional Individuals, 32*, 108–114. doi:
10.1177/0885728809336654

Cole, C.L., & Levinson, T.R. (2002). Effects of within-
activity choices on the challenging behavior of children
with severe developmental disabilities. *Journal of Positive
Behavior Interventions, 4*(1), 29–37, 52.

Cook, B.G., & Cook, S.C. (2011). *Thinking and communicating clearly about evidence-based practices in special education.*
Arlington, VA: Division for Research, Council for Exceptional Children.

Copeland, S.R., & Hughes, C. (2002). Effects of goal setting on task performance of persons with mental retardation. *Education and Training in Mental Retardation and
Developmental Disabilities, 37*(1), 40–54.

Copeland, S.R., Hughes, C., Agran, M., Wehmeyer, M.L.,
& Fowler, S.E. (2002). An intervention package to support high school students with mental retardation in general education classrooms. *American Journal on Mental
Retardation, 107*(1), 32–45.

Davies, D.K., Stock, S.E., Holloway, S., & Wehmeyer, M.L.
(2010). Evaluating a GPS-based transportation device to
support independent bus travel by people with intellectual disability. *Intellectual and Developmental Disabilities,
48*(6), 454–463. doi: 10.1352/1934-9556-48.6.454

Davies, D.K., Stock, S.E., & Wehmeyer, M.L. (2002a).
Enhancing independent task performance for individuals with mental retardation through use of a handheld
self-directed visual and audio prompting system. *Education and Training in Mental Retardation and Developmental
Disabilities, 37*(2), 209–218.

Davies, D.K., Stock, S.E., & Wehmeyer, M.L. (2002b).
Enhancing independent time-management skills in individuals with mental retardation using a Palmtop personal
computer. *Mental Retardation, 40*(5), 358–365.

Davies, D.K., Stock, S.E., & Wehmeyer, M.L. (2003). A
Palmtop computer-based intelligent aid for individuals
with intellectual disabilities to increase independent decision making. *Research and Practice for Persons with Severe
Disabilities, 28*(4), 182–193. doi:10.2511/rpsd.28.4.182

DiGangi, S.A., Maag, J.W., & Rutherford, R.B. (1991). Self-
graphing of on-task behavior: Enhancing the reactive
effects of self-monitoring on on-task behavior and academic performance. *Learning Disability Quarterly, 14*(3),
221–230. doi:10.2307/1510851

Doss, B., & Hatcher, B. (1996). Self-determination as a family affair: Parents' perspectives on self-determination. In
D.J. Sands & M.L. Wehmeyer (Eds.), *Self-determination
across the lifespan: Independence and choice for people with
disabilities* (pp. 51–63). Baltimore, MD: Paul H. Brookes
Publishing Co.

Dunlap, G., dePerczel, M., Clarke, S., Wilson, D., Wright,
S., White, R., & Gomez, A. (1994). Choice making to
promote adaptive behavior for students with emotional
and behavioral challenges. *Journal of Applied Behavior
Analysis, 27*(3), 505–518.

Eisenman, L.T., & Chamberlin, M. (2001). Implementing self-determination activities: Lessons from schools.
Remedial and Special Education, 22(3), 138–147.

Erwin, E.J., Brotherson, M.J., Palmer, S.B., Cook, C.C.,
Weigel, C.J., & Summers, J.A. (2009). How to promote
self-determination for young children with disabilities:
Evidence-based strategies for early childhood practitioners and families. *Young Exceptional Children, 12*, 27–37.

Erwin, E.J., & Brown, F. (2003). From theory to practice: A contextual framework for understanding self-
determination in early childhood environments. *Infants
and Young Children, 16*, 77–87.

Everson, J.M., & Zhang, D. (2000). Person-centered planning: Characteristics, inhibitors, and supports. *Education
and Training in Mental Retardation and Developmental Disabilities, 35*(1), 36–43.

Falk, G.D., Dunlap, G., & Kern, L. (1996). An analysis of
self-evaluation and videotape feedback for improving the

peer interactions of students with externalizing and internalizing behavior problems. *Behavioral Disorders, 21*(4), 261–276.

Farrell, A., & McDougall, D. (2008). Self-monitoring of pace to improve math fluency of high school students with disabilities. *Behavior Analysis in Practice, 1*(2), 26–35.

Feldman, E., Kim, J.-S., & Elliott, S.N. (2011). The effects of accommodations on adolescents' self-efficacy and test performance. *Journal of Special Education, 45*(2), 77–88. doi:10.1177/0022466909353791

Field, S. (1996). Self-determination instructional strategies for youth with learning disabilities. *Journal of Learning Disabilities, 29*, 40–52.

Field, S., & Hoffman, A. (1999). The importance of family involvement for promoting self-determination in adolescents with autism and other developmental disabilities. *Focus on Autism and Other Developmental Disabilities, 14*(1), 36–41.

Field, S., & Hoffman, A. (2002a). Lessons learned from implementing the Steps to Self-Determination curriculum. *Remedial and Special Education, 23*(2), 90–98. doi: 10.1177/074193250202300205

Field, S., & Hoffman, A. (2002b). Preparing youth to exercise self-determination: Quality indicators of school environments that promote the acquisition of knowledge, skills, and beliefs related to self-determination. *Journal of Disability Policy Studies, 13*, 113–118.

Field, S., Martin, J.E., Miller, R., Ward, M.J., & Wehmeyer, M.L. (1998a). *A practical guide to teaching self-determination*. Reston, VA: Council for Exceptional Children.

Field, S., Martin, J.E., Miller, R., Ward, M.J., & Wehmeyer, M.L. (1998b). Self-determination for persons with disabilities: A position statement of the Division on Career Development and Transition. *Career Development for Exceptional Individuals, 21*, 113–128.

Field, S., Sarver, M.D., & Shaw, S.F. (2003). Self-determination: A key to success in postsecondary education for students with learning disabilities. *Remedial and Special Education, 24*, 339–349.

Figarola, P.M., Gunter, P.L., Reffel, J.M., Worth, S.R., Hummel, J., & Gerber, B.L. (2008). Effects of self-graphing and goal setting on the math fact fluency of students with disabilities. *Behavior Analysis in Practice, 1*(2), 36–41.

Flannery, B., Newton, S., Horner, R., Slovic, R., Blumberg, R., & Ard, W.K. (2000). The impact of person centered planning on the content and organization of individual supports. *Career Development for Exceptional Individuals, 23*(2), 123–137.

Forest, M., & Pearpoint, J. (1992). MAPS: Action planning. In J. Pearpoint, M. Forest & J.A. Snow (Eds.), *The inclusion papers: Strategies to make inclusion work* (pp. 52–56). Toronto, Ontario, Canada: Inclusion Press.

Frankland, H.C., Turnbull, A.P., Wehmeyer, M.L., & Blackmountain, L. (2004). An exploration of the self-determination construct and disability as it relates to the Dine (Navajo) culture. *Education and Training in Developmental Disabilities, 39*, 191–205.

Furby, L., & Beyth Marom, R. (1992). Risk taking in adolescence: A decision-making perspective. *Developmental Review, 12*(1), 1–44.

Gans, A.M., Kenny, M.C., & Ghany, D.L. (2003). Comparing the self-concept of students with and without learning disabilities. *Journal of Learning Disabilities, 36*, 287–295.

Gersten, R., Fuchs, L.S., Compton, D., Coyne, M., Greenwood, C., & Innocenti, M.S. (2005). Quality indicators for group experimental and quasi-experimental research in special education. *Exceptional Children, 71*(2), 149–164.

Goddard, Y.L., & Sendi, C. (2008). Effects of self-monitoring on the narrative and expository writing of four fourth-grade students with learning disabilities. *Reading and Writing Quarterly, 24*(4), 408–433.

Graham, S., MacArthur, C., & Schwartz, S. (1995). Effects of goal setting and procedural facilitation on the revising behavior and writing performance of students with writing and learning problems. *Journal of Educational Psychology, 87*(2), 230–240. doi:10.1037/0022-0663.87.2.230

Graham, S., MacArthur, C., Schwartz, S., & Page-Voth, V. (1992). Improving the compositions of students with learning disabilities using a strategy involving product and process goal setting. *Exceptional Children, 58*(4), 322–334.

Grigal, M., Neubert, D.A., Moon, S.M., & Graham, S. (2003). Self-determination for students with disabilities: Views of parents and teachers. *Exceptional Children, 70*, 97–112.

Hagopian, L.P., Long, E.S., & Rush, K.S. (2004). Preference assessment procedures for individuals with developmental disabilities. *Behavior Modification, 28*, 668–677. doi: 10.1177/0145445503259836

Halpern, A.S., Herr, C.M., Wolf, N.K., Lawson, J.D., Doren, B., & Johnson, M.D. (1995). *NEXT S.T.E.P.: Student transition and educational planning. Teacher manual.* Eugene: University of Oregon.

Hart, D., Grigal, M., & Weir, C. (2010). Expanding the paradigm: Postsecondary education options for individuals with autism spectrum disorder and intellectual disabilities. *Focus on Autism and Other Developmental Disabilities, 25*(3), 134–150. doi:10.1177/1088357610373759

Hasazi, S.B., Johnson, D.R., Thurlow, M., Cobb, B., Trach, J., Stodden, B., . . . Grossi, T. (2005). Transitions from home and school to the roles and supports of adulthood. In K.C. Lakin & A.P. Turnbull (Eds.), *National goals and research for persons with intellectual and developmental disabilities* (pp. 65–92). Washington, DC: American Association on Mental Retardation and the Arc of the United States.

Holburn, S. (2002). How science can evaluate and enhance person-centered planning. *Research and Practice for Persons with Severe Disabilities, 27*(4), 250–260. doi:10.2511/rpsd.27.4.250

Horner, R.H., Carr, E.G., Halle, J., McGee, G., Odom, S., & Wolery, M. (2005). The use of single-subject research to identify evidence-based practice in special education. *Exceptional Children, 71*(2), 165–179.

Houghton, J., Bronicki, G.B., & Guess, D. (1987). Opportunities to express preferences and make choices among students with severe disabilities in classroom settings. *Journal of The Association for Persons with Severe Handicaps, 12*, 18–27.

Huebner, E.S., Ash, C., & Laughlin, J.E. (2001). Life experiences, locus of control, and school satisfaction in adolescence. *Social Indicators Research, 55*(2), 167–183.

Hughes, C., Copeland, S.R., Agran, M., Wehmeyer, M.L., Rodi, M.S., & Presley, J.A. (2002). Using self-monitoring to improve performance in general education high school classes. *Education and Training in Mental Retardation and Developmental Disabilities, 37*(3), 262–272.

Hughes, C., Copeland, S.R., Wehmeyer, M.L., Agran, M., Cai, X., & Hwang, B. (2002). Increasing social interaction between general education high school students and their peers with mental retardation. *Journal of Developmental and Physical Disabilities, 14*(4), 387–402.

Hughes, C., Korinek, L., & Gorman, J. (1991). Self-management for students with mental retardation in public school settings: A research review. *Education and Training in Mental Retardation, 26*(3), 271–291.

Hughes, C., Rung, L.L., Wehmeyer, M.L., Agran, M., Copeland, S.R., & Hwang, B. (2000). Self-prompted communication book use to increase social interaction among high school students. *Journal of The Association for Persons with Severe Handicaps, 25*(3), 153–166.

Individuals with Disabilities Education Act Amendments (IDEA) of 1997, PL 105-17, 20 U.S.C. §§ 1400 *et seq.*

Individuals with Disabilities Education Improvement Act (IDEA) of 2004, PL 108-446, 20 U.S.C. §§ 1400 *et seq.*

Izzo, M.V., & Lamb, P. (2003). Developing self-determination through career development activities: Implications for vocational rehabilitation counselors. *Journal of Vocational Rehabilitation, 19*, 71–78.

Janiga, S.J., & Costenbader, V. (2002). The transition from high school to postsecondary education for students with learning disabilities: A survey of college service coordinators. *Journal of Learning Disabilities, 35*, 462–479.

Johnson, L., Graham, S., & Harris, K.R. (1997). The effects of goal setting and self-instruction on learning a reading comprehension strategy: A study of students with learning disabilities. *Journal of Learning Disabilities, 30*(1), 80–91. doi:10.1177/002221949703000107

Jolivette, K., Wehby, J.H., & Canale, J. (2001). Effects of choice-making opportunities on the behavior of students with emotional and behavioral disorders. *Behavior Disorders, 26*, 131–145.

Joseph, L.M., & Eveleigh, E.L. (2011). A review of the effects of self-monitoring on reading performance of students with disabilities. *Journal of Special Education, 45*(1), 43–53. doi:10.1177/0022466909349145

Joyce, B., & Weil, M. (1980). *Models of teaching* (2nd ed.). Upper Saddle River, NJ: Prentice Hall.

Kalyanpur, M., & Harry, B. (2012). *Cultural reciprocity in special education: Building family–professional relationships.* Baltimore, MD: Paul H. Brookes Publishing Co.

Karvonen, M., Test, D.W., Wood, W.M., Browder, D., & Algozzine, B. (2004). Putting self-determination into practice. *Exceptional Children, 71*, 23–41.

Kern, L., Vorndran, C.M., Hilt, A., Ringdahl, J.E., Adelman, B.E., & Dunlap, G. (1998). Choice as an intervention to improve behavior: A review of the literature. *Journal of Behavioral Education, 8*(2), 151–169.

Klassen, R.M., & Lynch, S.L. (2007). Self-efficacy from the perspective of adolescents with LD and their specialist teachers. *Journal of Learning Disabilities, 40*(6), 494–507. doi:10.1177/00222194070400060201

Konrad, M., Fowler, C.H., Walker, A.R., Test, D.W., & Wood, W.M. (2007). Effects of self-determination interventions on the academic skills of students with learning disabilities. *Learning Disability Quarterly, 30*, 89–113.

LaCava, P.G., & Shogren, K.A. (2012). *Evidence-based practice and autism spectrum disorders: The intersection of research, practice and policy.* Paper presented at the 136th Annual Meeting of the American Association on Intellectual and Developmental Disabilities, Charlotte, NC.

Lancioni, G.E., O'Reilly, M.F., & Oliva, D. (2002). Engagement in cooperative and individual tasks: Assessing the performance and preferences of persons with multiple disabilities. *Journal of Visual Impairment and Blindness, 96*, 50–53.

Lee, S.H., Simpson, R.L., & Shogren, K.A. (2007). Effects and implications of self-management for students with autism: A meta-analysis. *Focus on Autism and Other Developmental Disabilities, 22*, 2–13.

Lee, S.H., Wehmeyer, M.L., Palmer, S.B., Soukup, J.H., & Little, T.D. (2008). Self-determination and access to the general education curriculum. *Journal of Special Education, 42*(2), 91–107.

Lee, Y., Wehmeyer, M.L., Palmer, S.B., Williams-Diehm, K., Davies, D.K., & Stock, S.E. (2012). Examining individual and instruction-related predictors of the self-determination of students with disabilities: Multiple regression analyses. *Remedial and Special Education, 33*, 150–161. doi:10.1177/0741932510392053

Lehmann, J.P., Bassett, D.S., & Sands, D.J. (1999). Students' participation in transition-related actions: A qualitative study. *Remedial and Special Education, 20*(3), 160–169. doi: 10.1177/074193259902000307

Locke, E.A., & Latham, G.P. (1990). *A theory of goal setting and task performance.* Upper Saddle River, NJ: Prentice Hall.

Locke, E.A., & Latham, G.P. (2002). Building a practically useful theory of goal setting and task motivation: A 35-year odyssey. *American Psychologist, 57*(9), 705–717.

Locke, E.A., & Latham, G.P. (2006). New directions in goal-setting theory. *Current Directions in Psychological Science, 15*, 265–268. doi:10.1111/j.1467-8721.2006.00449.x

Lohrmann-O'Rourke, S., Browder, D.M., & Brown, F. (2000). Guidelines for conducting socially valid systematic preference assessments. *Journal of The Association for Persons with Severe Handicaps, 25*, 42–53.

Lohrmann-O'Rourke, S., & Gomez, O. (2001). Integrating preference assessment within the transition process to create meaningful school-to-life outcomes. *Exceptionality, 9*, 157–174.

Mace, F.C., Belfiore, P.J., & Hutchinson, J.M. (Eds.). (2001). *Operant theory and research on self-regulation* (2nd ed.). Mahwah, NJ: Lawrence Erlbaum Associates.

Machalicek, W., O'Reilly, M.F., Beretvas, N., Sigafoos, J., & Lancioni, G.E. (2007). A review of interventions to reduce challenging behavior in school settings for students with autism spectrum disorders. *Research in Autism Spectrum Disorders, 1*, 229–246.

Mancina, C., Tankersley, M., Kamps, D., Kravits, T., & Parrett, J. (2000). Reduction of inappropriate vocalizations for a child with autism using a self-management treatment program. *Journal of Autism and Developmental Disorders, 30*(6), 599–606.

Martin, J.E., Huber Marshall, L., & Sale, P. (2004). A 3-year study of middle, junior high, and high school IEP meetings. *Exceptional Children, 70*(3), 285–297.

Martin, J.E., Huber Marshall, L., & Wray, D. (2004). *Choose and take action: Finding the right job for you.* Longmont, CO: Sopris West Educational Services.

Martin, J.E., & Marshall, L.H. (1995). ChoiceMaker: A comprehensive self-determination transition program. *Intervention in School and Clinic, 30*, 147–156.

Martin, J.E., Marshall, L.H., Maxson, L., & Jerman, P. (1993). *Self-directed IEP: Teacher's manual.* Colorado Springs: Center for Educational Research, University of Colorado.

Martin, J.E., Marshall, L.H., Maxson, L., & Jerman, P. (1996). *Self-directed IEP* (2nd ed.). Longmont, CO: Sopris West Educational Services.

Martin, J.E., Mithaug, D.E., Cox, P., Peterson, L.Y., Van Dycke, J.L., & Cash, M.E. (2003). Increasing self-determination: Teaching students to plan, work, evaluate, and adjust. *Exceptional Children, 69,* 431–447.

Martin, J.E., Mithaug, D.E., Husch, J.V., Frazier, E.S., & Marshall, L.H. (2003). The effects of optimal opportunities and adjustments on job choices of adults with severe disabilities. In D.E. Mithaug & D.K. Mithaug (Eds.), *Self determined learning theory: Construction, verification, and evaluation* (pp. 188–205). Mahwah, NJ: Lawrence Erlbaum Associates.

Martin, J.E., Mithaug, D.E., Oliphint, J.H., Husch, J.V., & Frazier, E.S. (2002). *Self-directed employment: A handbook for transition teachers and employment specialists.* Baltimore, MD: Paul H. Brookes Publishing Co.

Martin, J.E., Van Dycke, J.L., Christensen, W.R., Greene, B.A., Gardner, J.E., & Lovett, D.L. (2006). Increasing student participation in IEP meetings: Establishing the self-directed IEP as an evidenced-based practice. *Exceptional Children, 72,* 299–316.

Martin, J.E., Van Dycke, J.L., Greene, B.A., Gardner, J.E., Christensen, W.R., Woods, L.L., & Lovett, D.L. (2006). Direct observation of teacher-directed IEP meetings: Establishing the need for student IEP meeting instruction. *Exceptional Children, 72,* 187–200.

Martin, J.E., Woods, L.L., Sylvester, L., & Gardner, J.E. (2005). A challenge to self-determination: Disagreement between the vocational choices made by individuals with severe disabilities and their caregivers. *Research and Practice for Persons with Severe Disabilities, 30,* 147–153.

Mason, C., Field, S., & Sawilowsky, S. (2004). Implementation of self-determination activities and student participation in IEPs. *Exceptional Children, 70,* 441–451.

Mazzotti, V.L., Test, D.W., Wood, C.L., & Richter, S.M. (2012). Effects of computer-assisted instruction on students' knowledge of postschool options. *Career Development for Exceptional Individuals, 33,* 25–40.

Mazzotti, V.L., Wood, C.L., Test, D.W., & Fowler, C.H. (2012). Effects of computer-assisted instruction on students' knowledge of the Self-Determined Learning Model of Instruction and disruptive behavior. *Journal of Special Education, 45*(4), 216–226.

McGlashing-Johnson, J., Agran, M., Sitlington, P., Cavin, M., & Wehmeyer, M.L. (2003). Enhancing the job performance of youth with moderate to severe cognitive disabilities using the Self-Determined Learning Model of Instruction. *Research and Practice for Persons with Severe Disabilities, 28*(4), 194–204.

Michaels, C.A., & Ferrara, D.L. (2006). Promoting postschool success for all: The role of collaboration in person-centered transition planning. *Journal of Educational and Psychological Consultation, 16*(4), 287–313.

Miner, C., & Bates, P. (1997). The effect of person centered planning activities on the IEP/transition planning process. *Education and Training in Developmental Disabilities, 32,* 105–112.

Mithaug, D.E. (1993). *Self-regulation theory: How optimal adjustment maximizes gain.* Westport, CT: Praeger Publishers/Greenwood Publishing Group.

Mithaug, D.E. (1996). *Equal opportunity theory.* Thousand Oaks, CA: Sage Publications.

Mithaug, D.E., Campeau, P.L., & Wolman, J.M. (2003). Assessing self-determination prospects among students with and without disabilities. In D.E. Mithaug, D.K. Mithaug, M. Agran, J.E. Martin, & M.L. Wehmeyer (Eds.), *Self determined learning theory: Construction, verification, and evaluation* (pp. 61–76). Mahwah, NJ: Lawrence Erlbaum Associates.

Mooney, P., Ryan, J.B., Uhing, B.M., Reid, R., & Epstein, M.H. (2005). A review of self-management interventions targeting academic outcomes for students with emotional and behavioral disorders. *Journal of Behavioral Education, 14*(3), 203–221. doi:10.1007/s10864-005-6298-1

Mount, B. (1991). *Person-centered planning: A sourcebook of values, ideals, and method to encourage person-centered development.* New York, NY: Graphic Futures.

National Autism Center. (2009). *Evidence-based practice and autism in the schools: A guide to providing appropriate interventions to students with autism spectrum disorders.* Randolph, MA: Author.

Nelson, J.M., & Manset-Williamson, G. (2006). The impact of explicit, self-regulatory reading comprehension strategy instruction on the reading-specific self-efficacy, attributions, and affect of students with reading disabilities. *Learning Disability Quarterly, 29*(3), 213–230. doi: 10.2307/30035507

Newman, B., Buffington, D.M., & Hemmes, N.S. (1996). Self-reinforcement used to increase the appropriate conversation of autistic teenagers. *Education and Training in Mental Retardation and Developmental Disabilities, 31*(4), 304–309.

Nota, L., Ferrari, L., Soresi, S., & Wehmeyer, M. (2007). Self-determination, social abilities and the quality of life of people with intellectual disability. *Journal of Intellectual Disability Research, 51,* 850–865. doi:10.1111/j.1365-2788.2006.00939.x

Nowicki, S., & Strickland, B.R. (1973). A locus of control scale for children. *Journal of Consulting and Clinical Psychology, 40,* 148–154.

Odom, S.L., Brantlinger, E., Gersten, R., Horner, R.H., Thompson, B., & Harris, K.R. (2005). Research in special education: Scientific methods and evidence-based practices. *Exceptional Children, 71*(2), 137–148.

Office of Special Education and Rehabilitative Services. (1989). *National conference on self-determination: 29 recommendations.* Washington, DC: Author.

O'Neill, R.E., Horner, R.H., Albin, R., Storey, K., & Sprague, J.R. (1997). *Functional assessment and program development for behavior problems.* Pacific Grove, CA: Brooks/Cole.

Page-Voth, V., & Graham, S. (1999). Effects of goal setting and strategy use on the writing performance and self-efficacy of students with writing and learning problems. *Journal of Educational Psychology, 91*(2), 230–240. doi: 10.1037/0022-0663.91.2.230

Palmer, S.B. (2010). Self-determination: A life-span perspective. *Focus on Exceptional Children, 42*(6), 1–16.

Palmer, S.B., Wehmeyer, M.L., Gipson, K., & Agran, M. (2004). Promoting access to the general curriculum by teaching self-determination skills. *Exceptional Children, 70,* 427–439.

Pauley, C.A. (1998). The view from the student's side of the table. In M.L. Wehmeyer & D.J. Sands (Eds.), *Making it happen: Student involvement in education planning, decision making and instruction* (pp. 123–128). Baltimore, MD: Paul H. Brookes Publishing Co.

Pearpoint, J., O'Brien, J., & Forest, M. (1995). *PATH: A workbook for planning positive possible futures* (2nd ed.). Toronto, Ontario, Canada: Inclusion Press.

Powers, L.E., Turner, A., Matuszweski, J., Wilson, R., & Loesch, C. (1999). A qualitative analysis of student involvement in transition planning. *Journal for Vocational Special Needs Education, 21,* 18–26.

Prizant, B.M. (2011, Fall). The use and misuse of evidence-based practice: Implications for persons with ASD. *Autism Spectrum Quarterly,* 34–49.

Rehabilitation Act of 1973, PL 93-112, 29 U.S.C. §§ 701 *et seq.*

Reid, D.H., Parsons, M.B., & Green, C.W. (1991). *Providing choices and preferences for persons who have severe handicaps.* Morganton, NC: Habilitative Managment Consultants.

Reinecke, D.R., Newman, B., & Meinberg, D.L. (1999). Self-management of sharing in three pre-schoolers with autism. *Education and Training in Mental Retardation and Developmental Disabilities, 34*(3), 312–317.

Rogers, L.A., & Graham, S. (2008). A meta-analysis of single subject design writing intervention research. *Journal of Educational Psychology, 100*(4), 879–906. doi: 10.1037/0022-0663.100.4.879

Rotter, J.B. (1966). Generalized expectancies for internal versus external control of reinforcement. *Psychological Monographs, 80,* 244–248.

Rumrill, P.D., Jr. (1999). Effects of social competence training program on accommodation request activity, situational self-efficacy, and Americans with Disabilities Act knowledge among employed people with visual impairments and blindness. *Journal of Vocational Rehabilitation, 12*(1), 25–31.

Sailor, W., Dunlop, G., Sugai, G., & Horner, R. (2009). *Handbook of positive behavior support.* New York, NY: Springer.

Schalock, R.L., Borthwick-Duffy, S., Bradley, V., Buntix, W.H.E., Coulter, D.L., Craig, E.P.M., . . . Yeager, M.H. (2010). *Intellectual disability: Definition, classification, and systems of support* (11th ed.). Washington, DC: American Association on Intellectual and Developmental Disabilities.

Schalock, R.L., Brown, I., Brown, R., Cummins, R.A., Felce, D., Matikka, L., . . . Parmenter, T. (2002). Conceptualization, measurement, and application of quality of life for persons with intellectual disabilities: Report of an international panel of experts. *Mental Retardation, 40*(6), 457–470.

Schalock, R.L., Luckasson, R., Bradley, V., Buntinx, W., Lachapelle, Y., Shogren, K.A., . . . Wehmeyer, M.L. (2012). *User's guide for the 11th edition of intellectual disability: Diagnosis, classification and systems of support.* Washington, DC: American Association on Intellectual and Developmental Disabilities.

Schunk, D.H., & Zimmerman, B.J. (2007). Influencing children's self-efficacy and self-regulation of reading and writing through modeling. *Reading and Writing Quarterly: Overcoming Learning Difficulties, 23*(1), 7–25. doi:10.1080/10573560600837578

Self-Advocates Becoming Empowered. (1996). *SABE definition of self-determination.* Retrieved June 26, 2012, from http://www.sabeusa.org/user_storage/File/sabeusa/Position%20Statements/39_%20Self-Determination.pdf

Seybert, S., Dunlap, G., & Ferro, J. (1996). The effects of choice making on the problem behaviors of high school students with intellectual disabilities. *Journal of Behavioral Education, 6,* 49–65.

Shevin, M., & Klein, N.K. (1984). The importance of choice-making skills for students with severe disabilities *Journal of The Association for Persons with Severe Handicaps, 9,* 159–166.

Shogren, K.A. (2010). *Social validity interview data.* Unpublished manuscript.

Shogren, K.A. (2011). Culture and self-determination: A synthesis of the literature and directions for future research and practice. *Career Development for Exceptional Individuals, 34,* 115–127. doi: 10.1177/0885728811398271

Shogren, K.A. (2012). Hispanic mothers' perceptions of self-determination. *Research and Practice for Persons with Severe Disabilities, 37,* 170-184.

Shogren, K.A., Bovaird, J.A., Palmer, S.B., & Wehmeyer, M.L. (2010). Examining the development of locus of control orientations in students with intellectual disability, learning disabilities, and no disabilities: A latent growth curve analysis. *Research and Practice for Persons with Severe Disabilities, 35,* 80–92.

Shogren, K.A., & Broussard, R. (2011). Exploring the perceptions of self-determination of individuals with intellectual disability. *Intellectual and Developmental Disabilities, 49*(2), 86–102. doi:10.1352/1934-9556-49.2.86

Shogren, K.A., Faggella-Luby, M., Bae, S.J., & Wehmeyer, M.L. (2004). The effect of choice-making as an intervention for problem behavior: A meta-analysis. *Journal of Positive Behavior Interventions, 6*(4), 228–237.

Shogren, K.A., Lang, R., Machalicek, W., Rispoli, M., & O'Reilly, M.F. (2011). Self-versus teacher management of behavior for elementary school students with Asperger syndrome: Impact on classroom behavior. *Journal of Postive Behavior Interventions, 13,* 87–96. doi: 10.1177/1098300710384508

Shogren, K.A., Lopez, S.J., Wehmeyer, M.L., Little, T.D., & Pressgrove, C.L. (2006). The role of positive psychology constructs in predicting life satisfaction in adolescents with and without cognitive disabilities: An exploratory study. *Journal of Positive Psychology, 1,* 37–52.

Shogren, K.A., Palmer, S.B., Wehmeyer, M.L., Williams-Diehm, K., & Little, T.D. (2012). Effect of intervention with the Self-Determined Learning Model of Instruction on access and goal attainment. *Remedial and Special Education, 33,* 320-330. doi:10.1177/0741932511410072

Shogren, K.A., & Plotner, A.J. (2012). Characteristics of transition planning for students with intellectual disability and autism: Data from the National Longitudinal Transition Study-2. *Intellectual and Developmental Disabilities, 50,* 16-30. doi:10.1352/1934-9556-50.1.16

Shogren, K.A., & Turnbull, A.P. (2006). Promoting self-determination in young children with disabilities: The critical role of families. *Infants and Young Children, 19,* 338–352.

Shogren, K.A., Wehmeyer, M.L., Palmer, S.B., Rifenbark, G.G., & Little, T.D. (2012). *Postschool outcomes of youth with disabilities: The impact of self-determination.* Manuscript submitted for publication.

Shogren, K.A., Wehmeyer, M.L., Palmer, S.B., Soukup, J.H., Little, T.D., Garner, N., & Lawrence, M. (2007). Examining individual and ecological predictors of the self-determination of students with disabilities. *Exceptional Children, 73,* 488–509.

Shogren, K.A., Wehmeyer, M.L., Palmer, S.B., Soukup, J.H., Little, T.D., Garner, N., & Lawrence, M. (2008). Understanding the construct of self-determination: Examining the relationship between The Arc's Self-Determination Scale and the AIR Self-Determination Scale. *Assessment for Effective Intervention, 33,* 94–107. doi: 10.1177/1534508407311395

Simpson, R., de Boer-Ott, S.R., Griswold, D., Myles, B.S., Byrd, S.E., Ganz, J., . . . Adams, L.G. (2005). *Autism spectrum disorders: Interventions and treatments for children and youth.* Thousand Oaks, CA: Corwin Press.

Smith, J.D., & Wehmeyer, M.L. (2012). *Good blood bad blood: Science, nature and the myth of the Kallikaks.* Washington, DC: American Association on Intellectual and Developmental Disabilities.

Snell, M.E., & Brown, F. (2006). *Instruction of students with severe disabilities* (6th ed.). Upper Saddle River, NJ: Pearson Prentice Hall.

Stafford, A.M., Alberto, P.A., Fredrick, L.D., Heflin, L.J., & Heller, K.W. (2002). Preference variability and the instruction of choice making with students with severe intellectual disabilities. *Education and Training in Mental Retardation and Developmental Disabilities, 37,* 70–88.

Stancliffe, R.J. (2001). Living with support in the community: Predictors of choice and self-determination. *Mental Retardation and Developmental Disabilities Research Reviews, 7,* 91–98. doi:10.1002/mrdd.1013

Sugai, G., & Horner, R. (2010). Schoolwide positive behavior supports: Establishing a continuum of evidence-based practices. *Journal of Evidence-Based Practices for Schools, 11*(1), 62–83.

Swain, K.D. (2005). CBM with goal setting: Impacting students' understanding of reading goals. *Journal of Instructional Psychology, 32*(3), 259–265.

Test, D.W., Fowler, C.H., Brewer, D.M., & Wood, W.M. (2005). A content and methodological review of self-advocacy intervention studies. *Exceptional Children, 72*(1), 101–125.

Test, D.W., Fowler, C.H., Richter, S.M., White, J., Mazzotti, V., Walker, A.R., . . . Kortering, L. (2009). Evidence-based practices in secondary transition. *Career Development for Exceptional Individuals, 32*(2), 115–128.

Test, D.W., Fowler, C.H., Wood, W.M., Brewer, D.M., & Eddy, S. (2005). A conceptual framework of self-advocacy for students with disabilities. *Remedial and Special Education, 26,* 43–54.

Test, D.W., Mason, C., Hughes, C., Konrad, M., Neale, M., & Wood, W.M. (2004). Student involvement in individualized education program meetings. *Exceptional Children, 70*(4), 391–412.

Test, D.W., Mazzotti, V., Mustian, A.L., Fowler, C.H., Kortering, L., & Kohler, P. (2009). Evidence-based secondary transition predictors for improving postschool outcomes for students with disabilities. *Career Development for Exceptional Individuals, 32,* 160–181.

Test, D.W., & Neale, M. (2004). Using the self-advocacy strategy to increase middle graders' IEP participation. *Journal of Behavioral Education, 13,* 135–145. doi: 10.1023/B:JOBE.0000023660.21195.c2

Thoma, C.A., Baker, S.R., & Saddler, S.J. (2002). Self-determination in teacher education: A model to facilitate transition planning for students with disabilities. *Remedial and Special Education, 23,* 82–89. doi: 10.1177/074193250202300204

Thoma, C.A., & Getzel, E.E. (2005). "Self-determination is what it's all about:" What post-secondary students with disabilities tell us are important considerations for success. *Education and Training in Developmental Disabilities, 40*(3), 234–242.

Thoma, C.A., Nathanson, R., Baker, S.R., & Tamura, R. (2002). Self-determination: What do special educators know and where do they learn it? *Remedial and Special Education, 23,* 242–247.

Thompson, J.R., Bradley, V., Buntinx, W.H.E., Schalock, R.L., Shogren, K.A., Snell, M.E., . . . Yeager, M.H. (2009). Conceptualizing supports and the support needs of people with intellectual disability. *Intellectual and Developmental Disabilities, 47*(2), 135–146.

Thompson, J.R., Bryant, B.R., Campbell, E.M., Craig, E.P.M., Hughes, C.M., Rotholz, D.A., . . . Wehmeyer, M.L. (2004). *Supports Intensity Scale: Users manual.* Washington, DC: American Association on Intellectual and Developmental Disabilities.

Thompson, J.R., Wehmeyer, M.L., & Hughes, C. (2010). Mind the gap! Implications of a person-environment fit model of intellectual disability for students, educators, and schools. *Exceptionality, 18*(4), 168–181.

Trainor, A. (2005). Self-determination perceptions and behaviors of diverse students with LD during the transition planning process. *Journal of Learning Disabilities, 38,* 233–248.

Turnbull, A.P., Blue-Banning, M.J., Anderson, E.L., Turnbull, H.R., Seaton, K.A., & Dinas, P.A. (1996). Enhancing self-determination through group action planning. In D.J. Sands & M.L. Wehmeyer (Eds.), *Self-determination across the lifespan: Independence and choice for people with disabilities* (pp. 237–256). Baltimore, MD: Paul H. Brookes Publishing Co.

Turnbull, A.P., & Turnbull, H.R. (n.d.). *Group action planning as a strategy for getting a life.* Lawrence, KS: Beach Center on Disability.

Turnbull, A.P., & Turnbull, H.R., III. (1996). Group action planning as a strategy for providing comprehensive family support. In L.K. Koegel, R.L. Koegel, & G. Dunlap (Eds.), *Positive behavioral support: Including people with difficult behavior in the community.* (pp. 99–114). Baltimore, MD: Paul H. Brookes Publishing Co.

Turnbull, A.P., & Turnbull, H.R. (1997). Self-determination within a culturally responsive family systems perspective. In L.E. Powers, G.H.S. Singer & J. Sowers (Eds.), *On the road to autonomy: Promoting self-competence in children and youth with disabilities* (pp. 195–220). Baltimore, MD: Paul H. Brookes Publishing Co.

Turnbull, A.P., Turnbull, H.R., Erwin, E.E., Soodak, L.C., & Shogren, K.A. (2010). *Families, professionals, and exceptionality: Positive outcomes through partnership and trust* (6th ed.). Upper Saddle River, NJ: Merrill Prentice Hall.

Valenzuela, R.L., & Martin, J.E. (2005). Self-directed IEP: Bridging values of diverse cultures and secondary education. *Career Development for Exceptional Individuals, 28,* 4–14.

Van Laarhoven, T., Kraus, E., Karpman, K., Nizzi, R., & Valentino, J. (2010). A comparison of picture and video prompts to teach daily living skills to individuals with autism. *Focus on Autism and Other Developmental Disabilities, 25*(4), 195–208. doi:10.1177/1088357610380412

Van Reusen, A.K., & Bos, C.S. (1994). Facilitating student participation in the individualized education programs through motivation strategy instruction. *Exceptional Children, 60,* 466–475.

Van Reusen, A.K., Bos, C.S., Schumaker, J.B., & Deshler, D.D. (1994). *The self-advocacy strategy for education and transition planning.* Lawrence, KS: Edge Enterprises.

Wagner, M., Newman, L., Cameto, R., Garza, N., & Levine, P. (2005). *After high school: A first look at the postschool experiences of youth with disabilities. A report from the National Longitudinal Transition Study–2.* Menlo Park, CA: SRI International.

Walker, A.R., & Test, D.W. (2011). Using a self-advocacy intervention on African American college students' ability to request academic accommodations. *Learning Disabilities Research and Practice, 26*(3), 134–144.

Ward, M.J., & Kohler, P.D. (1996). Promoting self-determination for individuals with disabilities: Content and process. In L.E. Powers, G.H.S. Singer, & J. Sowers (Eds.), *On the road to autonomy: Promoting self-competence in children and youth with disabilities* (pp. 275–290). Baltimore, MD: Paul H. Brookes Publishing Co.

Wehman, P. (2013). *Life beyond the classroom: Transition strategies for young people with disabilities* (5th ed.). Baltimore, MD: Paul H. Brookes Publishing Co.

Wehmeyer, M.L. (1993). Perceptual and psychological factors in career decision-making of adolescents with and without cognitive disabilities. *Career Development for Exceptional Individuals, 16,* 135–146.

Wehmeyer, M.L. (1994a). Employment status and perceptions of control of adults with cognitive and developmental disabilities. *Research in Developmental Disabilities, 15,* 119–131.

Wehmeyer, M.L. (1994b). Perceptions of self-determination and psychological empowerment of adolescents with mental retardation. *Education and Training in Mental Retardation and Developmental Disabilities, 29,* 9–21.

Wehmeyer, M.L. (1997). Self-determination as an educational outcome: A definitional framework and implications for intervention. *Journal of Developmental and Physical Disabilities, 9,* 175–209.

Wehmeyer, M.L. (2003a). A functional theory of self-determination: Definition and categorization. In M.L. Wehmeyer, B. Abery, D.E. Mithaug, & R. Stancliffe (Eds.), *Theory in self-determination: Foundations for educational practice* (pp. 174–181). Springfield, IL: Charles C. Thomas Publishing Co.

Wehmeyer, M.L. (2003b). A functional theory of self-determination: Model overview. In M.L. Wehmeyer, B. Abery, D.E. Mithaug, & R. Stancliffe (Eds.), *Theory in self-determination: Foundations for educational practice* (pp. 182-201). Springfield, IL: Charles C. Thomas Publishing Co.

Wehmeyer, M.L. (2005). Self-determination and individuals with severe disabilities: Re-examining meanings and misinterpretations. *Research and Practice for Persons with Severe Disabilities, 30,* 113–120.

Wehmeyer, M.L. (2011). *The Adolescent Self-Determination Scale–Short Form: Administration and scoring procedures.* Lawrence: Kansas University Center for Developmental Disabilities.

Wehmeyer, M.L., Abery, B.H., Zhang, D., Ward, K., Willis, D., Hossain, W.A., . . . Walker, H.M. (2011). Personal self-determination and moderating variables that impact efforts to promote self-determination. *Exceptionality, 19,* 19–30. doi:10.1080/09362835.2011.537225

Wehmeyer, M.L., Agran, M., & Hughes, C. (2000). A national survey of teachers' promotion of self-determination and student-directed learning. *Journal of Special Education, 34,* 58–68.

Wehmeyer, M.L., Agran, M., Hughes, C., Martin, J.E., Mithaug, D., & Palmer, S. (2007). *Promoting self-determination in students with developmental disabilities.* New York, NY: Guilford Press.

Wehmeyer, M.L., Baker, D.J., Blumberg, R., & Harrison, R. (2004). Self-determination and student involvement in functional assessment: Innovative practices. *Journal of Positive Behavior Interventions, 6*(1), 29–35.

Wehmeyer, M.L., Bersani, H., Jr., & Gagne, R. (2000). Riding the third wave: Self-determination and self-advocacy in the 21st century. *Focus on Autism and Other Developmental Disabilities, 15*(2), 106–115.

Wehmeyer, M.L., Field, S., Doren, B., Jones, B., & Mason, C. (2004). Self-determination and student involvement in standards-based reform. *Exceptional Children, 70,* 413–425.

Wehmeyer, M.L., Gragoudas, S., & Shogren, K.A. (2006). Self-determination, student involvement, and leadership development. In P. Wehman (Ed.), *Life beyond the classroom: Transition strategies for young people with disabilities* (4th ed., pp. 41–69). Baltimore, MD: Paul H. Brookes Publishing Co.

Wehmeyer, M.L., & Kelchner, K. (1995). *The Arc's Self-Determination Scale.* Arlington, TX: The Arc National Headquarters.

Wehmeyer, M.L., & Kelchner, K. (1996). Perceptions of classroom environment, locus of control and academic attributions of adolescents with and without cognitive disabilities. *Career Development for Exceptional Individuals, 19,* 15–29.

Wehmeyer, M.L., Kelchner, K., & Richards, S. (1996). Essential characteristics of self-determined behavior of individuals with mental retardation. *American Journal on Mental Retardation, 100,* 632–642.

Wehmeyer, M.L., Lawrence, M., Kelchner, K., Palmer, S.B., Garner, N., & Soukup, J. (2004). *Whose future is it anyway? A student-directed transition planning process.* Lawrence: Beach Center on Disability and Kansas University Center on Developmental Disabilities.

Wehmeyer, M.L., Little, T.D., Lopez, S.J., & Shogren, K.A. (2011). *Adolescent Self-Determination Assessment–Short Form.* Lawrence: Kansas University Center for Developmental Disabilities.

Wehmeyer, M.L., & Palmer, S.B. (2003). Adult outcomes for students with cognitive disabilities three-years after high school: The impact of self-determination. *Education and Training in Developmental Disabilities, 38*, 131–144.

Wehmeyer, M.L., Palmer, S.B., Agran, M., Mithaug, D.E., & Martin, J.E. (2000). Promoting causal agency: The Self-Determined Learning Model of Instruction. *Exceptional Children, 66*(4), 439–453.

Wehmeyer, M.L., Palmer, S.B., Lee, Y., Williams-Diehm, K., & Shogren, K. (2011). A randomized-trial evaluation of the effect of whose future is it anyway? On self-determination. *Career Development for Exceptional Individuals, 34*(1), 45–56. doi:10.1177/0885728810383559

Wehmeyer, M.L., Palmer, S.B., Shogren, K.A., Williams-Diehm, K., & Soukup, J. (2012). Establishing a causal relationship between interventions to promote self-determination enhanced student self-determination. *Journal of Special Education, 46*, 195–210. doi: 10.1177/0022466910392377

Wehmeyer, M.L., & Schwartz, M. (1997). Self-determination and positive adult outcomes: A follow-up study of youth with mental retardation or learning disabilities. *Exceptional Children, 63*, 245–255.

Wehmeyer, M.L., Shogren, K.A., Palmer, S.B., Williams-Diehm, K., Little, T.D., & Boulton, A. (2012). Impact of the Self-Determined Learning Model of Instruction on student self-determination: A randomized-trial placebo control group study. *Exceptional Children, 78*, 135–153.

Wehmeyer, M. L., Yeager, D., Bolding, N., Agran, M., & Hughes, C. (2003). The effects of self-regulation strategies on goal attainment for students with developmental disabilities in general education classrooms. *Journal of Developmental and Physical Disabilities, 15*, 79-91.

Weston, C., & Went, F. (1999). Speaking up for yourself: Description and evaluation of an assertiveness training group for people with learning disabilities. *British Journal of Learning Disabilities, 27*(3), 110-115. doi: 10.1111/j.1468-3156.1999.tb00099.x

What Works Clearinghouse. (2008). *WWC procedures and standards handbook: Version 2.0*. Retrieved from http://ies.ed.gov/ncee/wwc/references/idocviewer/doc.aspx?docid=19&tocid=1

White, G.W., & Vo, Y.T.H. (2006). Requesting accommodations to increase full participation in higher education: An analysis of self-advocacy training for postsecondary students with learning and other disabilities. *Learning Disabilities: A Multidisciplinary Journal, 14*(1), 41–56.

Whitehurst, G.J. (2002). *Evidence-based education*. Retrieved from www.ies.ed.gov/director/pdf/2002_10.pdf

Whitman, T.L. (1990). Self-regulation and mental retardation. *American Journal on Mental Retardation, 94*(4), 347–362.

Williams, R.R. (1989). Creating a new world of opportunity: Expanding choice and self-determination in lives of Americans with severe disability by 1992 and beyond. In R. Perske (Ed.), *Proceedings from the National Conference on Self-Determination* (pp. 1–5). Minneapolis, MN: Institute on Community Integration.

Wolman, J., Campeau, P., Dubois, P., Mithaug, D., & Stolarski, V. (1994). *AIR Self-Determination Scale and user guide*. Palo Alto, CA: American Institutes for Research.

Wood, C.L., Kelley, K.R., Test, D.W., & Fowler, C.H. (2010). Comparing audio-supported text and explicit instruction on students' knowledge of accommodations, rights, and responsibilities. *Career Development for Exceptional Individuals, 33*(2), 115–124. doi: 10.1177/0885728810361618

Wood, W.M., Fowler, C.H., Uphold, N., & Test, D.W. (2005). A review of self-determination interventions with individuals with severe disabilities. *Research and Practice for Persons with Severe Disabilities, 30*, 121–146. doi: 10.2511/rpsd.30.3.121

Wood, W.M., & Test, D.W. (2001). *Final performance report: Self-determination synthesis project*. Charlotte: University of North Carolina.

Zhang, D. (2001). Self-determination and inclusion: Are students with mild mental retardation more self-determined in regular classrooms? *Education and Training in Mental Retardation and Developmental Disabilities, 36*, 357–362.

Zhang, D. (2005). Parent practices in facilitating self-determination skills: The influences of culture, socioeconomic status, and children's special education status. *Research and Practice for Persons with Severe Disabilities, 30*, 154–162.

Zimmerman, B.J. (2000). *Attaining self-regulation: A social cognitive perspective*. San Diego, CA: Academic Press.

Zimmerman, B.J., & Kitsantas, A. (1997). Developmental phases in self-regulation: Shifting from process goals to outcome goals. *Journal of Educational Psychology, 89*(1), 29–36. doi: 10.1037/0022-0663.89.1.29

Zimmerman, B.J., & Kitsantas, A. (1999). Acquiring writing revision skill: Shifting from process to outcome self-regulatory goals. *Journal of Educational Psychology, 91*(2), 241–250. doi: 10.1037/0022-0663.91.2.241

Zimmerman, B.J., & Kitsantas, A. (2005). Homework practices and academic achievement: The mediating role of self-efficacy and perceived responsibility beliefs. *Contemporary Educational Psychology, 30*(4), 397–417. doi: 10.1016/j.cedpsych.2005.05.003

For Further Information

ONLINE

National Gateway to Self-Determination (http://www.aucd.org/ngsd)

Provides videos, resource guides, and publications on self-determination across the life span. Self-advocates share their experiences with self-determination and its meaning in their lives.

National Secondary Transition Technical Assistance Center (http://www.nsttac.org/)

Provides information on evidence-based practices in transition, including self-determination. The Lesson Plan Starters tab has lesson plans on student-focused planning that can be used to teach students skills to participate in transition planning and develop self-determination skills that are research based.

I'm Determined.org (http://www.imdetermined.org/)

Provides information, training materials, and resources for students, families, and teachers. Includes modules on self-determination and its history in the disability field, films on self-determination and student involvement, tools to promote goal setting and attainment, and downloadable templates that can be used in practice. The Life Lines section provides a multitude of self-determination lesson plans collected from practicing teachers.

Zarrow Center for Learning Enrichment (http://www.ou.edu/content/education/centers-and-partnerships/zarrow.html)

Provides free self-determination assessment tools for download, including the AIR Self-Determination Scales and The Arc Self-Determination Scale that are described in Chapter 2, as well as instructional materials to promote self-determination.

National Center on Secondary Education and Transition (http://www.ncset.org/)

Includes tools for teachers, parents, and students. The Youthhood portion of the web site is a tool for students to engage and learn about self-determination and the transition process. There are also publications and tools for use by parents and professionals on self-determination and transition.

CURRICULA TO PROMOTE STUDENT INVOLVEMENT IN TRANSITION PLANNING AND THE IEP MEETING

ChoiceMaker Self-Determination Transition Curriculum (Martin & Marshall, 1995)

- Includes 1) a criterion-referenced assessment tool, 2) lessons on choosing goals, 3) the self-directed IEP, and 4) lessons on taking action.

- The lessons on choosing goals teach students to identify their interests, skills, limits, and goals. The Self-Directed IEP lessons teach students leadership skills to participate in their IEP meeting (see Table 6.1). The lessons on taking action teach students to break long-range goals into smaller goal schedules.

- The Choosing Goals, Self-Directed IEP, and Taking Action lessons can be purchased and used separately.

- Available for purchase from Sopris Learning.

Whose Future Is it Anyway? (Wehmeyer, Lawrence et al., 2004)

- Includes 36 sessions introducing students to the concept of transition and transition planning, including 1) self- and disability-awareness, 2) making decisions about transition-related outcomes, 3) identifying and securing community resources to support transition services, 4) writing and evaluating transition goals and objectives, 5) effectively communicating in small groups, and 6) developing skills to become an effective team member, leader, or self-advocate.

- Available for purchase from the Attainment Company and includes a student reader, workbook, instructor guide, and software.

Next S.T.E.P.: Student Transition and Educational Planning (Halpern et al., 1995)

- Includes 16 lessons that are organized into four units: 1) getting started—overview of transition planning, 2) self-exploration and self-evaluation, 3) developing goals and qctivities, and 4) putting a plan into place.

- Includes the transition skills inventory, a 72-item rating instrument assessing how well the student is doing in four transition areas: (1) personal life, (2) jobs, (3) education and training, and (4) living on one's own. Students complete this assessment during the self-exploration and self-evaluation unit.

- Available for purchase from PRO-ED and includes a teacher's manual, student workbook, and instructional videos.

The Self-Advocacy Strategy (Van Reusen et al., 1994)

- Includes seven instructional areas and lesson plans focused on teaching students to participate in planning meetings: 1) orient and make commitments, 2) describe, 3) model and prepare, 4) verbal practice, 5) group practice and feedback, 6) individual practice and feedback, and 7) generalization.

- Students learn the I PLAN strategy during the describe phase to implement throughout the phases.
- Available for Purchase from Edge Enterprises.

Index

Page references followed by *f* or *t* indicate figures or tables, respectively.

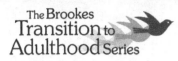

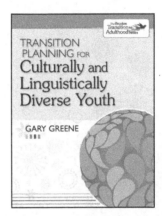